FROM SINAI TO SUNDAY
Old Testament Studies from Jeff Griffin's Sermons

I0520550

Claude F. Mariottini

Ancient Path Press
Plainfield, Illinois

Jeff Griffin
Senior Pastor, The Compass Church
Naperville, Illinois

FROM SINAI TO SUNDAY
Old Testament Studies from Jeff Griffin's Sermons

Published by Ancient Path Press
Plainfield, Illinois

This book occasionally cites additional English Bible translations when they better convey nuances of the underlying Hebrew text; these translations are identified where they occur.

The content of this book is based on sermons delivered by Jeff Griffin, Senior Pastor of The Compass Church in Naperville, Illinois, and is used with his gracious permission.

Library of Congress Control Number: 2025923702

ISBN 979-8-9938752-0-0 (Paperback)
ISBN 979-8-9938752-1-7 (Hardback)
ISBN 979-8-9938752-2-4 (Kindle Edition)

To Jeff Griffin,
who, like Ezra of old,
"has set his heart to study the Law of the LORD,
and to do it and to teach his statutes" (Ezra 7:10 ESV),
bringing the riches of the Old Testament to life for God's people.

CONTENTS

PART 4 – DAVID

PART 5 – JOEL

PART 6 – ESTHER

LIST OF ABBREVIATIONS

AB	Anchor Bible
ABD	*Anchor Bible Dictionary.* Edited by David Noel Freedman. 6 vols. New York: Doubleday, 1992.
AC	After Christ
ANET	James B. Pritchard, ed. *Ancient Near Eastern Texts Relating to the Old Testament*, 3rd ed. Princeton, NJ: Princeton University Press, 1969.
ASOR	*American Schools of Oriental Research*
BC	Before Christ
BSac	*Bibliotheca Sacra*
CSB	Christian Standard Bible
DRA	The Douay-Rheims 1899 American Edition
ESV	English Standard Version
GWN	God's Word to the Nations
Int	*Interpretation*
JNES	*Journal of Near Eastern Studies*
JSOT	*Journal for the Study of the Old Testament*
KJV	King James Version
LXX	Septuagint
MT	Masoretic Text
NAB	New American Bible
NET	New English Translation
NIV	New International Version
NJB	New Jerusalem Bible
NLT	New Living Translation
NRSV	New Revised Standard Version
PEQ	*Palestine Exploration Quarterly*
RSV	Revised Standard Version
TNK	Jewish Publication Society TANAKH 1985
VT	*Vetus Testamentum*

ACKNOWLEDGEMENTS

The author expresses gratitude to Jeff Griffin,
Senior Pastor of The Compass Church,
for permission to adapt his sermons for publication.
His faithful preaching of the Old Testament
inspired this collection.

JEFF GRIFFIN

In a time when Old Testament preaching has become rare in American pulpits, my pastor, Jeff Griffin, Senior Pastor of The Compass Church in Naperville, Illinois, stands out as a notable exception. His deep love and appreciation for the Old Testament, along with his unique ability to make ancient texts resonate with modern congregations, offer a refreshing return to the core scriptures of our faith.

A Pastor's Journey to the Old Testament

Jeff Griffin's journey into pastoral ministry happened unexpectedly. Originally a pre-med student at Wheaton College, Jeff felt God's guiding hand toward ministry, which led him to pursue a degree in theology at Trinity Evangelical Divinity School. This educational background equipped him with the scholarly tools needed to understand the complexities of Old Testament literature, but it was his pastoral heart that transformed dry exegesis into lively proclamation.

Since becoming Senior Pastor of The Compass Church in 2014, Jeff has demonstrated his commitment to Scripture through his dedication to expository preaching, alternating between Old and New Testament series. This balanced method ensures that his congregation receives the whole counsel of Scripture, rather than a New Testament-heavy diet that characterizes much of modern evangelical preaching.

The Art of Old Testament Exposition

What makes Jeff unique is not just his willingness to preach from the Old Testament but also the way he does it. He begins and ends with the biblical text, allowing Scripture to speak for itself instead of using it as a springboard for unrelated topics. This text-focused approach ensures that congregants engage with the true message of the Old Testament rather than superficial applications or allegorical interpretations that miss the historical and literary context.

Jeff's sermon series has explored the wide range of Old Testament literature: the prophetic books of Jonah, Hosea, and Joel; the narrative stories of Abraham, Jacob, and Elijah; the wisdom writings of Job; the historical accounts of Hezekiah's reign; the beloved story of Ruth, and many others. Each series demonstrates his commitment to allowing these ancient texts to speak to the modern church without imposing artificial connections or distorting their original meaning.

Archaeological Illumination

One of Jeff's most notable traits is his use of archaeological discoveries in his preaching. This method makes the ancient world feel real to modern audiences, helping to connect the time and culture gap between biblical times and today. His work with the Oriental Institute at the University of Chicago demonstrates his dedication to historical accuracy.

The memorable incident with the *lmlk* jar during his Hezekiah series shows Jeff's creative use of visual aids and experiential learning. Whether building a replica of the Ark of the Covenant with church members or securing authentic artifacts for illustration, he understands that effective Old Testament preaching must help congregants visualize and connect with the material culture of ancient Israel.

The Master Storyteller

Jeff's gift as a storyteller greatly improves his Old Testament preaching. He weaves personal stories and historical accounts into his sermons, creating links between ancient times and today. These stories serve as entry points, helping listeners connect with biblical stories that might otherwise seem distant or unimportant.

His willingness to share personal stories—such as running out of gas on the way to a wedding, taking his son on a roller coaster, and recounting local history about Wheaton and Naperville—shows his understanding that effective communication needs vulnerability and relatability. These modern stories build emotional and experiential bonds that prepare hearts to receive the deeper truths of Scripture.

Making Ancient Texts Contemporary

Perhaps Jeff's greatest strength is his ability to show how the Old Testament directly speaks to twenty-first-century believers. His sermon on Sennacherib's letter to Hezekiah (2 Kings 19:10–13) demonstrates this talent. While most pastors avoid such obscure texts, Jeff finds in them strong examples of faith under pressure that connect with modern Christians facing their own threats and challenges.

His treatment of Joel's prophecy relates to modern experiences of hardship and suffering, demonstrating how the prophet's call to return to God during times of calamity remains powerful for believers today. Through Jeff's explanation, Joel's ancient words become a relevant guide for handling personal and community crises.

The story of Esther receives special attention as Jeff emphasizes themes of courage in impossible situations, faithfulness in oppressive times, and God's providence at work through human choices. These themes extend beyond their ancient Persian background to address the fears, challenges, and moral dilemmas faced by modern believers.

A Rare Commitment

Jeff's dedication to Old Testament preaching helps fill a significant gap in modern evangelical worship. Too often, pastors see the Old Testament only as background for New Testament themes or focus on moral lessons while missing its theological depth. Jeff's approach honors both the historical context of these texts and their ongoing relevance for Christian growth.

His methodology shows that faithful Old Testament preaching does not have to be outdated or irrelevant. By combining thorough exegesis with creative presentation and modern application, he demonstrates how these ancient texts continue to influence Christian discipleship and community life.

The Old Testament Speaks to the Church

Through Jeff's ministry, the Old Testament truly resonates with the church. His sermons show that the Old Testament is not just historical artifacts or moral lessons, but lively writings that speak to the deepest needs and struggles of today's believers. Whether dealing with suffering like Job, showing courage like Esther, or trusting God's faithfulness like Abraham, these ancient figures become mentors and examples for modern Christians.

Jeff's work reminds us that the God who called Israel, delivered the Hebrews from Egypt, gave them laws at Mount Sinai, and spoke through the prophets is the same God who calls, offers, and speaks to the church today. In an era when biblical literacy is declining and knowledge of the Old Testament is especially weak, pastors like Jeff provide an invaluable service to the body of Christ.

His dedication to allowing these texts to speak for themselves, enriched by archaeological insights and applied through pastoral wisdom, offers a blueprint for how the church can reclaim its Old Testament heritage. Through his faithful teaching, congregants come to realize that the God of the Old Testament is not distant or irrelevant, but is personally involved in their daily challenges, choices, and spiritual growth.

In Jeff's hands, the Old Testament becomes what it was always meant to be: not just a collection of ancient stories, but the living Word of God that speaks hope, challenge, and transformation to his people across every generation.

A Collaborative Ministry

From Sinai to Sunday captures the unfolding of this book's central conviction: that the God who spoke from Mount Sinai speaks still to his people gathered on Sunday morning. The title of the book moves us from the dramatic moment of divine revelation in the wilderness, when God established his covenant with Israel and gave them his law, to the contemporary worship of the church. It suggests that the Old Testament is not merely ancient history or a religious book, but a living word that continues to address believers in their present circumstances. The studies in this book show that the same God who shaped the lives of people in ancient Israel is actively shaping his church through Scripture on every Lord's Day.

The biblical studies in *From Sinai to Sunday* showcase a unique partnership between a pastor and a scholar. While these studies are rooted in the sermons Jeff delivered at The Compass Church, they are not just transcriptions of his messages. Instead, each study builds on the core ideas and concepts Jeff shared from the pulpit and expands them into detailed biblical explorations suitable for both personal reflection and group study.

This collaborative approach reflects the essence of effective ministry itself, the dynamic interaction between pastoral proclamation and scholarly development, between the spoken word that meets the immediate needs of a congregation and the written word that can reach a broader audience seeking to understand God's truth.

A Pastor's Heart

Throughout this work, Jeff is addressed by his first name, reflecting both the warmth of friendship and the accessibility that characterizes his ministry. This informal approach reflects the culture at The Compass Church, where no one refers to their pastor as "Griffin." He is simply "Jeff" to every member of the congregation, a testament to his approachable leadership style and his genuine availability to his people.

This accessibility is more than just casual familiarity; it reflects a deeper pastoral philosophy. Jeff genuinely makes himself available to every church member, embodying the biblical model of pastoral care that views ministry not as a professional distance but as a relational calling. His willingness to be known simply as "Jeff" shows his understanding that effective pastoral ministry requires both authority and approachability, as well as scholarly preparation and personal connection.

A Shared Hope

Both Jeff and I share a common hope for our readers: that by exploring the stories of Old Testament figures, modern believers will gain a fresh outlook on their own spiritual journeys. These ancient stories are not kept just for history but as living examples of faith in practice.

When readers face their own impossible circumstances, they can learn from Esther's courage in risking death. When going through seasons of suffering and hardship, they can draw strength from Joel's call to return to God. When grappling with doubt or delayed promises, they can find encouragement in Abraham's faith and Ruth's loyalty.

The primary objective of these studies is to demonstrate that the God who was active in the lives of patriarchs, prophets, and ordinary believers throughout Israel's history remains active today. The same divine character that supported Elijah during depression, guided Ruth through uncertainty, and defended Hezekiah against overwhelming odds continues to work in the lives of twenty-first-century believers.

These biblical figures are more than just historical examples; they become mentors in faith, guiding modern Christians on how to trust and wait on the God whose faithfulness surpasses every generation. Through their stories, readers learn that the challenges they face are not unique, that the God they serve is not distant, and that the faith they aim to develop has been tested and proven by countless believers who came before.

In this way, Jeff's pulpit ministry extends beyond the walls of The Compass Church to serve the broader body of Christ, demonstrating once again that when the Old Testament is faithfully proclaimed and carefully studied, it truly speaks to the church.

The biblical studies in this book are based on sermon series preached by Jeff Griffin, Senior Pastor of The Compass Church in Naperville, Illinois. The original audio sermons and additional biblical resources are available at www.thecompass.net.

PART 1

JOSEPH

INTRODUCTION

WHIPLASH: A STUDY OF JOSEPH'S LIFE

My pastor, Jeff Griffin, Senior Pastor of The Compass Church in Naperville, Illinois, delivered a series of sermons about the life of Joseph. In sharing Joseph's story, Jeff titled the series "Whiplash" and likened Joseph's life to a roller coaster.

Jeff's sermons explore the ups and downs, the twists and turns of Joseph's life. Jeff uses a roller coaster to illustrate Joseph's journey. When a person follows God, life will have its highs and lows; it is not a straight path. When God controls our lives, we will experience both ups and downs, good times and bad, and unexpected twists and turns.

Joseph's life was like a roller coaster. The series title "Whiplash" points to the sudden shifts in Joseph's life that brought years of suffering and humiliation, ultimately resulting in his exaltation in a foreign land.

The Roller Coaster Journey of Joseph

Joseph's life began as his father's favorite son. From being the favorite, Joseph was sold into slavery in Egypt. Starting as a favored slave in his master's house, he eventually became a prisoner in an Egyptian dungeon. However, from a prisoner, Joseph was exalted and became Pharaoh's counselor, the second most powerful person in Egypt.

Through all the twists and turns, ups and downs, God was in control of Joseph's life. A key theme in Joseph's story is divine providence. God was working behind the scenes, providing, guiding, and shaping Joseph's story in the most unexpected ways. Like a roller coaster, Joseph was securely attached to the tracks because his life was in God's hands.

Life is like a roller coaster. Our futures are filled with unexpected twists and turns. I have developed this series of studies on Joseph based on Jeff's sermons. These studies will examine the life of Joseph and show us how to navigate life's ups and downs.

Along with these seven studies based on Jeff's sermons, I will present two additional studies that highlight Joseph's struggles. The first study focuses on "Joseph's Coat of Many Colors." Joseph's coat serves as the spark that ignited jealousy among his brothers. The second study, "How Can Someone Sell His Own Brother to the Egyptians?" examines how Joseph was sold into slavery in Egypt by his brothers.

Additional Studies: Understanding the Deeper Themes

Study 1: Joseph's Coat of Many Colors

The Symbol That Started It All

Joseph's distinctive coat was more than just clothing—it was a clear symbol of his father's favoritism and his brothers' exclusion. This study examines how material symbols can foster division and how even well-intentioned favoritism can harm family relationships.

Study 2: How Can Someone Sell His Own Brother to the Egyptians?

Understanding the Depths of Human Betrayal

Joseph's brothers' decision to sell him into slavery shows one of the most shocking betrayals in Scripture. This study examines how sin can proliferate, how jealousy can lead to violence, and how intense emotions can break family ties. Yet even this worst betrayal fits into God's plan of redemption.

The Seven Sermons: A Journey Through Joseph's Life

Jeff delivered seven powerful sermons tracing Joseph's incredible journey from being the favored son to becoming an Egyptian ruler. Each sermon examines a different challenge in life and highlights God's faithfulness through them all.

1. Joseph: Family Dysfunction

The Beginning of the Roller Coaster

Joseph's story starts in a deeply troubled family. As Jacob's favorite son, born to his beloved wife Rachel, Joseph faced the resentment and jealousy of his brothers. This sermon examines how family favoritism, sibling rivalry, and poor parenting choices can create toxic environments that lead us into life's unexpected turns. Yet even in dysfunction, God's plans begin to unfold.

2. Joseph: Career Success

Rising to the Top of the First Hill

Despite being sold into slavery, Joseph quickly rises to prominence in Potiphar's house. This sermon explores how Joseph maintained his integrity and work ethic even in the most challenging circumstances. His success as a slave shows that our attitude and character are more important than our circumstances.

3. Joseph: Overcoming Temptation

The Sharp Turn That Tests Everything

When Potiphar's wife tried to seduce Joseph, he faced a moment that would forever shape his character. This message explores strategies for managing temptation when no one is watching and the consequences appear minor. Joseph's refusal and the false accusation that followed teach us about the cost of integrity.

4. Joseph: Impacting Others

Using Your Position to Lift Others Up

Even in prison, Joseph continued to serve others and utilize his God-given gifts to interpret dreams. This sermon emphasizes the importance of making a positive impact, regardless of our circumstances. Joseph's ministry to the cupbearer and baker shows that our influence depends not on our position but on our desire to serve.

5. Joseph: Enduring Hardship

The Long, Dark Valleys

Joseph spent years in prison for a crime he did not commit. This sermon explores how to maintain faith and hope during prolonged periods of suffering and injustice. Joseph's patient endurance shows us how to trust God's timing even when His purposes are not clear.

6. Joseph: Relational Conflict

When the Past Comes Back

When Joseph's brothers came to Egypt seeking food during the famine, Joseph faced his greatest relational challenge. This sermon examines how to handle conflict with people who have wronged us, especially family members. Joseph's example shows us how to restore relationships rather than seek revenge.

7. Joseph: Extending Forgiveness

The Ultimate High Point

The climax of Joseph's story occurs when he reveals his identity to his brothers and offers total forgiveness. This sermon highlights the power of forgiveness to transform not only relationships but entire family legacies. Joseph's view that "God meant it for good" teaches us how to reframe our suffering.

The Divine Providence Theme

Throughout Joseph's story, we observe a consistent theme of divine providence: God working behind the scenes to fulfill his purposes through both good and bad circumstances in life. Like passengers on a roller coaster, we might not understand the track's design during each twist and turn, but we can trust that a loving Engineer guides an intentional design.

Joseph's declaration to his brothers, "You intended to harm me, but God intended it for good to accomplish what is now being done, the saving of many lives" (Genesis 50:20 NIV), serves as the central truth of his entire journey. What appeared to be a series of unfortunate events was actually God's carefully planned strategy to save not only Joseph's family but also whole nations from famine.

Conclusion

Jeff and I hope these studies will help you handle the ups and downs of daily life. When you experience the sudden shifts of life, remember Joseph's example. The same God who guided Joseph through his roller coaster journey is with you in yours.

Whether you are at the peak of success or facing tough times, whether you are being tempted, going through hardships, or dealing with relationship issues, Joseph's story reminds us that we are never alone on this path. God is not only with us; he is the one who created the way.

As you study these lessons, may you find the faith to trust God's providence, the strength to uphold your character, and the grace to forgive those who have wronged you. Most importantly, may you realize that even in life's most shocking moments of upheaval, God is working all things together for good for those who love him and are called according to his purpose.

As you read these studies, remember that your own story, like Joseph's, remains securely in God's capable hands, even when the ride feels overwhelming. The same God who guided Joseph through slavery, false imprisonment, and ultimate exaltation continues to write beautiful stories of redemption and purpose in the lives of those who trust him today.

CHAPTER 1

JOSEPH'S COAT OF MANY COLORS

The story of Joseph and his unique garment is one of the most well-known and misunderstood tales in biblical literature. It has fascinated people for centuries, inspiring many artistic works, from ancient commentaries to modern plays. However, beneath this familiar story lies a complex web of translation issues, cultural contexts, and scholarly debates that underscore the nuanced nature of biblical interpretation.

The story of Joseph begins with a statement that highlights the special place he held in his father's home: "Now Israel loved Joseph more than any other of his children, because he was the son of his old age" (Genesis 37:3). This opening declaration immediately sets up the central tension that will drive the entire story, introducing themes of favoritism, jealousy, and divine providence that run throughout the Joseph cycle.

The Context of Favoritism

When the story begins, Joseph is only seventeen years old, but he already holds a unique and privileged position within Jacob's household. The special place Joseph had in his father's house was not simply random; it grew from deeply personal and emotional reasons. Joseph was the firstborn son of his beloved wife Rachel, the woman Jacob loved more than her sister Leah (Genesis 29:18), Jacob's first wife. This favoritism was rooted in the complex marriage arrangements that marked Jacob's earlier life, in which he was tricked into marrying Leah before he was allowed to marry his true love, Rachel.

The dynamics of this polygamous household created an environment ripe for conflict. Rachel's long period of barrenness, followed by the joy of Joseph's birth and the subsequent birth of Benjamin, meant that these two sons held a special place in Jacob's heart that his other ten sons could never occupy. The emotional investment Jacob had in Rachel naturally extended to her children, creating an imbalance that would have far-reaching consequences for the entire family structure.

Jacob's favoritism was the cause of the bitterness between Joseph and his brothers, creating a pattern of family dysfunction that would last for generations. The favoritism was not just emotional; it was also evident in clear ways that the other family members could not ignore or hide. The text gives two main reasons for the negative feelings Joseph's brothers had toward him, each reflecting a different part of the growing family crisis.

The Sources of Brotherly Animosity

The first reason for the rising tension was that Joseph would bring reports to his father, informing him about what his brothers were doing: "Joseph told his father about the bad things his brothers were doing" (Genesis 37:2 GWN). This behavior, whether driven by genuine concern, youthful naivety, or a feeling of moral duty, made Joseph seem like an informant within the family. Or, as another translation puts it with even stronger language: "He accused his brethren to his father of a most wicked crime" (Genesis 37:2 DRA).

This behavior suggests several possibilities about Joseph's character and his role in the family. He might have genuinely been concerned about his brothers' actions and felt it was his duty to inform their father. Alternatively, his actions could reflect the privileged position he held, which gave him access to his father's attention and a sense of responsibility for family matters that his brothers did not share. The ambiguity in the text allows for multiple interpretations, but the result was clear: Joseph's brothers saw him as a spy and a threat to their independence.

The second reason for the brothers' hatred of Joseph was undeniable evidence of Jacob's favoritism: "Now Israel loved Joseph more than any other of his children" (Genesis 37:3). This love was not hidden or subtle but openly displayed, humiliating and marginalizing the other sons. It is possible that Jacob saw traits in Joseph —such as intelligence, spiritual sensitivity, or leadership ability —that reminded him of his younger self.

The psychological impact of such obvious favoritism cannot be overstated. In ancient Near Eastern culture, where family status determined inheritance rights, social standing, and future prospects, Jacob's preferential treatment of Joseph signified more than just an emotional slight; it threatened the very foundational aspects of the brothers' identity and security within the family structure.

Perhaps Jacob loved Joseph so profoundly because of the great love he had for Rachel, Joseph's mother, and this love continued to go beyond her death to include her children. However, this favoritism did not sit well with his other sons, creating a toxic environment of competition and resentment: "Joseph's brothers saw that their father loved him more than any of them. They hated Joseph and couldn't speak to him on friendly terms" (Genesis 37:4 GWN). The Hebrew text suggests that the brothers could not even speak to Joseph peacefully, showing that the family discord had reached a point where everyday communication had broken down.

The Symbolic Garment

Jacob showed his love and affection for Joseph most visibly and symbolically by giving him a special garment: "a coat of many colours" (Genesis 37:3 KJV). This gift was more than just an expression of paternal love; it was a public statement of Joseph's higher status within the family. This garment set Joseph apart from and above his brothers, marking him as different and superior in their father's eyes.

The practice of wearing distinctive clothing was a recognized tradition in ancient cultures, used to indicate rank, status, and authority. By providing Joseph with this special garment, Jacob was making a statement that extended beyond the family to the broader community. Everyone who saw Joseph wearing this unique clothing would understand his privileged position, and this public display of his status would have been deeply humiliating to his brothers.

This special distinction given to Joseph only worsened the hatred his brothers felt toward him, making him a more obvious target for their anger. The garment served as a constant reminder of their father's favoritism and how they saw themselves as less important. Every time Joseph wore this unique clothing, it emphasized the hierarchy that placed him above them, despite his younger age and their greater experience.

The Translation Controversy

The nature of Joseph's garment has been the subject of much discussion and disagreement among biblical scholars, translators, and interpreters for centuries. Popular imagination envisions Joseph's garment as a technicolor robe. This idea inspired cultural phenomena such as "Joseph and the Amazing Technicolor Dreamcoat," a musical with lyrics by Tim Rice and music by Andrew Lloyd Webber. This widespread belief has become so deeply ingrained in Christian and popular culture that it often overshadows scholarly efforts to understand the text's original meaning.

However, a detailed examination of the original Hebrew text and comparative linguistic analysis suggest that the color of the garment Jacob gave to Joseph was unlikely to have been the distinguishing feature. The idea that Joseph's coat had many colors came from a mistranslation that happened during the ancient translation process, specifically in the Septuagint (LXX), the Greek translation of the Hebrew Bible made in the third and second centuries BC.

The Septuagint (LXX) translates the words in Genesis 37:3 as "multicolored tunic." The English translation of the Septuagint by Lancelot C. L. Brenton renders Genesis 37:3 as follows: "And Jacob loved Joseph more than all his sons, because he was to him the son of old age; and he made for him a coat of many colors" (Genesis 37:3). The Vulgate adopted the Septuagint translation, the Latin version of the Bible translated by Jerome in the late fourth and early fifth centuries AC. The influence of these early translations was significant, as they laid the groundwork for later vernacular translations during the medieval and early modern periods.

The King James Bible, first published in 1611, followed the Septuagint tradition by translating the Hebrew words as "coat of many colours." Due to its significant impact on English-speaking Christianity, this translation became deeply ingrained in the religious mindset of millions of believers. The poetic and memorable phrase "coat of many colours" captured the imagination in a way that more precise but less vivid translations might not have.

Linguistic Analysis and Scholarly Debate

The Hebrew words behind the expression "coat of many colours" are *ketōnet passîm*, a phrase with an uncertain and disputed meaning that has challenged biblical scholars for generations. The complexity of this linguistic puzzle is evident in the wide variety of translations offered by different English versions of the Bible. The English translations differ significantly in how they translate *ketōnet passîm*, reflecting the ongoing scholarly uncertainty about its precise meaning.

This is how various versions of the Bible translate this Hebrew expression, demonstrating the range of scholarly opinion:

NRSV: "A long robe with sleeves." **KJV**: "A coat of many colours." **NIV**: "A richly ornamented robe." **CJB**: "A long-sleeved robe." **NAB**: "A long tunic." **NJB**: "A decorated tunic."

These different translations of the two Hebrew words demonstrate that scholars still disagree on the meaning of this expression, despite centuries of research and analysis. The variation in translation methods reflects different priorities: some translations focus on literal translation of each word, others emphasize cultural and contextual factors, and others aim to convey the likely functional meaning of the garment in its ancient context.

The interpretive challenge is made more difficult by the fact that the two words appear again in 2 Samuel 13:18 to describe a special garment worn by the daughters of kings: "Now [Tamar] was wearing a long robe with sleeves; for this is how the virgin daughters of the king were clothed in earlier times" (2 Samuel 13:18). This parallel usage provides important contextual information, as it links the *ketōnet passîm* to royal or noble status, indicating that the garment's importance lies not in its color, but in its social and political meaning.

Since the word *ketōnet passîm* is used in this royal context, the various Bible versions translate these two words as they did in Genesis 37:3, maintaining consistency in their interpretive approach. This parallel usage strongly suggests that the garment was associated with high social status, royal prerogatives, or ceremonial functions rather than simply being notable for its colorful appearance.

Mesopotamian Parallels and Archaeological Evidence

In his influential commentary on Genesis, E. A. Speiser used Mesopotamian literature and archaeological evidence to clarify the meaning of this complex expression. His approach marked a significant advancement in biblical studies by aiming to understand Hebrew terminology within the larger context of ancient Near Eastern culture and language. He wrote:

Cuneiform inventories may shed light on the garment in question. Among various types of clothing listed in the texts, there is one called *kitû pišannu*. The important thing there, besides the close external correspondence with the Heb. phrase, is that the article so described was a ceremonial robe which could be draped around statues of goddesses, and had various gold ornaments sewed onto it (Speiser 1964:290).

Speiser's comparative approach opened new avenues for understanding the Hebrew text by placing it within the broader cultural context of the ancient Near East. The Mesopotamian parallel he identified suggested that the garment in question was not simply an article of clothing but a ceremonial or religious object associated with divine or royal status. This interpretation would align with the garment's appearance in the context of royal daughters in 2 Samuel 13:18.

Therefore, the translations that use the phrase "ornamented robe" (NIV) or "decorated tunic" (NJB) follow Speiser's suggestion, which highlights the garment's decorative and ceremonial features rather than its color. This method indicates that the Hebrew text describes a garment characterized by its ornamentation, craftsmanship, or symbolic meaning rather than by its multiple colors.

Those versions that translate the two Hebrew words as "long sleeve" follow a different interpretive tradition, one rooted in Jewish exegesis that understands the word *pas* (as in *passîm*) to mean the palm of the hand. This interpretation emphasizes the garment's unusual construction, which completely covers the hands, making it unsuitable for manual labor and, therefore, a symbol of higher social status.

Critical Evaluation and Alternative Approaches

Speiser believed that Mesopotamian religious traditions might explain the two Hebrew words, based on an article by A. Leo Oppenheim, "The Golden Garments of the Gods," published in the *Journal of Near Eastern Studies* 8 (1949): 172–193. Oppenheim's study of ancient Mesopotamian religious practices offered valuable comparative material for understanding Hebrew terminology, but his work also showed the limitations of using such comparative approaches.

In his discussion of the garments used to dress the images of the goddesses, Oppenheim acknowledged that the meaning of the *pišannu* garment is not entirely clear, even within its Mesopotamian context. This admission highlights the inherent difficulties in using comparative linguistic evidence to resolve textual ambiguities. While such parallels can provide valuable insights, they cannot always provide definitive answers to interpretive questions.

In his commentary on 2 Samuel, P. Kyle McCarter critiqued Speiser's view, dismissing it because of the difficulty in conclusively linking the Mesopotamian garments with those mentioned in Genesis 37 and 2 Samuel 13. McCarter's skepticism exemplifies a more cautious approach to comparative linguistics, one that acknowledges the limitations of drawing conclusions from superficial similarities between languages and culturesSince the word *pas* can mean "extremities," referring to either hands or feet, McCarter developed an alternative interpretation that emphasizes the garment's unique construction rather than its decoration. He believed that the words *ketōnet passîm* refer to a garment that reaches the extremities of the body. He wrote: "It follows that *ketōnet passîm* means 'gown extending to the extremities'—i.e., hands or feet, since it is plural and not dual—and thus 'long gown with sleeves'" (McCarter 1984:319).

McCarter's interpretation highlights the garment's practical features, its unusual length, and the addition of sleeves, which would have set it apart from typical working clothes of the time. This view, adopted by many modern translations, shows a balance between linguistic accuracy and interpretive caution.

Social and Cultural Implications

Since the *ketōnet passîm* was a garment worn by the daughters of kings, as shown in 2 Samuel 13:18, it was likely associated with individuals of royal status, high-ranking palace officials, or those holding an elevated position in society. This connection to royalty and social prominence offers important insight into the meaning of Jacob's gift to Joseph.

The social implications of Jacob's gift go far beyond personal affection. In ancient Near Eastern society, clothing was a primary indicator of social status, occupation, and authority. By giving Joseph a garment linked to royalty, Jacob was making a public statement about his son's rank within the family and his hopes for Joseph's future role.

The fact that Jacob gave Joseph a *ketōnet passîm* indicates that he treated Joseph as a royal person, above all his other sons. This treatment would have had profound implications not only for family dynamics but also for the broader community's perception of Joseph and his brothers. The garment served as a visible symbol of Jacob's intentions regarding inheritance, succession, and family leadership.

The garment's royal associations also foreshadow Joseph's eventual rise to power in Egypt, where he would indeed hold a position comparable to royalty as Pharaoh's chief administrator. From a literary perspective, the *ketōnet passîm* serves as an early indication of Joseph's destined greatness, even as it immediately creates the conditions for his temporary downfall.

The Persistence of Popular Interpretation

Considering the scholarly consensus that *ketōnet passîm* means "a long robe with sleeves," a garment worn by royalty, how should we interpret Joseph's supposed coat of many colors? The phrase "coat of many colors" is so deeply embedded in the minds of Christians and the general public that it will be nearly impossible to convince them that Joseph did not have a technicolor coat.

This continued popular interpretation, despite scholarly correction, highlights several key factors in the transmission and reception of biblical texts. First, the King James Version's translation has had such a profound cultural impact that its language has become the standard for many believers, regardless of subsequent scholarly advancements. Second, the vivid and memorable image of a multicolored coat appeals to the imagination in ways that more accurate but less dramatic translations do not.

The popularity of cultural adaptations like "Joseph and the Amazing Technicolor Dreamcoat" has helped solidify the multicolored interpretation in the public mind. These artistic adaptations, while taking some liberties with the biblical story, have introduced the Joseph narrative to audiences who might not otherwise be familiar with it, but they have also reinforced misunderstandings about its original message.

Educational and pastoral challenges arise from this situation. Religious educators and clergy must carefully balance honoring cherished traditions with promoting an accurate understanding of biblical texts. The tension between widespread familiarity and scholarly precision highlights larger questions about how academic biblical studies connect with religious practice.

Conclusion and Implications

Thus, many people may eventually be convinced through careful study and explanation that Joseph had a coat with long sleeves, even though they will continue to believe that Joseph had a multicolored coat with long sleeves. This compromise reflects the difficulty of replacing deeply rooted cultural interpretations entirely, even when scholarly evidence clearly points elsewhere.

The story of Joseph's garment highlights several key principles for biblical interpretation and translation. First, it emphasizes the importance of understanding biblical texts within their original cultural and linguistic contexts rather than depending solely on later translation traditions. Second, it shows how translation decisions made centuries ago can continue to affect interpretation long after their initial basis has been questioned or abandoned.

Third, the ongoing debate over *ketōnet passîm* highlights the inherent limitations of biblical interpretation. Even with access to comparative linguistic evidence, archaeological materials, and sophisticated analytical methods, some textual questions may remain unresolved. Scholarly humility entails acknowledging these limitations while continually striving for the most accurate understanding possible.

The story of Joseph's garment also raises important questions about the relationship between academic scholarship and popular religious understanding. While scholars have a responsibility to pursue accurate interpretation, they must also consider how their findings can be communicated effectively to broader audiences without completely undermining cherished traditions.

Ultimately, this chapter emphasizes the ongoing importance of biblical scholarship for modern faith communities. By deepening our understanding of the original meaning and importance of biblical texts, scholarly research can enhance rather than diminish the spiritual and theological significance of these ancient stories. The true meaning of Joseph's *ketōnet passîm*—as a symbol of royal status and divine election—might be even more theologically meaningful than the popular image of a colorful coat.

Viewing Joseph's garment as a royal robe rather than just a colorful coat ties the story more closely to themes of divine providence, chosen status, and the fulfillment of God's promises common throughout the biblical narrative. In this way, correct interpretation does not lessen the text's importance but uncovers deeper levels of meaning that might otherwise go unnoticed.

CHAPTER 2

HOW CAN SOMEONE SELL
HIS OWN BROTHER TO THE EGYPTIANS?

"Then Judah said to his brothers, 'What profit is it if we kill our brother and conceal his blood? Come, let us sell him to the Ishmaelites, and not lay our hands on him, for he is our brother, our own flesh.' And his brothers agreed. When some Midianite traders passed by, they drew Joseph up, lifting him out of the pit, and sold him to the Ishmaelites for twenty shekels. And they took Joseph to Egypt" (Genesis 37:26–28).

The biblical story of Joseph's sale into slavery raises a profound moral question: How could his brothers sell their own flesh and blood into slavery in Egypt? This act of betrayal, driven by hatred and jealousy, reveals both the depths of human evil and the mysterious ways of divine providence.

The Roots of Fraternal Hatred

Joseph's tragic fate stemmed from deep-rooted family dysfunction in Jacob's household. Joseph was Jacob's favorite son because he was the son of Rachel, the woman Jacob truly loved (Genesis 29:18), and because "he was the son of his old age" (Genesis 37:3). Joseph held a special position that caused resentment among his brothers. Jacob's favoritism was clearly shown in the special garment he made for Joseph: "a long robe with sleeves" (Genesis 37:3).

This preferential treatment, along with Joseph's role as an informant who reported his brothers' misdeeds to their father (Genesis 37:2), created an atmosphere of intense hostility. The brothers' hatred was so deep that they could no longer have polite conversations with Joseph, with every interaction tainted by their barely concealed rage.

One day, when Joseph's brothers were tending their father Jacob's flock in Dothan, Joseph went toward where his brothers were. As he got closer, his brothers saw him from a distance. They mockingly said, "Here comes that dreamer" (Genesis 37:19). Then, the brothers plotted to kill him.

The brothers grabbed Joseph, stripped him of his special robe, and put him into an empty cistern to die a slow death. His older brother Reuben intervened and said to his brothers, "Let's not kill him" (Genesis 37:21 GWN). As they sat down to eat, they saw a caravan of Ishmaelites coming from Gilead on their way to Egypt. So, Judah, Joseph's brother, said to his brothers, "Let us not hurt him, because he is our brother, our own flesh and blood" (Genesis 37:27). His brothers agreed with Judah's proposition. They took Joseph out of the cistern and sold him to the Ishmaelites for twenty shekels of silver (Genesis 37:28). The Ishmaelites took Joseph to Egypt to be sold as a slave.

Joseph did not go to Egypt willingly. His brothers sold him to the Ishmaelites for twenty shekels of silver. The Ishmaelites then sold Joseph to Potiphar to serve as a slave in his house.

Historical Context: The Slave Trade to Egypt

The biblical story closely resembles ancient Near Eastern records. In his article, "How Can Someone Sell His Own Fellow to the Egyptians?" Ignacio Márquez Rowe points out that few cuneiform texts mention selling people into Egyptian slavery. He explains that during famines in the ancient Near East, men, women, and children sold themselves into slavery to survive (Rowe 2004:337). This is reflected in Egypt during the famine in Joseph's time. Joseph helped the Egyptians endure the famine, and in gratitude, they told him, "You have saved our lives; may it please my lord, we will be slaves to Pharaoh" (Genesis 47:25).

Rowe states that selling slaves to Egypt "finds many parallels in the cuneiform documentation," even though the evidence for "the way in which slaves were acquired in Egypt" is very limited. He cites a legal text from Ugarit (Rowe 2004:338), written in alphabetic cuneiform, which mentions that debtors who fail to pay their debts will be sold as slaves to Egypt.

If they (the debtors) leave for [another] country, they (the sureties) will pay 1,000 shekels of silver; and if they do not pay the 1,000 (shekels of silver), they will be sold to Egypt.

The person who fails to pay a debt, such as the sureties, is accountable for the debt. As a result, the penalty for unpaid debt was that the individual would be sold into slavery in Egypt.

Rowe discusses an Akkadian letter in which "the sender requests from the governor of Ugarit to intervene on his behalf concerning the redemption of his own slaves 'from the hands of Hehea the Egyptian.'" The letter does not specify why these individuals were sold into slavery in Egypt. Rowe suggests that they were sold either through a legal transaction or because they were captured after escaping from their master's house (Rowe 2004:338).

Rowe mentions another document that describes the fate of a man from Ugarit who was wrongly sold into slavery in Egypt (Rowe 2004:340). The governor of Ugarit wrote a letter to the king of Siyannu asking for the man's immediate release. The document includes a response to the request "in which the responsible king reports the observant release and delivery of the man of Ugarit into the hands of the person who would bring him back to his original condition or place." The document also contains the governor of Ugarit's reply, in which he mentions "the mutual duty to observe their agreement concerning misappropriation and sale of their subjects." Rowe translates the governor's reply as follows:

Now, as for you, should (some day) a subject of mine be sold there (i.e. in Ugarit) to the Egyptians, seize him and send him back to me (too)! Otherwise, you will set unseemly things between us. Indeed, how can someone sell his own fellow to the Egyptians?

In light of the governor's response, Rowe writes, "The rhetorical question addressed by the ruler of Siyannu, 'How can a man sell his own fellow to the Egyptians?', eloquently shows that the ideal or ethical rules of behavior were far from being followed by his, or his neighbor's, subjects. As a matter of fact, who has not asked himself over and over again in reading the story of Joseph, 'How could the sons of Jacob sell their own brother to Egypt?'" (Rowe 2004:342).

Rowe concludes, "This small group of cuneiform texts we have presented here is not a random sample but all that is so far available attesting to the sale of Levantine people, namely Ugaritians, to the Egyptians. We must admit, however, that despite the limited character of the evidence, the general historical and social picture it reveals, including some important details, is undoubtedly significant when compared to the description of Joseph's sale in the book of Genesis. The first general remark that can be made is that by the thirteenth and twelfth centuries before our era, there was a considerable demand for slaves in Egypt and a relatively important transfer of them from the Levant" (Rowe 2004:341).

Four Factors Behind the Brothers' Decision

In light of the parallels cited above, we ask again, "How could Joseph's brothers sell their own flesh and blood to the Egyptians? The text provides four reasons why Joseph's brothers sold him to Egypt.

Family Dysfunction

The toxic environment within Jacob's household created conditions ripe for such betrayal. Parental favoritism often breeds sibling rivalry, which can ultimately erupt into violence. The brothers' hatred for Joseph was so consuming that they felt no moral compunction about condemning him to a life of brutal servitude.

Financial Motivation

Second, it was for money. Joseph's brothers sold him to the Ishmaelites for twenty shekels of silver. According to Leviticus 27:5, twenty shekels was the price for a male slave between the ages of five and twenty years. According to Exodus 21:32, the price of an adult slave was thirty shekels. Since Joseph was only seventeen years old when he was sold to the Egyptians (Genesis 37:2), he was sold as a minor; thus, he was worth only twenty shekels. Jacob's brother got rid of the one they hated and made some profit in the process of getting rid of their brother. As Wenham writes, "For shepherds who might expect to earn, if employed by others, about eight shekels a year, the sale of Joseph represented a handy bonus" (Wenham 1994: 429).

Economic Demand

Third, it was because there was a great need for slaves in Egypt. It is not known when Joseph was sold to Egypt. If the exodus is dated to the 13th century BC, it is possible that Joseph came to Egypt during the Second Intermediate Period (1802–1550 BC), when the Thirteenth Dynasty ruled Egypt. It is also possible that Merneferre was the pharaoh at that time. Merneferre was the longest-reigning pharaoh of the Thirteenth Dynasty and a notable pyramid builder. The pyramid building required slave labor.

Israel spent four hundred years in Egypt. As slaves in Egypt, the Israelites built two supply cities for pharaoh, Pithom and Rameses (Exodus 1:11). Egypt was known as "the house of slavery" (Exodus 20:2) and "the iron furnace" (Deuteronomy 4:20). The Egyptians "were ruthless in all the tasks that they imposed" on their slaves" (Exodus 1:14). Rowe says that "to have been sentenced to slavery in Egypt in the Late Bronze Age stood for one of the most, if not the most, severe punishment, possibly comparable to, or worse than, imprisonment. It meant, therefore, forced and extremely dull and heavy labor" (Rowe 2004:343).

Divine Providence

Perhaps most significantly, the brothers' evil intentions became the instrument of God's sovereign plan. Through their treachery, Joseph was positioned to save not only Egypt during the coming famine but also his own family—the very people who had betrayed him. When Joseph later revealed his identity to his brothers, he explained: "You intended to harm me, but God intended it for good to accomplish what is now being done, the saving of many lives" (Genesis 50:20).

The Joseph narrative illustrates the profound mystery of divine providence—how God works through human evil to accomplish his purposes. The brothers' hatred and greed, the Ishmaelites' commercial opportunism, and Potiphar's need for household staff all became instruments in God's plan to preserve his covenant people during the great famine.

This does not excuse the brothers' actions or minimize the reality of Joseph's suffering. Rather, it reveals how God's sovereignty operates through human choices, bringing good from evil without negating moral responsibility. The brothers remained accountable for their wickedness, even as God used their sin to accomplish his redemptive purposes.

The apostle Paul captured this principle when he wrote: "We know that for those who love God all things work together for good, for those who are called according to his purpose" (Romans 8:28 ESV). The Joseph story stands as one of Scripture's most compelling illustrations of this divine truth—that even the darkest human betrayals cannot thwart God's ultimate purposes.

Conclusion

How could Joseph's brothers sell their own flesh and blood into Egyptian slavery? The answer lies at the crossroads of human depravity and divine sovereignty. Driven by jealousy, hatred, and greed, the brothers committed an act of unconscionable betrayal. Yet even their evil deed became the means by which God would save many lives, including their own.

This ancient story continues to speak to every generation, reminding us that while human evil is real and its consequences severe, God's purposes ultimately prevail. In the mystery of providence, even the most heinous acts of betrayal can become instruments of redemption in the hands of a sovereign God.

CHAPTER 3

JOSEPH: FAMILY DYSFUNCTION

The story of Joseph stands apart from the narratives of Abraham, Isaac, and Jacob in several significant ways. While God renewed his covenant promise to Isaac and Jacob, no such direct renewal appears in Joseph's account. Unlike the patriarchs who experienced direct divine communication through theophanies and angelic messengers, God speaks to Joseph primarily through dreams and providential circumstances. Through a series of dramatic reversals, moments of triumph and tragedy, elevation and humiliation, God guides Joseph's journey from favored son to prime minister of Egypt.

Joseph's formative years unfolded within a deeply fractured family system. His story reveals the devastating effects of parental favoritism and sibling rivalry, which ultimately lead to betrayal and near fratricide. As Brueggemann insightfully observes, this is fundamentally "the story of one son having been loved too much, one father loving too much, and eleven brothers feeling loved too little" (Brueggemann 1982:300).

Joseph's Coat: A Symbol of Favoritism

Joseph's story begins with Jacob settling permanently in Canaan, the land where his ancestors Abraham and Isaac had lived as wanderers. Unlike his forebears, who led a nomadic life, Jacob put down roots to grow his family and expand his pastoral work. The family business focused on shepherding, and all of Jacob's sons took part in this, except Benjamin, who was still too young for such duties.

As the owner of extensive flocks, Jacob relied on his sons to manage his livestock. Joseph, seventeen years old at the time, worked alongside his brothers in tending their father's sheep. Joseph held a unique position in the family as the firstborn son of Rachel, Jacob's beloved wife. When Rachel died in childbirth while delivering Benjamin, Joseph became even more precious to his father as a living reminder of his cherished wife. The text explicitly states that Jacob "loved Joseph more than any of his other sons" because "he was the son of his old age" (Genesis 37:3).

Jacob's deep love for Joseph showed itself clearly: he gave him "a richly ornamented robe" (Genesis 37:3 NIV). The Hebrew phrase *ketōnet passîm* has puzzled scholars for centuries, leading to various translations. The King James Version, following the Septuagint, calls it "a coat of many colours," while the New Revised Standard Version describes it as "a long robe with sleeves," reflecting early Christian tradition.

The expression *ketōnet passîm* appears only once elsewhere in the Hebrew Bible, in 2 Samuel 13:18-19, where it describes the garment worn by Tamar, King David's daughter. This parallel suggests that Joseph's robe was indeed a garment of distinction, befitting royalty or nobility. The NIV's translation as "a richly ornamented robe" likely captures the essence of this special garment, which served as a visible symbol of Jacob's exceptional love for Joseph and his elevated status within the family hierarchy.

Joseph's Dreams: Divine Revelation Amid Family Strife

Jacob's household represented a complex web of relationships marked by division and tension. With two wives and two concubines, the family dynamic was inherently complicated. Joseph, as the son of Jacob's most beloved wife, became the target of his brothers' intense hatred, a hatred so profound that the biblical narrative emphasizes it three times for dramatic effect.

The pattern of favoritism plaguing Jacob's family had deep roots. As Wenham observes, "Favoritism has a long pedigree in Jacob's family. Isaac loved Esau more than Jacob, Rebekah loved Jacob more than Esau, and most pertinently, Jacob loved Rachel more than Leah (25:28; 29:30). His old love for Rachel is now transferred to Joseph, Rachel's son" (Wenham 1994:424). When the brothers witnessed their father's preferential treatment of Joseph, their resentment intensified to the point where they could no longer maintain even basic civility toward him.

The brothers' animosity toward Joseph stemmed partly from his role as an informant. Joseph regularly "brought their father a bad report about them" (Genesis 37:2 NIV), chronicling his brothers' misconduct while they tended the flocks away from home. Some commentators have criticized Joseph as a mere tattletale, with Wenham suggesting that "Joseph misrepresented his brothers to his father, his father believed him, and his brothers hated him for his lies" (Wenham 1994:424). Hamilton similarly speculates that "for some undisclosed reason, Joseph maligned his brothers to Jacob" (Hamilton 1995:383).

However, a more charitable interpretation arises when we consider that Jacob specifically asked for these reports. When sending Joseph to check on his brothers, Jacob told him to "come back and bring me a report" (Genesis 37:14). Joseph was carrying out his father's direct order by giving accurate accounts of his brothers' activities in the field. Instead of malicious gossip, Joseph's reports probably showed genuine concerns about his brothers' work ethic and behavior. Sadly, his faithful obedience to his father's wishes only made his brothers' resentment worse.

The situation reached a crisis point when Joseph experienced his first prophetic dream. In this vision (Genesis 37:5–8), Joseph saw his brothers' grain sheaves bowing down to his sheaf in the field. When Joseph shared this dream, "they hated him even more for his dreams and his words" (Genesis 37:8). The dream's obvious implication, that Joseph would one day rule over his brothers, struck them as insufferably arrogant.

Joseph's second dream proved even more provocative (Genesis 37:9–10). This time, the sun, moon, and eleven stars bowed down before him, clearly representing his parents and brothers submitting to his authority. Even Jacob rebuked Joseph for this dream, though the text notes that he "kept the matter in mind," suggesting he recognized its potential significance.

Why would Joseph share these inflammatory dreams with his already hostile family? Rather than displaying arrogance or naivety, Joseph likely understood that these were divine revelations requiring disclosure. As Brueggemann explains, "Though hidden in the form of a dream, silent and not at all visible, the listener will understand that the dream is the unsettling work of Yahweh." Joseph recognized that God intended for his family to know these things because "his dream will save the whole family. Without Joseph, there is no future" (Brueggemann 1982: 298–299).

These dreams were prophetic visions revealing God's sovereign plan for Jacob's family. As Isaiah declares, Yahweh orchestrates history to accomplish his redemptive purposes: "I am God, and there is no other; I am God, and there is no one like me, declaring the end from the beginning and from ancient times things not yet done, saying, 'My purpose shall stand, and I will fulfill my intention'" (Isaiah 46:9–10). Joseph's dreams foreshadowed events that would ultimately preserve his entire family and advance God's covenant promises.

Joseph Sold into Egypt: From Favored Son to Slave

Despite Joseph's good intentions in sharing his divine revelations, his words were met with hostility. His brothers saw the dreams as threats to their status and pride, unable to accept submitting to their hated younger brother. Their solution was simple and cruel: eliminate the dreamer to destroy his dreams.

The opportunity for revenge presented itself when Jacob sent Joseph to check on his brothers, who were grazing the flocks near Shechem. Following his usual routine, Jacob instructed Joseph to assess his sons' well-being and the condition of the livestock, then "come back and bring me a report" (Genesis 37:14). Joseph had completed this task before, but his earlier reports only increased his brothers' hostility.

When Joseph arrived at Shechem, he discovered his brothers had moved on to Dothan. A helpful stranger directed him to their new location, unknowingly facilitating the unfolding drama. As Joseph approached Dothan, his brothers spotted him from a distance and immediately began plotting his demise. Their contemptuous greeting, "Here comes that dreamer" (literally "master of dreams" in Hebrew), dripped with sarcasm and malice.

The brothers' immediate reaction reveals the depth of their dysfunction: "Come now, let's kill him" (Genesis 37:20 GWN). Their murderous intent focused specifically on destroying Joseph's dreams: "and we shall see what will become of his dreams" (Genesis 37:20). They believed that killing the dreamer would prevent the dreams' fulfillment, demonstrating their fundamental misunderstanding of divine sovereignty.

Reuben, Jacob's firstborn, intervened to prevent immediate bloodshed. Rather than openly opposing his brothers, he proposed what appeared to be an alternative method of disposal: "Don't shed any blood. Throw him into this cistern here in the desert" (Genesis 37:22 NIV). The cistern, a dry water storage pit, would become Joseph's tomb, allowing him to die slowly from exposure and dehydration while technically avoiding the guilt of direct murder.

Reuben's true motivation, however, was to save Joseph's life. His secret plan was to return later to rescue Joseph from the cistern and restore him to their father. Unfortunately, this noble intention was thwarted by subsequent events.

After stripping Joseph of his ornate robe and casting him into the empty cistern, the brothers callously sat down to eat while their brother faced death nearby. Their meal was interrupted by the sight of an approaching caravan, Ishmaelite merchants traveling the trade route to Egypt. Judah, seizing the moment, proposed a more profitable solution: "What will we gain if we kill our brother and cover up his blood? Come, let's sell him to the Ishmaelites" (Genesis 37:26–27 NIV).

The transaction was quickly completed. Joseph was sold for twenty pieces of silver, the standard price for a young slave, and the caravan continued toward Egypt with their human cargo. The brothers had eliminated their problem while turning a profit, demonstrating their complete moral bankruptcy.

When Reuben returned to execute his rescue plan, he discovered the empty cistern and realized Joseph was gone. His reaction, tearing his clothes in grief and despair, showed genuine anguish over the failed rescue attempt. The brothers then collaborated on an elaborate deception to explain Joseph's disappearance to their father. They slaughtered a goat, soaked Joseph's distinctive robe in its blood, and presented the evidence to Jacob with the false suggestion that a wild animal had killed Joseph.

Jacob's response to the fabricated news was devastating. Despite his children's attempts to comfort him, he remained inconsolable, declaring his intention to "I will go to my grave mourning for my son" (Genesis 37:35 NLT). The family's dysfunction had reached its tragic culmination, leaving a father broken by grief and brothers bound together by their shared secret.

Providence Through Adversity

Joseph's story is one of the most powerful in the Old Testament about human flaws turned around by divine intervention. Through this tale, we see how favoritism, jealousy, and sibling rivalry cause havoc in a family. Joseph's early life, marked by his brothers' hatred, threats of death, and eventual betrayal into slavery, could have broken many people.

Yet Joseph's dreams pointed toward a future that transcended present circumstances. The very hatred and jealousy that led to his enslavement would ultimately serve God's purposes for preserving Jacob's family and advancing his covenant promises. Through the brothers' evil intentions, God orchestrated events that would position Joseph to save not only his family but also entire nations from famine.

The presence of God with Joseph throughout his trials shows that divine providence often works through human dysfunction and evil rather than despite them. Amid family betrayal and personal hardships, Joseph experienced God's protection and guidance, paving the way for one of history's most remarkable stories of redemption and reconciliation. The dysfunctional family that nearly destroyed Joseph would ultimately be preserved and blessed through the very son they aimed to eliminate.

The Old Testament Speaks to the Church

On August 22, 2021, my pastor, Jeff Griffin, senior pastor of The Compass Church in Naperville, Illinois, delivered a compelling sermon on Genesis 37:1–36, entitled "Joseph – Family Dysfunction." Drawing from the rich narrative of Joseph's early life, Jeff challenged the congregation to see beyond the surface-level family drama to discover profound truths about God's sovereignty and grace.

In his sermon conclusion, Jeff addressed the universal reality of family dysfunction while offering hope through divine providence. He acknowledged that while family life is one of God's most beautiful gifts, it also presents some of life's most significant challenges. Every family, regardless of socioeconomic status, cultural background, or spiritual maturity, struggles with relational difficulties, unmet expectations, and broken trust. Joseph's family serves as both a warning and a source of encouragement for believers navigating their own family challenges.

From Joseph's tumultuous early experiences, Jeff extracted three transformative lessons that speak directly to contemporary family struggles and individual spiritual journeys.

Lesson One: God's Sovereignty Over Imperfect Families

The first lesson Jeff emphasized is perhaps the most liberating for believers struggling with family shame: God can and will use imperfect families to accomplish his purposes in the world. This truth shatters the myth that God only works through pristine, harmonious families with perfectly ordered relational dynamics.

Jacob's household was a masterclass in dysfunction. Favoritism, deception, jealousy, and attempted murder marked their interactions. Yet this broken family became the foundation for the nation of Israel, God's chosen instrument of reconciliation and blessing to all nations. The twelve sons who conspired against Joseph ultimately became the patriarchs of the twelve tribes, carrying God's covenant promises to future generations.

This reality offers profound comfort to believers who come from troubled backgrounds or who currently struggle with family

47

relationships. God's redemptive plan does not require perfect families; it transforms imperfect ones. The same divine grace that worked through Jacob's dysfunctional household continues to operate in contemporary families marked by addiction, abuse, neglect, or relational breakdown. God's purposes are not thwarted by human failure but often advanced through it.

Modern believers need not wait until their families achieve relational perfection before expecting God to work through them. Instead, they can trust that God's power is often most clearly displayed through broken vessels, demonstrating that his grace is sufficient for every human weakness and family dysfunction.

Lesson Two: Understanding the Roots of Relational Conflict

The second lesson Jeff highlighted addresses the primary source of conflict within Joseph's family: sibling rivalry and its devastating consequences. This ancient problem continues to plague contemporary families, manifesting as competition, jealousy, and resentment among family members.

Joseph's brothers' jealousy was not just about a colorful coat or special treatment; it reflected deeper issues of identity, security, and belonging. They saw Joseph's dreams as threats to their own importance and future hopes. When Joseph shared his visions of greatness, his brothers took them as arrogant boasting rather than divine messages. Their growing hatred eventually led them to consider murder, showing how unchecked jealousy can destroy family bonds and cause devastating outcomes.

This pattern occurs in many families today. Children often vie for their parents' attention and approval. Siblings compare achievements, looks, and life situations. Adult children feel inadequate when others appear more successful or fortunate. These patterns can last for decades, causing deep wounds and broken relationships.

Jeff's insight urges believers to reflect on their own hearts for feelings of jealousy and competition. Instead of seeing others' blessings as threats to their worth, Christians are encouraged to rejoice in each other's successes and rely on God's unique plan for everyone. The solution to sibling rivalry, whether literal or figurative, comes from recognizing a secure identity in Christ and appreciating God's abundant grace for all his children.

Lesson Three: God's Individual Plans Within Corporate Purposes

The third lesson Jeff drew from Joseph's story reveals a profound truth about divine election and blessing: God has specific plans for each person, even when his purposes appear to favor one person over others. This principle addresses one of the most challenging aspects of family dynamics, the apparent inequality of divine blessing and calling.

Throughout biblical history, God's pattern involved selecting specific individuals for particular roles and responsibilities. Abraham was chosen from among his brothers to receive the covenant promise. Isaac, rather than Ishmael, inherited the patriarchal blessing. Jacob, not Esau, carried forward the divine promise. This pattern of divine selection often causes tension and resentment among family members who feel overlooked or undervalued.

In Joseph's case, his brothers' jealousy partly came from their belief that God had chosen their younger brother over them. They viewed Joseph's dreams as proof of divine favoritism that threatened their own importance and future. Their response was to try to stop God's plan by harming Joseph, showing a fundamental misunderstanding of divine sovereignty and grace.

However, Jeff's crucial insight shows that God's blessing of Joseph did not mean he had forgotten or abandoned his brothers. When Jacob blessed his sons in Genesis 49, he revealed God's specific plans for each of them. They would become the leaders of the twelve tribes of Israel, each with unique roles and responsibilities in God's redemptive plan. Their apparent disadvantage was actually part of a larger divine strategy that included them as key participants.

Joseph's special blessing, receiving the birthright that typically belonged to the firstborn, came through his two sons, Ephraim and Manasseh, who became separate tribes in Israel. This gave Joseph a double portion of the inheritance, fulfilling the Mosaic law regarding the firstborn's privilege (Deuteronomy 21:17). Meanwhile, Reuben, the actual firstborn, forfeited his birthright through moral failure (Genesis 49:3–4), demonstrating that God's blessings often transcend human expectations and traditional patterns.

Jeff concluded his message with a powerful application for contemporary believers: God has a unique plan for every person, and Christians should celebrate both their own journeys and those of others. This principle addresses the universal human tendency toward comparison and competition that can poison relationships and rob individuals of joy and contentment.

In our culture that values achievement, the urge to compare our worth to others' successes is especially strong. Social media amplifies this by showing curated glimpses of others' lives that seem more successful, blessed, or fulfilling than ours. Like Joseph's brothers, we can become consumed with envy over what others have, losing sight of God's unique plans for our own lives.

Jeff's counsel presents a different view: instead of stressing over others' blessings or comparing our situations to theirs, believers should concentrate on recognizing and embracing God's specific calling for their lives. Every person's story is valuable to God, designed with intentionality and purpose that go beyond human understanding.

This does not mean we should become self-absorbed or indifferent to others' well-being. Instead, it calls us to a mature faith that can both celebrate others' successes and remain confident in God's personal love and plans for our lives. When we truly understand that God's resources are unlimited and his love is personal, we can sincerely rejoice in others' blessings without feeling threatened or diminished.

Jeff's sermon on Joseph's family struggles offers hope for believers battling challenging family ties and personal feelings of inadequacy or jealousy. The message reminds us that God's plans are not upset by human mistakes but often move forward through them. Broken families can become channels of divine blessing. Sibling rivalry and relational conflicts, though painful, can be turned into chances for growth and reconciliation.

Most importantly, God's love and purposes are both corporate and individual. He works through families and communities while maintaining specific, loving plans for each person within those relationships. The challenge for contemporary believers is to trust in God's sovereignty while actively participating in his redemptive work through their own families and communities.

Joseph's story ultimately points toward the greater narrative of redemption that God continues to write through imperfect people and dysfunctional families. In Christ, we find both the security to celebrate others' blessings and the confidence to embrace our own unique calling, knowing that God's grace is sufficient for every family dysfunction and personal inadequacy we may face.

CHAPTER 4

JOSEPH: CAREER SUCCESS

The story of Joseph stands as one of the most compelling narratives in ancient literature, weaving together elements of betrayal, perseverance, and ultimate triumph. What captivates readers about Joseph's account is not merely its dramatic plot twists between good and evil, but rather the profound demonstration of divine providence working behind the scenes. God orchestrated the events of Joseph's life to accomplish his greater purpose: preparing a nation that would serve as his instrument for reconciling humanity to himself.

However, many readers fail to fully appreciate the extraordinary adversity Joseph endured before ascending to become Egypt's prime minister. Joseph was only seventeen years old (Genesis 37:2) when his brothers' treacherous actions led to his sale to traveling merchants. Thirteen long years would pass before he stood before Pharaoh at the age of thirty (Genesis 41:46) to offer his crucial counsel regarding the approaching famine.

During these thirteen transformative years, Joseph experienced profound loss and hardship. He was sold as a slave to Potiphar, one of Pharaoh's high-ranking officials who served as captain of the guard (Genesis 39:1). Later, he was imprisoned on false charges of sexual assault. Throughout this period, he lived as a foreigner in a culture vastly different from his own, stripped of his family, his freedom, and everything familiar. Confronted with such overwhelming adversities and deprived of his father's love, Joseph could easily have surrendered to despair and accepted his circumstances as unchangeable fate.

Joseph's Remarkable Career Journey

Despite years of enslavement and imprisonment in a dungeon, Joseph demonstrated extraordinary strength of character. He possessed an exceptional capacity for enduring hardship and an ability to thrive despite adversity. Throughout his ordeal, Joseph consistently proved himself a faithful servant to Potiphar and a trustworthy worker during his imprisonment. God's presence sustained Joseph, empowering him to succeed in every endeavor.

Throughout his lifetime, Joseph held four distinct positions, one in Canaan and three in Egypt. In each role, he achieved success by bringing a unique perspective to his responsibilities. Joseph approached every employment opportunity as a chance to demonstrate faithful service and to benefit others.

Joseph as Shepherd

Joseph's first position was in his father's enterprise. Jacob maintained large flocks, and Joseph fulfilled whatever duties his father assigned: "Joseph, being seventeen years old, was shepherding the flock with his brothers" (Genesis 37:2).

The Hebrew construction of this verse presents an intriguing ambiguity. The standard English translation renders it as "shepherding the flocks with his brothers," interpreting the Hebrew word *'et* as a preposition meaning "with." However, *'et* can also function as a direct object marker, which would yield the translation that Joseph "was shepherding his brothers."

The Hebrew text suggests that Jacob appointed Joseph as supervisor over his brothers. This interpretation explains why Jacob sent Joseph to check on his brothers' welfare and the condition of the flocks, then report back to him (Genesis 37:14). As Hamilton observes, "this verse provides an excellent introduction to the Joseph story. . . . What Joseph is doing during his teenage years is exactly what he will be doing in his adult life—caring and providing for those who are dependent on him" (Hamilton 1995:382).

Joseph as a Slave in Egypt

After merchants purchased Joseph, they "sold him in Egypt to Potiphar, one of Pharaoh's officials, the captain of the guard" (Genesis 37:36). Joseph began his Egyptian experience as a common slave acquired in the slave market. Initially serving as a household servant in Potiphar's residence, Joseph quickly distinguished himself through his competence and integrity. Recognizing Joseph's exceptional qualities as a faithful worker, Potiphar promoted him, making him overseer in his house and over all that he had (Genesis 39:5).

As estate manager for Potiphar, Joseph became a conduit of divine blessing. "The LORD blessed the Egyptian's house for Joseph's sake; the blessing of the LORD was on all that he had, in house and field" (Genesis 39:5).

Joseph as a Prisoner

A false accusation led to Joseph's imprisonment in the facility where Pharaoh's enemies were confined. Joseph entered prison as a common criminal, falling from a position of authority to one of complete humiliation. Yet even in these degrading circumstances, Joseph became a model prisoner and established a positive relationship with the warden. Recognizing Joseph's reliability and responsibility, the warden placed him "in charge of all the prisoners who were in prison" (Genesis 39:22). Remarkably, Joseph entered prison as a common criminal and emerged as the deputy warden.

Joseph as a Government Official

Joseph's elevation from prisoner to government official required considerable time, "two whole years" (Genesis 41:1). When summoned before Pharaoh, Joseph came as a dream interpreter (Genesis 41:15). After demonstrating his interpretive abilities, Joseph transitioned into the role of strategic consultant, presenting Pharaoh with a comprehensive plan for managing the coming famine. "The plan seemed good to Pharaoh and to all his officials" (Genesis 41:37 NIV). Impressed by Joseph's proposal, Pharaoh declared, "You shall be over my house, and all my people shall order themselves as you command; only with regard to the throne will I be greater than you" (Genesis 41:40). In this dramatic transformation, Joseph progressed from imprisoned dream interpreter to Egypt's second most powerful leader.

Working for Potiphar

Joseph arrived at Potiphar's household involuntarily, sold by his brothers to merchants who subsequently traded him in Egypt's slave market. His purchaser was likely a wealthy and influential government official, given his status and ownership of numerous slaves.

Joseph's new master, Potiphar, held the title "an officer of Pharaoh, the captain of the guard" (Genesis 39:1). This designation indicates not a minor servant but a high-ranking official who exercised significant administrative authority within the Egyptian government.

Most slaves in ancient slave markets were war captives or individuals who had sold themselves and their families to satisfy debts. Joseph's situation differed; he was sold purely for profit. Potiphar probably purchased Joseph for domestic duties or property maintenance work.

Upon entering Potiphar's service, Joseph was described as "a successful man" (Genesis 39:2). The Hebrew term literally translates to "a man who succeeds." Joseph's success stemmed from the fact that "the LORD was with him" (Genesis 39:3). The Genesis writer emphasizes twice that Yahweh accompanied Joseph (39:2, 3), and consequently, Yahweh blessed the Egyptian's house for Joseph's sake (Genesis 39:5).

When Potiphar observed that Yahweh was with Joseph and that everything he undertook prospered, he promoted Joseph from household servant to estate manager. The text does not specify how Potiphar "saw" Yahweh's presence with Joseph. Since Joseph understood that Yahweh had brought him to Egypt (Genesis 45:5), Potiphar may have witnessed Joseph's private worship practices.

Working for the Prison Warden

While serving in Potiphar's household, Joseph faced false accusations of attempted rape from his master's wife. This malicious charge resulted in Joseph's imprisonment. The Hebrew term for this prison, "the roundhouse," likely refers to a dungeon beneath the royal palace where Pharaoh's enemies were detained

(Genesis 39:20). Joseph's confinement underscored the seriousness of his alleged offense against a high-ranking official.

The biblical narrative twice emphasizes that Yahweh remained with Joseph during his imprisonment (Genesis 39:21, 23). While incarcerated, "The LORD reached out to him with his unchanging love and gave him protection" (Genesis 39:21 GWN). God's presence transformed the prison warden into Joseph's ally.

Joseph became an exemplary prisoner. The warden, recognizing Joseph's reliability and trustworthiness in managing prison affairs, "put Joseph in charge of all those held in the prison, and he was made responsible for all that was done there" (Genesis 39:22 NIV).

The foundation of Joseph's success, both in Potiphar's house and in prison, was Yahweh's abiding presence. Because Joseph acknowledged God's presence in his life, he approached his work diligently and served his masters faithfully.

Joseph succeeded in all his endeavors because "the LORD was with him" (Genesis 39:3). Von Rad noted that Yahweh's constant presence with Joseph "implies quite real protection and promotion in the matters of his external life, not, to be sure, protection from distress, but rather in the midst of distress" (von Rad 1973:367).

The Theology of Work

During Joseph's time in Egypt, he held various positions. Each position held significance in God's eyes because it contributed to his greater purpose of preparing a nation to collaborate with him in blessing all nations.

Work constitutes an essential element of God's design for creation. When God created humanity, he assigned humans the responsibility to continue the creative work he had initiated: "God created humankind in his image, in the image of God he created them; male and female he created them. God blessed them, and God said to them, 'Be fruitful and multiply, and fill the earth and subdue it; and have dominion over the fish of the sea and over the birds of the air and over every living thing that moves upon the earth'" (Genesis 1:27–28).

From creation's beginning, God intended his creatures to work: "The LORD God took the man and put him in the Garden of Eden to farm the land and to take care of it" (Genesis 2:15 GWN). God also commanded his people to work: "Six days you shall labor and do all your work" (Exodus 20:9).

God calls individuals and equips them with the skills and guidance they need for their vocations. He called Noah to build the ark, appointed Joseph to a position of political leadership in Egypt, and summoned Bezalel and Oholiab as master craftsmen, endowing them with the skills required for tabernacle construction (Exodus 31:1–6).

In his examination of work theology, William Messenger observes: "We must acknowledge God's command that everyone work to the degree they are able. God's command or call to work comes at the very beginning of the Bible, where God chooses to involve human beings in the work of creation, production, and sustenance. Work continues through to the very end of the Bible. There is work in the garden of Eden, and there is work in the New Heaven and New Earth" (Messenger 2011:171–172).

Joseph's career trajectory, from shepherd to slave, from prisoner to prime minister, illustrates how divine providence can transform even the most adverse circumstances into opportunities for service and success. His story demonstrates that faithful work, regardless of circumstances, becomes a vehicle for God's blessing and purpose. Through Joseph's varied professional experiences, we observe that meaningful work extends beyond personal advancement to encompass service to others and participation in God's redemptive plan for humanity.

The Old Testament Speaks to the Church

On August 29, 2021, my pastor, Jeff Griffin, Senior Pastor of The Compass Church in Naperville, Illinois, delivered a powerful sermon on Genesis 39:1–6, 20–23 titled "Joseph: Career Success."

In his sermon, Jeff emphasized that Joseph achieved success in every position he held, attributing this remarkable consistency to one fundamental truth: God was with him. While Joseph undoubtedly possessed a strong work ethic, the greatest key to his professional success was divine presence and partnership. Joseph understood that God was intimately involved in his work, playing a crucial role in everything he accomplished for his various masters.

Jeff identified three distinct yet interconnected roles that God played in Joseph's professional life, each offering profound insights for contemporary believers.

God as Joseph's Partner

The Lord stood alongside Joseph as his constant companion and co-worker, literally present right by his side, doing the work with him (Genesis 39:2, 21). This partnership proved especially meaningful given Joseph's circumstances. Far from his family, immersed in a foreign culture, and separated from his homeland, Joseph could have felt utterly alone and abandoned. Instead, he experienced God's tangible presence in his daily work environment.

This divine partnership transformed Joseph's workplace from a place of exile into a sanctuary of fellowship with the Almighty. Joseph did not just work for earthly masters; he worked alongside his Heavenly Father. This partnership offered comfort, guidance, and strength that no human relationship could provide, showing that God's presence can make any workplace holy, regardless of its challenges or limitations.

God as Joseph's Passion

The abiding presence of God in Joseph's life became the driving motivation behind his exceptional work performance. Conventional workplace motivators did not fuel Joseph's passion for excellence. He received no monetary compensation for his labor as a slave. His positions held no inherent nobility or prestige; he was, after all, merely a servant working for his masters.

Yet Joseph approached his work with extraordinary dedication and enthusiasm. The source of this passion was his recognition that he was ultimately serving God through his earthly responsibilities. The apostle Paul captured this profound truth in words that perfectly explain Joseph's work ethic: "Whatever you do, work at it with all your heart, as working for the Lord, not for men" (Colossians 3:23 NIV).

Joseph's example demonstrates that when we understand our work as service to God, our motivation shifts from external rewards to internal worship. Every task becomes an act of devotion, every responsibility an opportunity to honor the Lord. This divine passion enables believers to maintain excellence and integrity even under challenging circumstances or unrewarding positions.

God as Joseph's Power

The Lord served as Joseph's source of strength, providing the supernatural ability needed to excel in his responsibilities. Scripture clearly states that it was the LORD who made everything Joseph did prosper (Genesis 39:3, 23). Joseph's success was not merely the result of natural talent, favorable circumstances, or human effort; it was the direct result of divine empowerment.

This divine power manifested in multiple ways: wisdom to make sound decisions, favor with supervisors and colleagues, insight to solve complex problems, and resilience to overcome setbacks. When Joseph interpreted dreams, managed estates, or administered prison operations, he operated not in his own strength but through God's power working in and through him.

The recognition of God as his source of power kept Joseph humble in success and hopeful in adversity. He understood that his achievements were not personal accomplishments to boast about, but rather divine gifts to be stewarded faithfully.

Jeff concluded his sermon with a compelling challenge for contemporary Christians: invite God to become an active participant in your professional life. This invitation involves several practical commitments:

Dependence in Difficulty: Christians must learn to lean on God during challenging circumstances, stressful situations, and overwhelming demands. Rather than relying solely on human resources or personal strength, believers should turn to their heavenly Father for wisdom, peace, and supernatural provision.

Partnership in Power: Christians need to recognize their dependence on God's power to accomplish their daily tasks effectively. Whether leading meetings, serving customers, creating products, or solving problems, believers can access divine strength that transcends human limitations.

Integration of Faith: Christians should invite God into every aspect of their daily lives, including their professional responsibilities. Work should not be compartmentalized as a secular activity separate from spiritual life but rather understood as a sacred calling where faith and profession intersect.

Transformation Through Presence: When Christians genuinely invite God to be part of their work, Jeff emphasized, "everything changes." Divine presence transforms workplace relationships, decision-making processes, stress management, and overall job satisfaction. Work becomes worship, colleagues become ministry opportunities, and challenges become occasions for spiritual growth.

Joseph's example demonstrates that professional success, when rooted in divine partnership, passion, and power, becomes a testimony to God's faithfulness and a blessing to all those we serve. His story encourages modern believers to view their careers not merely as means of livelihood but as platforms for experiencing and expressing God's presence in the world.

The key to replicating Joseph's success lies not in emulating his techniques but in cultivating his relationship with God. When believers invite the Lord to be their partner, passion, and power in the workplace, they position themselves to experience the same divine favor and supernatural success that characterized Joseph's remarkable career journey.

CHAPTER 5

JOSEPH: OVERCOMING TEMPTATION

When Joseph arrived in Egypt as a slave, he was purchased by Potiphar, an influential Egyptian official, and became a servant in his household. The Lord blessed Joseph abundantly, and he quickly found favor with his master, who eventually placed him in charge of everything he owned. Joseph was young, handsome, and well-built (Genesis 39:6), qualities that would soon put him in a precarious situation, one that threatened to destroy his reputation, his relationship with his master, and potentially his very life.

Every day, people face temptations in various forms: food, money, sex, power, and countless others. Joseph encountered a temptation that seemed nearly irresistible. The crucial moment came down to a fundamental choice: would he surrender to desire or remain steadfast in his convictions? Would he betray the trust his master had placed in him by giving in to sexual temptation, or would he stay strong in his faith and remain faithful to God? Joseph's experience serves as a powerful paradigm for how to face temptation and achieve victory through God's help.

Joseph in Potiphar's House

The narrative in Genesis 39:1–5 provides insight into Joseph's life in Potiphar's household. After being transported to Egypt, the Ishmaelites sold Joseph as a slave to Potiphar, who served as both an important government official under Pharaoh and captain of the guard. Though Joseph had been torn from his family, he was not truly alone in Potiphar's house, "the LORD was with Joseph" (Genesis 39:2-3).

Because the LORD's presence was with Joseph, God prospered him and granted him success in everything he did for his master. Joseph's accomplishments were so impressive that even Potiphar could see them clearly. Potiphar realized that Joseph's God was with him and that this divine presence made everything Joseph touched successful. Although the biblical text does not explicitly explain how Potiphar recognized this spiritual truth, it's likely that Joseph's devotion to God was so evident that Potiphar could see the link between Joseph's faith and his extraordinary success.

Recognizing that his household's prosperity flowed directly from the blessing of Joseph's God, Potiphar promoted Joseph from a mere slave to a trusted servant with significant responsibility. He placed Joseph in charge of his entire household and all his possessions. "From that time on, the LORD blessed the Egyptian's household because of Joseph. The LORD's blessing extended to everything Potiphar owned, both in his house and in his fields" (Genesis 39:1–5).

Joseph was unmarried, well-built, and strikingly handsome (Genesis 39:6), physical attributes he had inherited from his mother Rachel, who "was lovely in form and beautiful" (Genesis 29:17). Joseph's attractive appearance caught the attention of Potiphar's wife, who was likely herself a beautiful woman of considerable wealth and social standing. Drawn to this handsome Hebrew servant, she began attempting to seduce him, boldly asking him to sleep with her.

Judah's Failure: A Contrasting Example

The story of Judah and Tamar (Genesis 38:1–26), a Canaanite woman, interrupts the flow of Joseph's narrative in Potiphar's house. This interruption serves a deliberate purpose: to demonstrate how two brothers, Judah and Joseph, handled similar situations involving temptation and sexual ethics in dramatically different ways.

Judah's moral failure began when he refused to fulfill his family obligations to Tamar. After Judah's son Er married Tamar and died without providing her with a son, Tamar became a childless widow living in her father-in-law's household. According to the Levirate law (Deuteronomy 25:5–10), Judah was responsible for giving Tamar his younger son in marriage so she could bear a child who would carry on her deceased husband's name and inherit his property.

Instead of honoring this responsibility, Judah sent Tamar back to her father's house (Genesis 38:11), ostensibly until his younger son matured enough for marriage. However, Judah never intended to follow through on this promise. His real plan was to leave Tamar permanently in her father's house, condemned to live as a celibate, childless widow.

When Tamar realized Judah's deception, she devised a plan to force the issue. After Judah's wife died, Tamar learned that he was traveling to Timnah for sheep shearing. She removed her widow's garments, veiled her face, and disguised herself as a prostitute, positioning herself along Judah's route.

When Judah thought he was engaging with a prostitute on the roadside, he did not realize it was his own daughter-in-law. This encounter led to Tamar's pregnancy. Later, when Judah found out Tamar was pregnant, he was furious and nearly had her put to death for adultery, only to realize, to his great shame, that he was the one who was the father.

Judah's moral failure was complete. In his attempt to satisfy sexual desire, he had committed incest with his own daughter-in-law while simultaneously failing in his family responsibilities. Faced with undeniable evidence of his hypocrisy, Judah was forced to acknowledge his sin: "She is more righteous than I am" (Genesis 38:26). In this moment of humiliation, God opened Judah's eyes to the full extent of his moral failure.

Joseph Faces Temptation

Joseph was seventeen years old when he arrived at Potiphar's house (Genesis 37:2) and thirty when he entered Pharaoh's service (Genesis 41:46). Since he spent more than two years in prison (Genesis 41:1), Joseph likely served in Potiphar's household for nearly a decade.

During this extended period, Potiphar's wife became sexually attracted to Joseph because of his physical appeal. Her approach was direct and persistent. She first propositioned him bluntly: "Come to bed with me" (Genesis 39:7 NIV). When Joseph refused, she did not accept his rejection. Later, she approached him again with the same explicit invitation: "Come to bed with me" (Genesis 39:12 NIV). When Joseph again refused her adulterous advance, Potiphar's wife physically grabbed his garment, attempting to force him into sexual relations. Joseph's response was immediate and decisive: he fled the house, leaving his garment in her hands.

Humiliated by Joseph's rejection and consumed with wounded pride, Potiphar's wife fabricated a story of attempted rape. She told the household servants that Joseph "came in here to sleep with me, but I screamed" (Genesis 39:14), using Joseph's abandoned garment as false evidence of her accusation.

Joseph Resists Temptation

Despite the considerable power Potiphar's wife wielded over her household and servants, her authority was insufficient to overcome Joseph's moral resolve. Though the temptation was immense and persistent, Joseph successfully resisted and refused to become a victim of sexual coercion.

Joseph's refusal to give in to his master's wife serves as a strong example of resisting temptation. Although he was single, far from family, and lacked freedom, his strength to resist seduction was based on wisdom, integrity, and unwavering faith. In turning down her advances, Joseph offered four solid reasons for his refusal.

First, Joseph recognized what he stood to lose. He told Potiphar's wife, "No one is greater in this house than I am. My master has withheld nothing from me except you, because you are his wife. How then could I do such a wicked thing and sin against God?" (Genesis 39:9). Joseph understood that he had achieved a position of remarkable trust and responsibility over nearly ten years of faithful service. An affair would destroy everything he had worked to build.

Second, Joseph considered the devastating impact on his master. Potiphar had withheld nothing from Joseph except his wife, and for obvious reasons. Joseph recognized that betraying this trust would cause profound pain to a man who had treated him with exceptional kindness and respect. The affair would represent the ultimate betrayal of Potiphar's confidence in him.

Third, Joseph understood that the affair constituted wickedness in God's sight. He explicitly called the proposed act "a wicked thing." Even in Egyptian society, where premarital sex was generally acceptable, adultery was condemned and severely punished. A married woman caught in adultery faced harsh consequences. Joseph's moral compass, shaped by his Hebrew heritage and relationship with God, clearly identified the proposed relationship as morally wrong.

Fourth, and most importantly, Joseph recognized that the affair would be "a sin against God." As a man of deep faith, Joseph lived with a constant awareness that God was present with him, watching, protecting, and blessing him every day. Joseph understood that a sexual relationship with Potiphar's wife went against God's will and would harm his relationship with him. His ability to resist temptation came directly from his close relationship with God.

When Potiphar's wife refused to accept Joseph's clear rejection, Joseph chose the wise course: he literally ran from the situation, leaving his garment behind. Ironically, a garment would again cause Joseph trouble, just as his special robe had created issues with his brothers years earlier. This time, the abandoned garment became false evidence in Potiphar's wife's fabricated accusation of attempted rape.

When she presented her story to Potiphar, claiming that Joseph had tried to assault her and fled when she screamed, leaving his garment as evidence (Genesis 39:18), the consequences Joseph had feared came to pass. Potiphar, deeply hurt and furious at what he believed was a betrayal of trust, had Joseph arrested and imprisoned in the same facility where the king's prisoners were held.

Joseph's experience demonstrates that victory over temptation is possible through wisdom, integrity, and faith in God. Unlike his brother Judah, who succumbed to sexual temptation and experienced devastating consequences, Joseph's steadfast commitment to his principles, even when facing severe personal cost, ultimately preserved his character and positioned him for God's greater purposes in his life. The temporary suffering caused by a false accusation could not compare to the lasting damage that moral compromise would have inflicted on Joseph's relationship with God and his own integrity.

The Old Testament Speaks to the Church

On September 5, 2021, my pastor, Jeff Griffin, Senior Pastor of The Compass Church, delivered a powerful sermon on Genesis 39:6–20 titled "Joseph: Overcoming Temptation."

In his sermon, Jeff emphasized a crucial truth that many overlook when facing moral challenges: the key to overcoming temptation lies in recognizing how much we stand to lose when we yield to it. This insight forms the cornerstone of Joseph's successful resistance and offers a practical framework for modern believers.

Jeff observed that when people face temptation, they often experience a kind of spiritual myopia; they cannot clearly see the devastating consequences that await them if they continue down that destructive path. This blindness to consequences is not accidental; it is one of temptation's most dangerous traits. People fail to fully understand the magnitude of the loss they will suffer and the chain of tragedies that will follow if they give in to temptation's pull.

A particularly striking element of Jeff's message was his insight into how temptation clouds our judgment. When people are facing temptation, he noted, they fail to think with the clarity and wisdom they would usually possess because they become overwhelmed by desire. This emotional and spiritual fog prevents them from making rational decisions based on long-term consequences rather than immediate gratification.

This observation helps explain why otherwise intelligent, principled people can make choices that seem incomprehensible to outside observers. The power of temptation lies not just in the appeal of what it offers, but in its ability to distort our perception of reality and narrow our focus to the immediate moment.

Jeff's sermon highlighted another sobering reality: yielding to temptation creates a destructive ripple effect that extends far beyond the individual making the choice. When someone succumbs to moral failure, it inevitably causes profound hurt across multiple spheres.

First, personal relationships suffer as trust is broken and intimacy is damaged. Second, families are devastated because the consequences of one person's choices impact spouses, children, and extended family members. Third, broader communities are affected as the fallout touches friends, colleagues, church members, and others who may be directly or indirectly connected to the situation.

This multi-layered impact highlights why Joseph's four-part reasoning was so thorough; he thought about not only his own well-being but also his master's, his relationship with God, and the moral integrity of his community.

Jeff presented the story of Joseph and his steadfast refusal to become involved with Potiphar's wife as more than just an ancient narrative; it is a powerful, practical lesson for anyone seeking to overcome temptation in their own life. Joseph's example demonstrates that victory over temptation is not only possible but achievable through the application of biblical principles that remain as relevant today as they were thousands of years ago.

The beauty of Joseph's approach lies in its clarity and replicability. By taking time to consider what he would lose, whom he would hurt, and how his actions would affect his relationship with God, Joseph created a framework that modern believers can apply to their own moral challenges. Jeff's sermon reminds us that, like Joseph, we have the resources we need to resist temptation and maintain our integrity, regardless of the circumstances we face.

Jeff's sermon on Joseph's victory over temptation provides both warning and hope. The warning is clear: temptation seeks to blind us to consequences and isolate us from the broader impact of our choices. The hope is equally clear: by following Joseph's example of carefully considering what we stand to lose and maintaining our focus on God's will, we can overcome even the most persistent and powerful temptations. Joseph's story remains a beacon of encouragement for all who seek to live lives of integrity and faithfulness in a world full of moral challenges.

CHAPTER 6

JOSEPH: IMPACTING OTHERS

Joseph's experience in Potiphar's household was marked by both remarkable success and profound disappointment. His time there proved rewarding as he made such a significant impact on Potiphar's life that his master entrusted him with complete authority over his entire household. Potiphar recognized that Joseph was a man devoted to his God, and he witnessed how the Lord blessed everything Joseph undertook.

However, Joseph's greatest trial emerged from his interaction with Potiphar's wife. Being a handsome young man, Joseph attracted the unwanted attention of his master's wife, who became infatuated with him and repeatedly propositioned him for sexual relations. When Joseph steadfastly refused her advances, maintaining his integrity and loyalty to both his master and his God, she falsely accused him of attempted rape. Despite likely believing in Joseph's innocence, Potiphar was compelled by his position in the Egyptian government to protect his wife's honor and reputation, resulting in Joseph's imprisonment.

Joseph in Prison

Though innocent of all charges and unjustly incarcerated, Joseph once again demonstrated his exceptional character by becoming a model prisoner. He was confined to the same prison that housed Pharaoh's political prisoners, as his alleged offense against a high-ranking official was considered a crime against Pharaoh himself.

Even in prison, Joseph was not abandoned, "the LORD was with him" (Genesis 39:21). God's presence sustained Joseph with his unchanging love and favor. The prison warden, observing Joseph's exemplary conduct, positive attitude, and natural leadership abilities, appointed him supervisor over all the prisoners. Joseph became "responsible for everything that they were doing" (Genesis 39:22 GWN).

After some time, two prominent Egyptian officials joined Joseph in prison: Pharaoh's cupbearer and the chief baker. The cupbearer held responsibility for Pharaoh's wine cellar and beverages, while the chief baker oversaw Pharaoh's kitchen staff and baked goods. Though the text does not specify their offense, it was evidently serious enough to warrant confinement in the royal prison. Given their high-ranking positions, the warden assigned them to Joseph's personal care (Genesis 40:4).

The Cupbearer's Dream

One night, both the cupbearer and the baker experienced vivid dreams that left them deeply troubled. When Joseph came to attend to them the following morning, he immediately noticed their distressed expressions. Demonstrating his characteristic compassion, Joseph asked, "Why are your faces so sad today?" (Genesis 40:7). When they explained their predicament, having received dreams they could not interpret, Joseph assured them that God could reveal the meaning of their dreams.

When Joseph mentioned God's ability to interpret dreams, he used the Hebrew word *elohim*, meaning "God" or "gods." In Egypt's polytheistic culture, the officials may have assumed Joseph referred to one of Egypt's many deities. However, Joseph was specifically invoking the one true God of the Hebrews, not the false gods of Egypt.

The cupbearer shared his dream: "In my dream I saw a vine in front of me, and on the vine were three branches. As soon as it budded, it blossomed, and its clusters ripened into grapes. Pharaoh's cup was in my hand, and I took the grapes, squeezed them into Pharaoh's cup and put the cup in his hand" (Genesis 40:9–11).

Joseph's Interpretation

Joseph confidently interpreted the dream: "Within three days Pharaoh will lift up your head and restore you to your position, and you will put Pharaoh's cup in his hand, just as you used to do when you were his cupbearer" (Genesis 40:13). Joseph assured the cupbearer that this favorable interpretation would certainly come to pass because God had revealed it to him.

Seizing this opportunity, Joseph made a heartfelt plea for the cupbearer to remember him after his restoration and intercede with Pharaoh for his release. Joseph presented two compelling arguments for his innocence: First, he had been kidnapped from the land of the Hebrews (the term "Hebrew" in the Old Testament often designates someone as a foreigner or outsider, emphasizing Joseph's status as a victim rather than a criminal). Second, he had committed no crime deserving imprisonment and was completely innocent of the charges against him.

The Chief Baker's Dream

Encouraged by the favorable interpretation given to his colleague, the chief baker eagerly shared his own dream, hoping for similar good news. He recounted: "On my head were three baskets of bread. In the top basket were all kinds of baked goods for Pharaoh, but the birds were eating them out of the basket on my head" (Genesis 40:16–17).

Joseph's Interpretation

Unfortunately, Joseph had to deliver devastating news to the baker. The three baskets symbolized three days, after which Pharaoh would execute him by beheading, impale his body on a pole, and leave it for birds to eat — a gruesome fate that would deny him a proper burial.

Three days later, on Pharaoh's birthday, both predictions came to pass exactly as Joseph had foretold. Pharaoh hosted a grand banquet for his officials and courtiers, during which he summoned both prisoners. The cupbearer was restored to his former position and resumed serving Pharaoh, while the chief baker was executed by hanging, precisely as Joseph had predicted.

The fulfillment of these prophecies demonstrated that God was indeed with Joseph and had granted him the supernatural ability to interpret dreams. However, despite his promise, the cupbearer "did not remember Joseph; he forgot him" (Genesis 40:23). This forgetfulness, whether from reluctance to credit a Hebrew slave, fear of political consequences, or simple human frailty, left Joseph languishing in prison for two additional years, seemingly "forgotten by man and God" (Brueggemann 1982:325).

The cupbearer's amnesia reflects a broader pattern in biblical history. Years later, "a new king arose over Egypt who did not know Joseph" (Exodus 1:8), and the Egyptians forgot how Joseph had saved their nation from devastating famine.

Joseph in Pharaoh's Court

Two years after the cupbearer's restoration, Pharaoh experienced two disturbing dreams on the same night. In the first dream, he saw seven healthy, fat cows followed by seven sickly, emaciated cows. In the second dream, he witnessed seven full, healthy heads of grain, then seven thin heads scorched by the east wind.

These dreams greatly troubled Pharaoh, leading him to summon all of Egypt's magicians and wise men the next morning. Despite their renowned wisdom and supposed supernatural powers, none could interpret the meaning of the dreams. It was only then that the cupbearer remembered Joseph and his extraordinary gift.

The crisis at hand finally jogged the cupbearer's memory. He recognized that Joseph had made a lasting impact on his life through his accurate interpretation and godly character. He confessed to Pharaoh that he had met a Hebrew slave in prison who possessed extraordinary abilities in dream interpretation, while also acknowledging his failure to keep his promise to Joseph.

Joseph was hastily summoned from prison, but before appearing before Pharaoh, he underwent necessary preparation. He shaved (or was shaved, according to the Septuagint) and changed into appropriate clothing. This grooming was culturally significant: Semites typically wore beards, while Egyptians were clean-shaven, so Joseph adopted Egyptian customs out of respect for Pharaoh.

When Pharaoh told Joseph, "I have heard it said of you that when you hear a dream you can interpret it" (Genesis 41:15), Joseph immediately deflected personal credit. He humbly clarified that he possessed no inherent ability to interpret dreams; only God could reveal their meaning, and God would provide Pharaoh with the correct interpretation.

Joseph's Interpretation

Joseph explained that Pharaoh's two dreams were really one message repeated for emphasis. God was showing that Egypt would have seven years of extraordinary abundance followed by seven years of severe famine. The repetition indicated that "the matter has been firmly decided by God, and God will do it soon" (Genesis 41:32).

Joseph's interpretation deeply impressed Pharaoh, who asked his officials, "Can we find anyone like this man, one in whom is the spirit of God?" (Genesis 41:38). Recognizing divine wisdom in Joseph, Pharaoh appointed him as second-in-command over all Egypt, granting him authority to implement whatever measures necessary to prepare for the coming crisis.

Following his appointment, Pharaoh gave Joseph an Egyptian name: Zaphenath-paneah. While scholars debate its exact meaning, it likely signifies "God speaks, and he lives" or "revealer of secrets." Pharaoh also arranged Joseph's marriage to Asenath, daughter of Potiphera (Mariottini 1992: 5:427), priest of On (Heliopolis). This union produced two sons, Manasseh and Ephraim, who would later become two of the twelve tribes of Israel.

Through these events, Joseph's journey from Hebrew slave to Egyptian prime minister demonstrates how God can transform even the most unjust circumstances into opportunities for his people to impact entire nations and fulfill his greater purposes.

The Old Testament Speaks to the Church

On September 12, 2021, my pastor, Jeff Griffin, Senior Pastor of The Compass Church, delivered a powerful sermon on Genesis 40:1—41:44 titled "Joseph: Impacting Others."

In his sermon, Jeff masterfully highlighted how Joseph's life created ripple effects of influence throughout Egyptian society. Joseph's impact was not merely circumstantial but deeply spiritual, rooted in his unwavering relationship with God even in the most challenging circumstances.

Impact on Potiphar. Joseph made such a profound impression on his master that Potiphar became convinced God was blessing his household specifically because of Joseph's presence. This recognition led Potiphar to entrust Joseph with complete authority over all his possessions, an extraordinary level of trust between master and slave.

Impact on the Prison Warden. Even in confinement, Joseph's character and demeanor so impressed the prison warden that he appointed Joseph to be in charge of all the prisoners. Joseph's integrity and leadership qualities were evident regardless of his circumstances.

Impact on Pharaoh's Cupbearer. Joseph's accurate interpretation of the cupbearer's dream, combined with his compassionate care during their shared imprisonment, made such a lasting impression that the cupbearer was willing to stake his reputation by recommending Joseph to Pharaoh as a reliable interpreter of divine revelations.

Impact on Pharaoh. Perhaps most remarkably, Joseph so impressed Egypt's most powerful ruler that Pharaoh appointed him as the second-highest official in the entire kingdom. Pharaoh recognized that Joseph possessed divine wisdom and was uniquely qualified to guide Egypt through the coming crisis.

The common thread throughout these relationships was that Joseph had a profound spiritual impact on people because God's presence was unmistakably evident in his life.

Four Principles for Spiritual Impact

In his sermon, Jeff extracted four practical principles from Joseph's life that modern Christians can apply to make a meaningful spiritual impact on others:

Principle 1: Recognize God's Activity in Your Life

Joseph maintained an acute awareness of God's presence and activity, regardless of his circumstances. Scripture repeatedly emphasizes that "the LORD was with Joseph," twice during his service in Potiphar's house and twice during his imprisonment. Joseph's remarkable success stemmed from his unwavering belief that God was present with him, whether he served as a slave or languished as a prisoner.

Joseph understood that even his eventual encounter with Pharaoh was part of God's sovereign plan. He recognized that God was orchestrating events behind the scenes, working through both favorable and adverse circumstances to accomplish his purposes. This perspective enabled Joseph to maintain hope and purpose even in the darkest moments.

Christians who recognize God's activity in their daily lives, both in blessings and trials, naturally radiate a confidence and peace that draws others' attention to the source of their strength.

Principle 2: Give Credit to God for Your Accomplishments

Joseph consistently deflected personal glory and directed credit to God for his abilities and successes. Potiphar clearly observed that Joseph prospered because God was with him. When interpreting dreams for both the cupbearer and Pharaoh, Joseph immediately clarified that he possessed no inherent power; only God could reveal the true meaning of their dreams.

This humility and God-consciousness made a profound impression on everyone Joseph encountered. Rather than promoting himself, Joseph used every opportunity to point others toward the true source of wisdom and blessing.

Christians can positively impact others by demonstrating that God's hand is at work in their lives through their work, relationships, and achievements. When others notice God's fingerprints on our lives, it opens natural opportunities for spiritual conversations.

Principle 3: Show Others That God Is Pursuing Them with Blessing

Joseph helped others understand that God was actively working in their lives for their benefit. He explained to the cupbearer that God was speaking directly to him through his dream, revealing his care and plans. Similarly, Joseph helped Pharaoh understand that God was warning him about the coming famine, not to frighten him, but because God cared deeply for both Pharaoh and the people of Egypt.

Joseph's entire journey to Egypt served as a demonstration of God's sovereignty and loving provision. Through Joseph's experience, both Egyptians and Hebrews could see that God was orchestrating events across nations and decades to preserve life and accomplish his greater purposes.

Christians can help others recognize that God is not distant or indifferent to their lives, but is actively pursuing them with love, care, and blessing. This perspective transforms how people view both their circumstances and their relationship with God.

Principle 4: Describe God Accurately to Those Who Don't Know Him

Joseph served as a faithful ambassador of the true God in a thoroughly pagan culture. Through his interpretation of Pharaoh's dreams, Joseph was essentially teaching Pharaoh about God's character, his wisdom, care, justice, and sovereignty. In a land filled with false gods and superstitions, Joseph presented the true God as he really is: loving, caring, all-knowing, and deeply involved in human affairs.

Joseph understood that people often have serious isconceptions about God's nature and intentions. Rather than assuming they understood, he took opportunities to reveal God's true character through both his words and his life.

Christians today encounter people with various misconceptions about God, seeing him as a distant, angry, unpredictable, or uncaring God. Like Joseph, we have opportunities to reveal God's true character through our lives and words, helping others discover that he is indeed loving, faithful, and deeply concerned about their well-being.

Jeff's sermon powerfully demonstrates that our greatest impact on others flows not from our talents, achievements, or personalities, but from the evident presence of God in our lives. Joseph's example shows that when we maintain intimate fellowship with God, give him credit for our successes, help others see his goodness in their circumstances, and accurately represent his character, we become instruments through which God can transform lives and even entire nations.

The question each believer must answer is: Are people drawn to God because of what they observe in my life? Joseph's legacy reminds us that our circumstances, whether favorable or challenging, are merely the stage upon which God demonstrates his faithfulness and love to a watching world.

CHAPTER 7

JOSEPH: ENDURING HARDSHIP

The investiture of Joseph as vizier of Egypt marked one of the highest moments in his extraordinary life. After Joseph interpreted Pharaoh's troubling dream, Pharaoh recognized his exceptional wisdom and promoted him to the second-highest position in the kingdom. Joseph was given authority over governmental affairs and made responsible for preparing the entire nation for the coming seven years of famine.

Pharaoh declared to Joseph, "You shall be over my house, and all my people shall order themselves as you command; only with regard to the throne will I be greater than you" (Genesis 41:40). The elaborate ceremony of installation described in Genesis closely mirrors rituals depicted in ancient Egyptian monuments, lending historical authenticity to the biblical account. Joseph's investiture included several significant rituals that demonstrated his newfound authority.

First, Pharaoh removed his signet ring and placed it on Joseph's finger. This ring served as the Pharaoh's official seal for signing important state documents. Second, Pharaoh clothed Joseph in robes of fine linen and placed a gold chain around his neck. The linen robe was characteristic of high-ranking government officials, while the golden chain identified him in his official capacity as Pharaoh's representative. Third, Pharaoh provided Joseph with a royal chariot, symbolizing his position as second-in-command throughout Egypt. Finally, Pharaoh granted Joseph comprehensive authority over the land, declaring that "no one anywhere in Egypt will lift a hand or foot without your permission" (Genesis 41:44 GWN).

Joseph's Journey Through Hardship

Joseph's rise to become Egypt's second most powerful leader came with great personal sacrifice. His life was marked by intense highs and lows, a cycle of gaining power followed by severe setbacks.

Before Joseph could enjoy the praise and honor of his elevated position, he faced years of betrayal, humiliation, imprisonment, and deep suffering.

The cyclical nature of Joseph's fortunes is evident throughout his story. In his father's household, he enjoyed the privileged status of Jacob's beloved son, only to be betrayed by his jealous brothers and sold into slavery in a foreign land. In Egypt, he rose to become manager of Potiphar's entire estate, trusted with all his master's possessions, only to be falsely accused of attempted rape by Potiphar's wife and stripped of his position.

This false accusation plunged Joseph into one of the darkest times of his life. He was imprisoned in a royal dungeon reserved for those who had committed crimes against Pharaoh or his officials. Yet even at his lowest, Joseph's character and abilities shone through as he was eventually put in charge of all the prisoners.

When Joseph interpreted the dreams of two fellow prisoners, Pharaoh's cupbearer and chief baker, he saw a spark of hope for freedom. He asked the cupbearer to remember him when he was restored to his position. However, this hope was dashed when the cupbearer forgot Joseph's kindness, leaving him to suffer in prison for two more painful years.

Joseph's Divine Restoration

Two years after the cupbearer's restoration, Pharaoh experienced disturbing dreams that none of Egypt's wise men, magicians, or counselors could interpret. The failure of these learned men suddenly reminded the cupbearer of the Hebrew prisoner who had accurately interpreted his own dream years earlier.

The cupbearer approached Pharaoh and recounted his prison experience, describing the young Hebrew who possessed remarkable interpretive abilities. Pharaoh immediately summoned Joseph from the dungeon. When brought before Egypt's ruler, Joseph humbly deflected credit for his gift, assuring Pharaoh that God alone could provide the proper interpretation of his dreams.

After hearing Pharaoh's dreams, Joseph revealed that both visions conveyed the same divine message: Egypt would experience seven years of unprecedented abundance followed by seven years of devastating famine. Joseph wisely counseled Pharaoh to appoint a capable administrator to oversee the preparation during the years of plenty, ensuring the nation's survival through the coming years of scarcity.

Pharaoh recognized that Joseph possessed "the spirit of God" and the wisdom necessary to save Egypt from the approaching catastrophe that threatened to devastate the nation. Without hesitation, Pharaoh appointed Joseph to oversee all Egyptian affairs and lead the preparations for the famine that was prophesied.

To demonstrate Joseph's authority to the Egyptian people and ensure their acceptance of this foreign leader, Pharaoh conducted the whole traditional installation ceremony. Additionally, Pharaoh sought to integrate Joseph, a Hebrew, fully into Egyptian society through several symbolic acts.

First, Pharaoh bestowed upon Joseph an Egyptian name: Zaphenath-Paneah (Genesis 41:45). While scholars debate the precise meaning, the name likely signifies "God speaks, and he lives." This new identity was intended to signal Joseph's complete assimilation into Egyptian culture. Significantly, however, this Egyptian name never appears again in Scripture, suggesting that while Joseph adopted Egyptian customs, he retained his Hebrew identity.

Second, Pharaoh arranged Joseph's marriage to Asenath, daughter of Potiphera, priest of On. The name Asenath means "She belongs to [the goddess] Neith." This marriage connected Joseph to one of Egypt's most influential priestly families. Potiphera's name means "He whom Re [the sun god] has given," and he served as priest in On, the center of solar worship in Egypt (later called Heliopolis by the Greeks).

With his new position, Egyptian name, and Egyptian wife, Joseph was thoroughly integrated into Egyptian society. Nevertheless, he never forgot his Hebrew heritage or that his success was a result of God's providence during years of adversity. This awareness is beautifully reflected in the names he chose for his sons.

The Significance of Joseph's Sons' Names

Joseph was seventeen when his brothers sold him into slavery (Genesis 37:2) and thirty when he entered Pharaoh's service (Genesis 41:46). During these thirteen formative years, Joseph endured tremendous hardships that taught him profound truths about life, suffering, and God's faithfulness, lessons that remain relevant across all ages and circumstances.

The first lesson Joseph learned was that all troubles are temporary. When his first son was born to Asenath, Joseph named him Manasseh, derived from the Hebrew verb *nāšâ*, meaning "He who makes forget" or "causing to forget." Joseph explained his choice: "God has made me forget all my hardship and all my father's house" (Genesis 41:51).

Joseph's reference to forgetting "his father's house" does not indicate that he had forgotten his family entirely. Instead, he had found healing from the painful memories of betrayal and rejection he experienced while living in his father's household. Joseph understood that with time and God's grace, the sharp pain of past wounds can fade, allowing one to embrace the present gifts God provides.

The second lesson Joseph learned was that one can remain productive and fruitful even in the midst of suffering. When his second son was born, Joseph named him Ephraim, from the Hebrew word *pārâ*, meaning "to be fruitful." Joseph declared, "God has made me fruitful in the land of my misfortunes" (Genesis 41:52).

Joseph's life exemplifies how God can bring fruitfulness from the most barren circumstances. In the house of Potiphar, God used Joseph's servitude to develop his administrative skills. Through his false imprisonment, God refined Joseph's character and prepared

82

him for greater service. Even his years in the dungeon positioned him to become Egypt's savior during the famine.

Joseph possessed natural strength of character, but that character was forged and refined in the furnace of adversity. God transformed Joseph's suffering into a means of helping countless people in need. His misfortunes became the very foundation for his ability to impact the lives of multitudes.

Joseph's story demonstrates that good often emerges from difficult circumstances, a truth later articulated by the apostle Paul: "We know that God causes everything to work together for the good of those who love God and are called according to his purpose for them" (Romans 8:28 NLT).

Through Joseph's example, we learn that hardship, while painful, can serve God's greater purposes. Troubles are temporary, healing is possible, and even in our darkest moments, God can make us fruitful for His glory and the benefit of others.

The Old Testament Speaks to the Church

On September 19, 2021, my pastor, Jeff Griffin, Senior Pastor of Compass Church in Naperville, Illinois, delivered a powerful sermon on Genesis 41:45–52 titled "Joseph: Enduring Hardship."

In his sermon, Jeff used Joseph's transformative experience in Egypt to illustrate a profound spiritual truth: hardship and misfortune, when surrendered to God's sovereign hand, can become instruments of his redemptive purpose. Rather than viewing suffering as meaningless or destructive, Jeff demonstrated how God can transform our most painful experiences into catalysts for positive impact and spiritual growth.

Jeff traced Joseph's journey through three distinct phases of adversity: his servitude in Potiphar's household, his unjust imprisonment, and his eventual elevation to serve Pharaoh, showing how each seeming setback was actually part of God's master plan. These experiences were not random acts of cruelty but divine preparation for Joseph's ultimate calling: bringing salvation to his family and deliverance to the people of Egypt during the devastating famine.

Jeff brought Joseph's ancient story into modern focus by sharing two compelling testimonies of individuals who discovered God's redemptive power through their own seasons of hardship.

The first example was Manny Mill, whose life exemplified how God can transform even our worst decisions into opportunities for ministry. Manny endured persecution under Cuba's communist regime and later faced imprisonment in the United States following a bank robbery conviction. It was within the walls of his prison cell that Manny encountered the transforming power of Jesus Christ, accepting him as Lord and Savior.

Following his release, Manny did not allow shame over his past to define his future. Instead, he channeled his prison experience into founding Koinonia House, a ministry specifically designed to reach inmates and ex-convicts with the gospel. God transformed Manny's criminal background into his greatest ministry asset, enabling him to connect authentically with those experiencing the very struggles he had once faced. Through Manny's story, we see how God can transform our deepest failures into bridges to reach others in similar circumstances.

The second example was Joseph himself, whose entire life narrative demonstrates the power of faithful endurance through extended seasons of suffering. Jeff emphasized how Joseph faced betrayal by his own brothers, humiliation through false accusations, and years of unjust imprisonment. Yet through each trial, Joseph maintained his faith and integrity.

Most significantly, Joseph's testimony was not limited to his words; it was permanently recorded in the names he chose for his sons. Through Manasseh ("God has made me forget all my hardship") and Ephraim ("God has made me fruitful in the land of my misfortunes"), Joseph declared two eternal truths: troubles are temporary, and God can bring extraordinary fruitfulness from our seasons of suffering.

Jeff concluded his message by acknowledging the universal reality of human suffering. Many people today are walking through valleys of pain, facing overwhelming hardships, and wrestling with circumstances that seem insurmountable. It is precisely in these challenging and difficult seasons that Joseph's story offers hope and direction.

Joseph's life teaches us invaluable lessons about God's character and his involvement in our circumstances. Through Joseph's example, we learn about God's faithful provision when resources seem scarce, his unconditional love when we feel abandoned, and his tender compassion when we are overwhelmed by life's storms.

Jeff emphasized that our most difficult seasons often become the backdrop for life's most significant discovery: the profound truth that God genuinely cares for us. When we are stripped of our self-reliance and human solutions, we are positioned to experience God's presence and provision in ways we might never have known otherwise.

This truth does not minimize the reality of pain or suggest that suffering is easy to endure. Instead, it offers hope that our current struggles are not the end of our story. Like Joseph, Manny Mill, and countless others throughout history, we can trust that God is working behind the scenes, weaving even our most painful experiences into his greater tapestry of redemption.

The message of Joseph's life remains as relevant today as it was thousands of years ago: in God's hands, no hardship is wasted, no suffering is meaningless, and no season of difficulty is beyond his ability to transform for our good and his glory.

CHAPTER 8

JOSEPH: RELATIONAL CONFLICT

After Joseph interpreted Pharaoh's dreams, predicting seven years of abundance followed by seven years of famine, he immediately traveled throughout Egypt to prepare for both seasons. During the years of plenty, he would gather and store grain; during the years of famine, he would distribute it to save lives (Genesis 41:46).

The Years of Plenty and Preparation

During the seven years of abundance, Egypt's land produced bountiful crops. Joseph implemented the strategy he had recommended to Pharaoh, systematically collecting surplus food from throughout the kingdom and storing it in cities across Egypt. The harvest was so abundant that Joseph accumulated grain "like the sands of the sea" (Genesis 41:49). During these prosperous years, before the famine arrived, Joseph became the father of two sons: Manasseh and Ephraim.

Droughts and famines were common occurrences in the ancient Near East. Abraham had fled to Egypt during a famine in Canaan (Genesis 12:10), while Isaac, facing a similar crisis, chose to go to Gerar in Philistine territory rather than Egypt (Genesis 26:1). Each patriarch responded differently to the same challenge, establishing a pattern of seeking refuge where food could be found.

The famine that struck during Joseph's administration was particularly severe. Genesis 41 emphasizes this severity by using the word "severe" three times and mentioning "famine" thirteen times. The drought was so devastating that "there was famine in every country" except Egypt. Thanks to Joseph's careful preparation, Egypt alone had food throughout the crisis (Genesis 41:54).

The Famine Reaches Canaan

The great famine also devastated Canaan, where Jacob and his family lived. When Jacob learned that grain was available for purchase in Egypt, he recognized the desperate situation his family was in. How he discovered Egypt's food supply remains unclear, though he may have assumed that the Nile's reliable waters would sustain Egyptian agriculture.

Frustrated by his sons' apparent inaction during this crisis, Jacob challenged them: "Why do you keep looking at one another?" (Genesis 42:1). His sons seemed unaware of Egypt's food availability, or perhaps they were reluctant to travel there because of their guilt over Joseph's fate. Despite their hesitation, Jacob commanded them to go to Egypt and buy food to prevent the family from starving.

Twenty years had passed since the brothers sold Joseph into slavery. As they prepared to reenter Joseph's life unknowingly, he was managing Egypt's famine relief efforts. During these two decades, Joseph had moved beyond his conflicts with his brothers, though he remained aware of their hatred toward him. The brothers had sold him to merchants because of his dreams of future greatness, leading to his enslavement in Potiphar's household.

After two decades in Egypt, Joseph had prospered remarkably. His journey from slave to prisoner to Egypt's second-highest official demonstrated his resilience and God's providence. However, the famine in Canaan was about to resurrect painful memories from his past. Unknown to Joseph, this same famine would bring his brothers back into his life.

The Brothers' Journey to Egypt

When Jacob's sons departed for Egypt, Jacob refused to let Benjamin, his youngest son, accompany them. Both Joseph and Benjamin were sons of Rachel, Jacob's beloved wife. Having already lost Joseph, Jacob feared that harm might befall Benjamin, leaving him bereft of both of Rachel's children.

Jacob's sons joined a large group of people traveling to Egypt to purchase food, as the famine was equally severe throughout the region. They came to buy provisions from the official responsible for Egypt's grain distribution, unaware that this official was Joseph, the brother they had betrayed and sold into slavery.

When the brothers appeared before the Egyptian grain administrator, they prostrated themselves before him, their faces touching the ground in respect for his high office. This act of submission fulfilled Joseph's prophetic dream from years earlier, when he had told them: "We were binding sheaves of grain out in the field when suddenly my sheaf rose and stood upright, while your sheaves gathered around mine and bowed down to it" (Genesis 37:7). When they had mockingly asked, "Are you really going to rule us?" (Genesis 37:8), they never imagined they would one day bow before the *šallîṭ* of Egypt—the governor or vizier who controlled the nation's affairs.

Recognition and Concealment

Joseph immediately recognized his brothers when they appeared before him. The physical features of Semitic peoples differed noticeably from those of Egyptians, as evidenced by ancient Egyptian artwork. The tomb paintings at Beni Hassan, for instance, show "distinctive skin tones or colors, hairstyles, dress, and other elements" that distinguished non-Egyptian peoples from native Egyptians (Mourad 2020:105–108).

However, Joseph's brothers failed to recognize him for several compelling reasons. First, they believed he was dead—over twenty years had passed since they sold him to Egyptian merchants. Second, Joseph had fully adopted Egyptian customs: he bore an Egyptian name, was clean-shaven in Egyptian fashion, spoke to them in Egyptian through an interpreter, and wore official Egyptian garments. To them, he appeared to be a native Egyptian official, not their Hebrew brother.

Testing His Brothers' Character

Upon seeing his brothers, Joseph "remembered the dreams that he had dreamed about them" (Genesis 42:9). Now that they had reentered his life, Joseph faced a crucial dilemma: How should he deal with them? Had they changed over the years? Did they still harbor hatred toward him? To answer these questions, Joseph devised a series of tests. While he may have felt some desire for retribution, his primary motivation was to determine whether his brothers had truly changed.

The First Test: Accusations of Espionage

Joseph's initial test involved speaking harshly to his brothers and accusing them of being spies. He repeatedly charged them with coming to Egypt to scout the land's defenses, forcing them to deny these accusations each time. When they claimed to be "honest men" (Genesis 42:11), Joseph resolved to test the truth of their assertion.

The Second Test: Demanding Benjamin's Presence

Joseph's second test was more personal: "This is how you will be tested . . . you will not leave this place unless your youngest brother comes here" (Genesis 42:15). He desperately wanted to see Benjamin, who had been merely a child when Joseph last saw him and was now a grown man with his own family. To verify their honesty, Joseph declared: "Let one of you go and bring your brother, while the rest of you remain in prison, so that your words may be tested" (Genesis 42:16).

To demonstrate his seriousness, Joseph imprisoned his brothers for three days in the same prison where he had spent years of his own life—the *mišmar* (Genesis 42:17). This confinement served dual purposes: it allowed his brothers to experience the horrors of imprisonment that he had endured, while increasing pressure on them to bring Benjamin to Egypt.

Joseph's ultimate goal was not punishment but reunion with his younger brother. After three days, he modified his terms: one brother would remain imprisoned while the others returned home with food for their families, but they must bring Benjamin back to secure their brother's release.

The Weight of Conscience

The conditions Joseph imposed forced his brothers to confront their past treachery: "They said to one another, 'Surely we are being punished because of our brother. We saw how distressed he was when he pleaded with us for his life, but we would not listen; that's why this distress has come upon us'" (Genesis 42:21 NIV). Joseph selected Simeon to remain in prison, binding him before his brothers' eyes before sending him away.

Simeon's imprisonment was strategically significant in Joseph's evaluation of his brothers' character. By forcing them to leave a brother behind in Egypt, Joseph was compelling them to relive their past abandonment of him. Their confession of guilt indicated that his strategy was working: they were beginning to understand the connection between their current suffering and their past sin.

Joseph then ordered his servants to fill his brothers' grain sacks, secretly return their payment money, and provide supplies for their journey home. Upon their return to Canaan, the brothers reported these events to Jacob, who adamantly refused to let Benjamin travel to Egypt. "You have deprived me of my children," Jacob lamented. "Joseph is no more and Simeon is no more, and now you want to take Benjamin. Everything is against me" (Genesis 42:36).

Jacob's heartbreak was evident, but his stubbornness meant that Simeon remained imprisoned in Egypt while the famine continued to ravage the land of Canaan. Eventually, desperation overcame Jacob's protective instincts. Faced with starvation, he reluctantly permitted Benjamin to accompany his brothers to Egypt, resignedly declaring: "As for me, if I am bereaved of my children, I am bereaved" (Genesis 43:14).

The Final Test and Revelation

When Joseph saw Benjamin among his returning brothers, he instructed his servants to prepare a feast. Simeon was released from prison, and Joseph dined with all his brothers. Once again, they "bowed to the ground before him" (Genesis 43:26), and Joseph inquired about their father's welfare.

Following the meal, Joseph's servants filled the brothers' grain sacks and, at Joseph's command, placed his silver cup in Benjamin's sack. After the brothers departed, Joseph sent his servants to pursue them and discover the "stolen" cup. When found, Joseph declared that the guilty party would become his slave while the others could return home freely (Genesis 44:10).

This final test created a scenario remarkably similar to Joseph's own experience. The brothers, already convicted of their past treatment of Joseph and fearful for their father's well-being, faced the prospect of abandoning another brother. How would Jacob react to losing yet another son?

Judah's Transformation

Judah, who had initially suggested selling Joseph into slavery, now demonstrated a remarkable transformation. Speaking to Joseph, he explained their family's desperate situation and his father's reaction to Simeon's imprisonment and Benjamin's required journey. Understanding what Benjamin's enslavement would do to Jacob, Judah made an extraordinary offer: "Please let your servant remain as a slave to my lord in place of the boy; and let the boy go back with his brothers" (Genesis 44:33).

This moment revealed the profound change in Judah's character. The man who had once profited from selling his brother now willingly offered to sacrifice his own freedom to save another brother.

91

The Moment of Reconciliation

When Judah finished speaking, Joseph recognized that his brothers had indeed changed. Overcome with emotion, he dismissed his servants and revealed his identity: "I am Joseph" (Genesis 45:3). His brothers were astonished—the brother they had hated and sold into slavery was now the powerful official before whom they had been bowing.

Joseph's emotional nature was evident throughout these encounters. He wept when he first saw his brothers (Genesis 42:24), when he saw Benjamin (Genesis 43:30), when he revealed himself (Genesis 45:2), when he embraced Benjamin (Genesis 45:14), when he kissed all his brothers (Genesis 45:15), when Jacob arrived in Egypt (Genesis 46:29), and when he mourned his father's death (Genesis 50:1).

A New Beginning

When Joseph revealed himself, embraced, and kissed his brothers, he was extending complete forgiveness for all the pain and suffering they had caused him. The evil of the past was erased, and a new relationship was beginning. That moment of tears, embraces, and kisses represented a historic reconciliation—not just between brothers, but between the past and the future, between human brokenness and divine restoration.

This powerful narrative demonstrates that even the deepest wounds can heal when genuine repentance meets gracious forgiveness, and that God can transform family conflict into beautiful reconciliation.

The Old Testament Speaks to the Church

On September 26, 2021, my pastor, Jeff Griffin, Senior Pastor of The Compass Church in Naperville, Illinois, delivered a powerful sermon on Genesis 42–49 titled "Joseph: Relational Conflict." The preceding essay draws from Jeff's insightful exposition of this remarkable biblical narrative.

In his sermon, Jeff drew on Joseph's life and his complex relationship with his brothers to develop five essential principles for navigating relational conflicts. These principles, drawn from Joseph's journey from victim to reconciler, offer practical wisdom for anyone seeking to heal broken relationships.

Five Principles for Resolving Relational Conflict

1. The Principle of Rationalization: Beware of Noble Motives

When dealing with conflicts, we must carefully examine our true motivations and beware of rationalization. People often convince themselves that they have noble motives for questionable actions, masking their real intentions behind seemingly righteous purposes.

Joseph exemplified this tendency. He genuinely desired to see his brothers again, particularly Benjamin, but he also harbored feelings of revenge for their betrayal. Joseph rationalized imprisoning his brothers by telling himself it was necessary to bring Benjamin to Egypt, when in reality, part of his motivation was to make them suffer as he had suffered. He convinced himself that harsh treatment would achieve his purposes, blending legitimate desires with vindictive impulses.

This rationalization trap is common in conflict situations. We may believe that treating others poorly is justified, that harsh words will "teach them a lesson," or that withholding forgiveness will somehow make things right. However, when we are honest with ourselves, we often discover mixed motives beneath our seemingly justified actions.

Before responding to conflict, we must examine our hearts honestly. Are we truly seeking reconciliation, or are we seeking revenge disguised as justice? Are our actions motivated by love and restoration, or by a desire to make the other person pay for their wrongs?

2. The Principle of Undeserved Kindness: Breaking the Cycle of Hostility

Joseph eventually recognized that leaving his brothers in prison was not the proper way to address his conflicts with them. Despite their betrayal and the years of pain they had caused him, Joseph chose to show kindness to his brothers, even though they clearly did not deserve it.

This undeserved kindness was remarkable because Joseph's brothers had made his life extraordinarily difficult. They had stripped him of his coat, thrown him into a pit, sold him into slavery, and allowed their father to believe he was dead. By any human standard, they deserved punishment, not kindness. Yet Joseph understood a profound truth: undeserved kindness is what breaks the cycle of hostility and opens the door to genuine reconciliation.

When we respond to hurt with more hurt, to betrayal with revenge, we perpetuate a destructive cycle. Only undeserved kindness has the power to interrupt this pattern and create space for healing.

In our conflicts, we must choose to show kindness even when others do not deserve it. This does not mean becoming a doormat or ignoring harmful behavior; instead, it means responding with grace rather than retaliation. Such kindness often disarms hostility and opens the door for genuine dialogue and reconciliation.

3. The Principle of Generosity: Going Beyond the Minimum

Joseph demonstrated remarkable generosity toward the very brothers who had treated him so poorly. His generosity was comprehensive and sacrificial: he provided them with food during a famine, secretly returned their payment money, and supplied additional provisions for their journey home. Joseph went far beyond what was required or expected, choosing abundance over scarcity in his dealings with those who had wronged him.

This generosity was not mere charity but a deliberate choice to bless those who had cursed him. Joseph could have sold them grain at full price and sent them away. Instead, he lavished unexpected gifts upon them, demonstrating that his heart had moved from bitterness to blessing.

When resolving conflicts, we should strive to be generous rather than merely fair. This might mean offering more patience than someone deserves, giving more grace than they have earned, or providing more help than they have requested. Such generosity often melts hard hearts and creates goodwill that facilitates reconciliation.

4. The Principle of Boundaries: Establishing Truth and Integrity

When handling conflicts, it is vital to set clear boundaries rooted in truth and integrity. When rebuilding a relationship amid conflict, it is important to honestly assess both attitudes and behavior.

Joseph's brothers claimed, "We are honest men" (Genesis 42:11), but their assertion was not entirely truthful; they were hiding how they treated Joseph and living with unconfessed guilt. Joseph wisely understood that healthy relationships cannot be based on deception or half-truths. Through his testing, he set boundaries that demanded honesty and true repentance before full reconciliation could occur.

Boundaries are not walls designed to keep people out; they are guidelines that create safe spaces for relationships to flourish. They require truth-telling, acknowledgment of wrongdoing, and genuine change in attitude and behavior.

When working toward reconciliation, we must insist on honesty and integrity. This means being truthful about what happened, acknowledging the harm caused, and demonstrating genuine change. Premature reconciliation without proper boundaries often leads to repeated cycles of hurt and disappointment.

5. The Principle of Courageous Affection: Embracing Vulnerability

In restoring his relationship with his brothers, Joseph courageously conveyed genuine affection to those who had once done him grave harm. When he finally revealed his identity, he did not maintain emotional distance or offer cold forgiveness. Instead, he embraced and kissed his brothers, demonstrating that he truly loved them despite their past betrayal.

This courageous affection required tremendous vulnerability. Joseph risked being hurt again, rejected, or misunderstood. Dealing with conflict always involves such vulnerability: we must be willing to open our hearts, express genuine feelings, and take emotional risks in the pursuit of restored relationships.

Forgiveness is not complete until it includes the courage to love again. This does not happen overnight, and it requires both wisdom and bravery. Joseph's tears, embraces, and expressions of love demonstrated that he had moved from mere forgiveness to complete restoration.

True reconciliation requires the courage to be vulnerable and to express genuine affection. We must be willing to risk our hearts again, to show love to those who have hurt us, and to be emotionally open as we reestablish broken relationships. This vulnerability, while risky, is essential for deep healing and authentic restoration.

Jeff's five principles, drawn from Joseph's remarkable journey, provide a roadmap for navigating relational conflicts with wisdom and grace. They challenge us to examine our motives, extend undeserved kindness, practice radical generosity, establish healthy boundaries, and courageously embrace the vulnerability required for genuine reconciliation.

These principles remind us that conflict resolution is not merely about solving problems but about transforming relationships. Like Joseph, we can choose to move from victim to victor, from bitterness to blessing, and from separation to reconciliation. The path is not easy, but it leads to the kind of restored relationships that reflect the heart of God himself.

CHAPTER 9

JOSEPH: EXTENDING FORGIVENESS

After Joseph brought his father and brothers to Egypt, he introduced his family to Pharaoh. Joseph presented his father and five of his brothers to the Egyptian ruler. When Pharaoh met with Joseph's brothers, he granted them permission to settle in the land of Goshen (Genesis 47:6). Subsequently, Joseph brought his father Jacob before Pharaoh and presented him personally.

The Death of Jacob

When Jacob stood before Pharaoh, the Egyptian king courteously inquired about his age. Jacob's response reflected the hardships he had endured throughout his life. He told Pharaoh, "The years of my pilgrimage are one hundred and thirty. My years have been few and difficult, and they do not equal the years of the pilgrimage of my fathers" (Genesis 47:9). Jacob blessed Pharaoh twice during their encounter. This blessing may reflect the customary practice of an elder blessing a younger person, but more significantly, Jacob was fulfilling the promise God made to Abraham that through him and his descendants, all peoples on earth would be blessed (Genesis 12:3).

Jacob arrived in Egypt at the age of one hundred and thirty. After reuniting with Joseph, he lived seventeen more years in Egypt, bringing his total lifespan to one hundred and forty-seven years (Genesis 47:28). Remarkably, Jacob had lived seventeen years with Joseph in Canaan (Genesis 37:2) and enjoyed another seventeen years with him in Egypt.

Following Jacob's death, Joseph requested that Egyptian physicians embalm his father (Genesis 50:2). The mummification process was lengthy and intricate, requiring forty days to complete. The total mourning period for Jacob lasted seventy days. Once the embalming was finished and the mourning concluded, Joseph, his family, and a delegation of Egyptian officials journeyed to Canaan to bury Jacob in the cave at Machpelah, as he had requested. Jacob was laid to rest beside his wife Leah in the ancestral burial cave (Genesis 49:31).

The Brothers' Fear of Joseph

After returning from Canaan, Joseph's brothers became consumed with fear that Joseph would punish them for their past cruelties. They were tormented by confusion regarding Joseph's intentions. They knew the magnitude of their crimes: they had hated him, sold him into slavery, and deceived their father about his fate. Yet since arriving in Egypt, Joseph had treated them with unexpected kindness.

The brothers believed that as long as their father lived, Joseph would refrain from taking action against them, assuming he would not want to cause their father additional grief. However, with Jacob now dead, they feared Joseph would finally seek revenge. Their persistent guilt and terror revealed that the brothers had never truly repented of their actions against Joseph.

Unable to face Joseph directly, the brothers sent him a message, whether through a messenger or in writing, the text does not specify. Their message read: "Your father left these instructions before he died: 'This is what you are to say to Joseph: I ask you to forgive your brothers the sins and the wrongs they committed in treating you so badly.' Now please forgive the sins of the servants of the God of your father" (Genesis 50:16–17).

Several troubling aspects arise from this message. Had the brothers ever admitted their deception to Jacob? Did their father know they had lied to him about Joseph's death? If Jacob had known the truth, he probably would have spoken to Joseph directly rather than through intermediaries. There is no evidence that Jacob was aware of his sons' treachery against Joseph. Clearly, driven by fear, the brothers fabricated these supposed instructions from their father. Having lied to Jacob years earlier (Genesis 37:32), they were now lying to Joseph.

In their fabricated message, the brothers acknowledged the gravity of their actions against Joseph. They admitted their behavior was criminal (mentioned twice), evil, and sinful. The fictitious instructions twice requested Joseph's forgiveness, and the brothers were so apprehensive that they appealed to "the God of your father" for mercy.

When Joseph received their message, tears filled his eyes, and "Joseph wept" (Genesis 50:17). The text does not explain why Joseph wept, but it is possible that after more than a decade, his brothers still could not believe he genuinely desired complete reconciliation. Joseph served a God who "forgives iniquity, transgression, and sin" (Exodus 34:7). As a faithful worshiper, Joseph was prepared to extend forgiveness to his brothers, whom he recognized as fellow "servants of the God" of his father.

Joseph Forgives His Brothers

Some time later, Joseph's brothers came to him in person (Genesis 50:18). When they appeared before Joseph, they wept and prostrated themselves at his feet. This marked the fourth time the brothers had bowed before Joseph, fulfilling the very dream they had once rejected and mocked (Genesis 37:7). Fearful of Joseph's potential retaliation, the brothers offered to become his slaves: "We are here as your slaves."

Joseph immediately reassured his brothers that they had no reason for fear. He would not seek revenge for their evil actions nor treat them as they had treated him. Joseph asked them, "Do not be afraid. Am I in the place of God?" (Genesis 50:19). His response implied that only God has the authority to bring retribution for wrongdoing.

While evil actions may deserve judgment, God alone is the ultimate avenger: "Vengeance belongs to me; I will repay" (Deuteronomy 32:35). God forgives iniquities, transgressions, and sins, though his forgiveness is conditional upon repentance. When Solomon prayed at the temple's dedication in Jerusalem, he appealed to God: "If they repent with all their heart and soul . . . then hear from heaven their prayer and forgive your people who have sinned against you" (2 Chronicles 6:38–39).

99

Joseph understood that behind all the evil his brothers had inflicted upon him, God had been orchestrating events to accomplish his divine purposes for their family. When Joseph first revealed his identity to his brothers, he told them, "God sent me before you to preserve for you a remnant on earth, and to keep alive for you many survivors. So it was not you who sent me here, but God" (Genesis 45:7–8). Now Joseph explained that although his brothers had intended evil, God had planned to bring good from their wicked actions. The good that emerged was "the survival of many people" (Genesis 50:20).

The years of suffering and humiliation Joseph endured as a slave and prisoner were used by God to save his family, the Egyptians, and countless others who came to Egypt to purchase grain. Ironically, the brothers who once sought to kill Joseph were now able to live because of the very treachery they had committed against him. Divine providence remains difficult to comprehend, but God's invisible hand was at work in Joseph's life to preserve lives. As Genesis 41:57 states, "All the world came to Joseph in Egypt to buy grain, because the famine became severe throughout the world."

Joseph continued to reassure his brothers that their fears were groundless. Having previously promised to provide for them (Genesis 45:11), he renewed his commitment: "I will provide for you and your children" (Genesis 50:21). Joseph's purpose was to calm their minds and eliminate every trace of fear they harbored toward him. He demonstrated his commitment through kind words, speaking directly "to their hearts."

Joseph's forgiveness was not merely verbal but practical and sustained. When he promised, "I will provide for you and your children" (Genesis 50:21), these were not empty words. Joseph backed his promise with actions throughout his lifetime. He was good to them, feeding their families and consistently caring for them. His forgiveness was proven through deeds, exemplifying the principle: "If your enemies are hungry, feed them; if they are thirsty, give them something to drink" (Romans 12:20).

Joseph also expressed his forgiveness through his manner of speaking to his brothers: "he spoke kindly to them" (Genesis 50:21). The Hebrew expression literally means "he spoke to their hearts." Joseph's tone and the gentleness of his words convinced his brothers of his sincerity. Finally, assured of Joseph's complete forgiveness, they could rest in peace, knowing their relationship with their brother was fully restored.

The Old Testament Speaks to the Church

On October 3, 2021, my pastor, Jeff Griffin, Senior Pastor of The Compass Church in Naperville, Illinois, delivered a powerful sermon on Genesis 50:15–26 titled "Joseph: Extending Forgiveness." The analysis above draws from Jeff's insightful exposition of this pivotal biblical passage.

Throughout his sermon, Jeff explored the profound dynamics of Joseph's relationship with his brothers, particularly focusing on the remarkable forgiveness Joseph extended despite years of betrayal and suffering. Jeff identified two fundamental reasons that enabled Joseph to forgive his brothers so completely.

First Foundation: God as the Ultimate Judge

First, Joseph recognized that ultimate judgment belongs to God alone. When his brothers pleaded for forgiveness, fearing retribution for their past wrongs, Joseph responded with a question that revealed his understanding of the God in whom he believed: "Am I in the place of God?" (Genesis 50:19). This rhetorical question demonstrated Joseph's humility and his recognition that vengeance is not his prerogative.

Jeff emphasized that God is both perfectly just and the righteous avenger of wrongs. As the Apostle Paul instructed believers: "Beloved, never avenge yourselves, but leave room for the wrath of God; for it is written, 'Vengeance is mine, I will repay, says the Lord'" (Romans 12:19). Joseph's ability to forgive stemmed from his deep faith and his understanding that as a believer in God, he was called to extend forgiveness rather than seek personal revenge.

This divine perspective freed Joseph from the burden of judgment, allowing him to respond with grace.

Second Foundation: God's Sovereign Providence

The second reason Joseph could forgive so readily was his profound understanding that God was sovereignly orchestrating the events of his life. Jeff highlighted how Joseph perceived God's hand at work even in the most painful circumstances. While his brothers had exercised their free will to commit terrible evil against him, God had mysteriously used their wicked actions to accomplish tremendous good, ultimately bringing salvation to many people.

Jeff underscored that God has a glorious, overarching plan for his creation and works through human actions, both good and evil, to accomplish his divine purposes. The evil that Joseph's brothers perpetrated was genuine and inexcusable. The suffering, pain, and humiliation Joseph endured as Potiphar's servant and as a prisoner were intensely real and deeply traumatic.

However, it was precisely through Joseph's role as a suffering servant that God saved not only the people of Egypt from starvation, but also countless others who came seeking grain during the widespread famine. This divine providence exemplifies the truth Paul later articulated: "We know that all things work together for good for those who love God, who are called according to his purpose" (Romans 8:28).

Jeff's sermon illuminated how Joseph's story serves as a powerful testament to both the necessity of forgiveness and the mysterious ways God can redeem even the most painful circumstances for his greater purposes. Joseph's example challenges believers to trust in God's sovereignty while extending the same grace they have received from their heavenly Father.

PART 2

GIDEON

INTRODUCTION

GIDEON: AGAINST ALL ODDS

Gideon, one of the twelve judges of Israel, was the son of Joash, the Abiezrite. Gideon lived in Ophrah, a village in the tribe of Manasseh. As we read Gideon's story, we find inspiration in the fact that God can use any person in times of adversity. We can also see a glimpse of ourselves in the life of Gideon, because, like Gideon, we sometimes are reluctant to accept the call of God to do what needs to be done through us.

From the time of Gideon's calling, through the deliverance of the people of Israel from the hands of their enemies, and through the completion of the work God commissioned him to do, we meet a man who lacked confidence that he could be used by God, a man who doubted that he could become a mighty warrior in the hands of God.

Although Gideon struggled with some aspects of his call, he believed God's promise that he would be with him. Confident that the Lord would fulfill his promise, Gideon obeyed the LORD and became the deliverer of Israel against the oppressive situation imposed upon the people by the heavy yoke of the Midianites and their allies.

Several valuable lessons can be gleaned from the story of Gideon. First, Gideon was not a warrior, and he was afraid of the Midianites. However, the Angel of the LORD spoke to him and called him "a mighty warrior." Because a humble Israelite man was willing to trust God, he was endowed with the Spirit of God and became the mighty warrior who delivered Israel.

Second, the LORD promised Gideon that he would be with him in his effort to save Israel from its oppressors. The promise of God's presence with Gideon was an affirmation that God was once again going to work through a weak vessel so that God's work could be accomplished in the world. But before Gideon could become

Israel's deliverer, he needed to learn to trust in God to provide what was necessary for him to achieve victory.

The story of Gideon shows the cycle of apostasy that plagues Israel throughout the period of the judges. This cycle of rebellion is reflected in the people's decision to worship Baal, the Canaanite storm god, and Asherah, the Canaanite goddess of fertility. Because of their apostasy, "the LORD delivered them into the hands of the Midianites for seven years" (Judges 6:1). When the people of Israel cried for help, God chose Gideon to deliver Israel from the oppression imposed upon the people by the Midianites.

This series of studies on Gideon will be done in partnership with my pastor, Jeff Griffin, Senior Pastor of The Compass Church in Naperville, Illinois. The studies will begin with an overview of Gideon's ministry as a judge, "Gideon, A Judge in Israel," followed by a study on Gideon's encounter with Yahweh, "Yahweh Waiting for Gideon." Then, I will write four studies based on Jeff's four sermons.

Jeff and I hope that these studies will help you gain a deeper understanding of Gideon's life. In addition, we hope that when you are confronted with challenges in your life, you will learn from Gideon, a man who defied all odds, was assigned the most impossible task, and yet succeeded and was victorious despite all odds being against him.

Gideon: Against All Odds

Study 1: Gideon: Against All Odds – Identity

When God's angel found Gideon hiding in a winepress, threshing wheat in secret to avoid Midianite raiders, the divine greeting was startling: "The LORD is with you, mighty warrior." Gideon saw himself as the least in his family, from the weakest clan in Manasseh, yet God saw something entirely different.

Study 2: Gideon: Against All Odds – Impact

From a frightened farmer to a deliverer of nations, Gideon's transformation illustrates how God uses ordinary people to accomplish extraordinary things. Despite his initial reluctance and repeated requests for signs, Gideon ultimately led Israel to victory over the oppressive Midianite coalition that had plagued the land for seven years.

Study 3: Gideon: Against All Odds – Dependence

Gideon's repeated requests for fleeces and signs reveal a man learning to depend on God rather than his own understanding or strength. When God systematically reduced his army from 32,000 to 300 men, the message became unmistakably clear: this victory would belong to the LORD alone, not to human might or military strategy. The bizarre battle plan of trumpets, torches, and clay jars further emphasized that Israel's deliverance would come through divine power, not conventional warfare.

Study 4: Gideon: Against All Odds – Courage

Courage is not the absence of fear; it is obedience in the face of fear. Gideon's journey from hiding in a winepress to boldly leading 300 men against a vast enemy army illustrates how God develops courage in his people through progressive steps of faith. Gideon's courage was not born from natural bravery but from growing confidence in God's character and faithfulness, reminding us that when God calls us to impossible tasks, he also provides the courage to accomplish them.

CHAPTER 10

GIDEON: A JUDGE IN ISRAEL

This chapter examines the role of Gideon as a military leader and judge in ancient Israel during a period of Midianite oppression. Through analysis of the biblical narrative in the book of Judges, this study explores the dual themes of military deliverance and religious reformation that characterize Gideon's leadership. While Gideon successfully addressed Israel's immediate military crisis, the underlying spiritual apostasy that precipitated foreign oppression remained unresolved, foreshadowing the cyclical pattern of decline that would plague Israel throughout the period of the judges.

Introduction

The period of the judges represents a turbulent epoch in Israel's early history, characterized by recurring cycles of apostasy, oppression, and divine deliverance. Among the prominent figures of this era, Gideon stands as a paradigmatic example of divinely appointed leadership confronting both external military threats and internal spiritual corruption. This chapter examines Gideon's role as both military commander and religious reformer, investigating how his leadership addressed the immediate crisis of Midianite oppression while failing to resolve the fundamental theological issues that plagued Israelite society.

Gideon's Identity and Historical Context

Gideon's name derives from the Hebrew root meaning "hewer" or "slasher" (Boling, 1992), reflecting his military function as a warrior-deliverer. The narrative assigns him the additional name Jerubbaal, meaning "Let Baal contend against him" (Judges 6:32), commemorating his destruction of his father's Baal altar. Significantly, the variant form Jerubbesheth appearing in 2 Samuel 11:21 represents a deliberate textual alteration, substituting *bosheth* ("shame") for the divine name Baal, thereby demonstrating later editorial rejection of Canaanite religious elements in Israelite nomenclature.

Gideon belonged to the clan of Abiezer within the tribe of Manasseh and lived in Ophrah, located in the strategic Jezreel Valley. This location put him at the heart of the Midianite attacks, which primarily impacted the territories of Manasseh and Ephraim. His father, Joash's, support of Baal worship shows how deeply Canaanite religious practices had entered Israelite society, even among tribal leaders.

The Midianite Crisis and Covenant Violation

The Midianite oppression occurred approximately forty years after the victory of Deborah and Barak over Sisera's Canaanite coalition (Judges 5:31). The narrative attributes these seven years of subjugation directly to Israel's covenant violation: "The Israelites did what was evil in the sight of the LORD, and the LORD gave them into the hand of Midian seven years" (Judges 6:1). This theological interpretation places the military crisis within the broader framework of Deuteronomic covenant theology (Endris 2008:173–195).

The invading force comprised multiple tribal confederations: the Midianites, Amalekites, and "people of the east." The Midianites, descendants of Abraham through Keturah (Genesis 25:1–2), were seminomadic peoples from western Arabia. The Amalekites, traditional enemies of Israel descended from Esau (Genesis 36:15–16), had previously allied with other adversaries against Israel. The identity of the "people of the east" remains debated, with scholars proposing either a collective designation for the Midianites and Amalekites or reference to additional eastern tribal groups, possibly the Kedemites.

Military and Economic Impact

The narrative describes the invading forces in exaggerated terms, comparing them to locust swarms and estimating their combined army at 135,000 warriors (Judges 8:10). Although this number might be an overstatement, it highlights how overwhelming the threat was. The invaders used methodical agricultural destruction, ruining crops and livestock to weaken Israel's economy. This tactic forced the Israelite people into caves and mountain hideouts, essentially leaving them to survive on very little (Malamat 1953: 61–65).

The Midianite oppression exemplifies the covenant curses outlined in Deuteronomy 28:50–51, which threatened foreign invasion as punishment for covenant violation. The systematic destruction of Israel's agricultural economy—grain, wine, oil, livestock— corresponds precisely to the threatened consequences of apostasy. The narrative thus presents the military crisis as divine judgment rather than mere historical circumstance.

Religious Syncretism and Idolatry

Israel's spiritual crisis manifested through the adoption of Canaanite religious practices, particularly Baal worship. The narrative identifies three elements of this syncretistic religion: the sacred oak at Ophrah associated with divination, the altar to Baal (the storm and fertility deity), and the Asherah pole representing the Canaanite fertility goddess. Joash's sponsorship of these cultic installations demonstrates how deeply Canaanite religion had penetrated Israelite society, reaching even the tribal leadership responsible for maintaining covenant fidelity.

Gideon's Divine Commission and Initial Reforms

Gideon's commission follows the classical pattern of biblical prophetic calling, which includes a divine appearance, initial reluctance, and confirmatory signs. The angel's declaration, "The LORD is with you, you mighty warrior" (Judges 6:12), establishes both divine presence and military vocation as central themes. God's command to "Go in the strength you have and save Israel" (Judges 6:14 NIV) explicitly links spiritual empowerment with military mission.

Significantly, Gideon's first act involves religious purification rather than military mobilization. The command to destroy his father's Baal altar and Asherah pole (Judges 6:25) establishes religious reform as the necessary foundation for military success. This sequence suggests that military victory depends primarily upon covenant restoration rather than strategic or tactical considerations.

Community Response and Religious Conflict

The community's hostile reaction to Gideon's iconoclastic activity reveals the depth of religious syncretism within Israelite society. Joash's defense of his son, "If he is a god, let him contend for himself" (Judges 6:31), demonstrates a sophisticated theological argument that effectively neutralizes Baal's claim to divine authority. This incident illustrates how religious reformation required not only individual courage but also community theological education.

Military Strategy and Divine Methodology

The narrative's emphasis on reducing Gideon's army from 32,000 to 300 warriors serves important theological purposes. This dramatic reduction ensures that victory cannot be attributed to human military prowess, thereby preserving divine prerogative and preventing Israelite boasting (Judges 7:2). The selection process, which dismisses the fearful and chooses those who remain alert while drinking, suggests that divine victory requires both courage and vigilance, rather than numerical superiority.

The battle strategy, which employed trumpets, torches, and empty jars, represents psychological warfare designed to create confusion and panic among the enemy forces. This approach reflects ancient Near Eastern military tactics, emphasizing reliance on divine intervention rather than conventional weapons. The success of this strategy validates the theological principle that "the battle belongs to the LORD" (1 Samuel 17:47).

Political and Social Consequences

Gideon's leadership required managing intertribal tensions, particularly between the tribes of Manasseh and Ephraim. The Ephraimites' complaint about exclusion from the initial battle

(Judges 8:1–3) reveals the political fragmentation that characterized Israel during the period of the judges. Gideon's diplomatic response, honoring Ephraim's contribution to the final victory, demonstrates political wisdom essential for maintaining a tribal coalition.

The people's offer of hereditary kingship to Gideon (Judges 8:22) and his subsequent refusal represent a crucial moment in Israel's political development. Gideon's response, "The LORD will rule over you" (Judges 8:23), affirms the theocratic principle that would later conflict with popular demand for monarchical government (1 Samuel 8). This incident foreshadows the theological tension between divine sovereignty and human political institutions that would characterize Israel's later history.

The Persistence of Spiritual Crisis

Despite Gideon's military success and initial religious reforms, the narrative concludes with Israel's return to Baal worship immediately following his death (Judges 8:33–35). This apostasy demonstrates that external reform, however dramatic, cannot address the fundamental human tendency toward idolatry without corresponding internal transformation. The cycle of apostasy-oppression-deliverance thus continues, revealing the temporary nature of purely human solutions to spiritual problems.

The narrator's concluding observation, "In those days there was no king in Israel; all the people did what was right in their own eyes" (Judges 21:25), provides an interpretive framework for understanding Israel's recurring spiritual and political crises. This assessment suggests that the absence of centralized authority contributed to moral and religious anarchy. However, the narrative maintains tension regarding whether human kingship represents a divine solution or human rebellion.

Theological Implications

Gideon's career illustrates both the necessity and insufficiency of human leadership in addressing covenantal crisis. While his military achievements provided temporary relief from foreign oppression, his inability to effect permanent spiritual transformation reveals the limitations of human deliverance. The narrative thus points beyond immediate historical circumstances toward the need for more fundamental divine intervention.

Conclusion

Gideon's role as judge in Israel demonstrates the complex relationship between military deliverance and spiritual reformation in ancient Israelite society. While his leadership successfully addressed the immediate crisis of Midianite oppression, the persistence of religious apostasy following his death reveals the fundamental inadequacy of human solutions to covenant violation. The narrative presents Gideon as a paradigmatic figure whose achievements and limitations illuminate both the necessity of divine intervention in human crisis and the ultimate insufficiency of temporal deliverance to address spiritual rebellion.

The cyclical pattern of apostasy, oppression, and deliverance that characterizes the period of the judges finds partial resolution in Gideon's career while simultaneously pointing toward its ultimate limitations. His refusal of kingship affirms theocratic principles while highlighting the tension between divine sovereignty and human political organization, a tension that would continue to challenge Israelite society. Thus, Gideon's legacy lies not merely in his military achievements but in his role as a transitional figure whose career both exemplifies and transcends the possibilities of human leadership within the covenant community.

The narrative's theological sophistication lies in its presentation of military and political events within the framework of covenant theology, demonstrating how historical circumstances serve didactic purposes in revealing divine character and human responsibility. Gideon's story thus functions not merely as a historical record but also as theological instruction on the relationship between divine sovereignty, human agency, and covenant fidelity in the ongoing drama of Israel's relationship with Yahweh.

CHAPTER 11

WAITING FOR GIDEON

The story of Gideon's commissioning in Judges 6 presents a notable theophanic encounter that reveals important theological insights about divine-human interaction in the Old Testament. This chapter examines the literary and theological aspects of Yahweh's patient approach to Gideon's needs, especially focusing on Yahweh's willingness to wait for a human response. Through detailed textual analysis, this chapter looks at how the Angel of Yahweh is identified with Yahweh himself, the slow process of recognizing divine presence, and what divine embodiment means in Old Testament theology.

The Context of Divine Intervention

The period of the Judges displays a recurring pattern of turning away from God, suffering, crying out for help, and being rescued in Israel's history. In this context, the story of Gideon's calling (Judges 6:11–24) stands out as a key example of God's divine presence, characterized by great patience and a willingness to meet people where they are. The Midianite oppression, which lasted seven years, had left Israel in severe poverty, causing the people to hide in caves and mountain strongholds while their enemies systematically destroyed their farms and resources.

The severity of the Midianite oppression cannot be overstated. The biblical text describes an enemy whose numbers "could not be counted" (Judges 6:5), arriving with livestock, tents, and camels in such quantity that they resembled locusts covering the land. This systematic devastation extended beyond mere military conquest to economic warfare, as the Midianites strategically timed their raids to coincide with harvest seasons, effectively strangling Israel's agricultural economy and reducing the population to subsistence living.

The divine response to Israel's cry for help follows an established pattern in Judges: first, prophetic confrontation addressing the root cause of oppression—Israel's abandonment of Yahweh for Canaanite deities—followed by the raising up of a deliverer. The prophet's message in Judges 6:8–10 explicitly connects Israel's suffering to their covenant unfaithfulness, establishing the theological foundation for subsequent divine intervention.

The Theophanic Encounter

The narrative presents a complex theological phenomenon in the identification of the Angel of Yahweh with Yahweh himself. This identification, observed throughout the Old Testament, suggests a sophisticated understanding of divine manifestation that transcends simple angelology. In Genesis 16:7–13, Hagar encounters the Angel of Yahweh, yet the text indicates that "Yahweh spoke to her." Similarly, in Genesis 22:11–12, the Angel of Yahweh prevents Abraham from sacrificing Isaac, while Yahweh himself is credited with the communication. The Exodus 3:2–4 account presents the same phenomenon, where the Angel of Yahweh appears to Moses in the burning bush, yet Yahweh speaks directly to him.

As Sasson observes, "The Hebrew God himself engages Gideon apparently without any physical changes to make his divinity obvious" (Sasson 2013:331). This seamless transition between the Angel of Yahweh and Yahweh himself suggests a theological understanding of divine presence that allows for both transcendence and immanence without contradiction.

The Commission and Resistance

Yahweh's commission to Gideon employs the emphatic Hebrew construction: "Go in this strength of yours, and you will rescue Israel from the power of Midian. Am I not sending you myself?" (Judges 6:14). The divine self-identification becomes more explicit as the dialogue progresses, particularly in Yahweh's assurance: "But I (*ehyeh*) will be with you" (Judges 6:16). The Hebrew *ehyeh* employed here directly echoes the divine self-revelation to Moses in Exodus 3:14: "God said to Moses, 'I AM WHO I AM'" (*ehyeh asher ehyeh*), establishing clear theological continuity between the two commissioning narratives.

Gideon's resistance follows a pattern familiar in biblical call narratives, presenting objections based on personal inadequacy and tribal insignificance. His claim that his clan is "the weakest in Manasseh" and that he is "the least in my family" (Judges 6:15) reflects both genuine humility and strategic rhetorical positioning common in ancient Near Eastern contexts.

The Sign and Divine Accommodation

Gideon's request for a sign represents more than mere skepticism; as Evans notes, "for Gideon the point of the sign is not to confirm the task but rather to validate God's identity" (Evans 2017:90). This distinction is crucial for understanding the theological function of signs in biblical narrative. Gideon seeks not confirmation of his mission but verification of his divine interlocutor's identity.

The most theologically significant aspect of this encounter lies in Yahweh's agreement to wait for Gideon's return with an offering. When Gideon proposed to bring an offering to Yahweh, Yahweh assured him, "I will remain until you return" (Judges 6:18). The Hebrew text employs the verb *yāšab*, meaning "to sit" or "to dwell," indicating not merely passive waiting but active accommodation to human temporal limitations. As Block translates: "I will sit [here] until you return" (Block 1999: 263), while Niditch renders it "I will sit still until you return" (Niditch 2008: 84).

The elaborate nature of Gideon's preparation—slaughtering and cooking a young goat, preparing bread from an ephah of flour (approximately ten pounds), and cooking the broth—would have required several hours. During this extended period, Yahweh remained seated under the oak tree, waiting for Gideon, demonstrating what Webb describes as "graciously accommodating himself to Gideon's need" (Webb 2012: 231).

The Consumption and Recognition

The miraculous consumption of the offering by fire emanating from the Angel's staff serves as the definitive sign of divine

115

presence. Gideon's response, "Alas, my Lord Yahweh! Now I have seen the Angel of Yahweh face to face" (Judges 6:22 NJB), reveals his sudden recognition of the gravity of his situation. The divine reassurance "Peace be with you; have no fear; you will not die" (Judges 6:23) addresses the common biblical motif that seeing God results in death, while Gideon's construction of an altar named "Yahweh-Shalom" ("Yahweh is Peace") memorializes both the encounter and the divine promise of peace.

Divine Embodiment in Hebrew Thought

The narrative raises important questions about divine embodiment in Hebrew theology. Contrary to later philosophical developments that emphasized divine incorporeality, the Old Testament consistently presents Yahweh in human form. As Hamori's study, When Gods Were Men: The Embodied God in Biblical and Near Eastern Literature, demonstrates, divine embodiment is a legitimate theological category in ancient Near Eastern and biblical thought rather than mere accommodation to a primitive understanding.

The text's matter-of-fact presentation of Yahweh's physical presence—sitting under a tree, waiting for Gideon to prepare a meal, eating food, engaging in extended conversation—suggests a theological worldview that does not perceive divine embodiment as problematic or contradictory to divine transcendence.

Divine Patience and Accommodation

The theological significance of Yahweh's willingness to wait for Gideon extends beyond mere narrative detail to reveal fundamental aspects of God's character. This patience represents not divine limitation but divine grace—the voluntary self-limitation of the infinite for the sake of finite human understanding and comfort. The divine accommodation serves pedagogical and relational purposes, allowing Gideon the time and space necessary to process his calling and prepare an appropriate response.

The Gideon narrative suggests a model of divine-human interaction characterized by patience, accommodation, and genuine dialogue rather than coercive command. Yahweh's willingness to engage Gideon's objections, provide reassurance, and wait for human response indicates a relational understanding of divine calling that honors human agency while maintaining divine sovereignty.

Conclusion

The account of Yahweh's encounter with Gideon presents a remarkable portrait of divine condescension and patience. The willingness of Yahweh, the transcendent God, to sit under an oak tree for several hours, waiting for a reluctant human servant to prepare an offering, reveals profound theological truths about divine character and the nature of divine-human relationship in Hebrew thought.

This narrative challenges both ancient and contemporary assumptions about divine impassibility and remoteness, presenting instead a God who actively accommodates divine action to human limitation and need. The theological implications extend beyond historical curiosity to fundamental questions about the nature of divine presence, the reality of divine embodiment, and the character of divine patience in human experience.

As the narrative concludes with Gideon's recognition—moving from knowing God "only by hearsay" to having "seen with my own eyes"—it establishes a paradigm for authentic religious experience that combines divine initiative with human responsiveness, mediated through patient divine accommodation to human temporal and psychological limitations.

CHAPTER 12

GIDEON: AGAINST ALL ODDS – IDENTITY

The narrative of Gideon in Judges 6 represents a pivotal moment in Israel's cyclical pattern of apostasy, oppression, and divine deliverance during the period of the Judges (Judges 2:11–19). This account, situated approximately four decades after the victory of Deborah and Barak over Sisera (Judges 4:1—5:31), illustrates the theological theme of divine election working against human expectations and circumstances. The Gideon narrative demonstrates how divine calling transcends human limitations and social status, revealing God's sovereign choice to work through unlikely instruments to accomplish his purposes.

The Midianite Oppression

Following forty years of peace after the defeat of Sisera (Judges 5:31), Israel once again abandoned their covenant relationship with Yahweh, engaging in the worship of Canaanite deities. This apostasy precipitated divine judgment in the form of Midianite oppression lasting seven years (Judges 6:1). The text presents this oppression not as arbitrary suffering but as covenantal consequence, demonstrating the direct correlation between Israel's spiritual fidelity and their political circumstances.

The Midianite oppression differed significantly from previous threats faced by Israel. Judges 6:2–5 describes a systematic economic and social devastation that forced the Israelites to abandon their settlements and seek refuge in mountainous terrain, caves, and fortified positions. The Midianites, allied with the Amalekites and eastern peoples, implemented what can be characterized as economic warfare, timing their incursions to coincide with harvest seasons to maximize agricultural disruption.

The biblical text emphasizes the overwhelming nature of this threat through several literary devices. First, the numerical superiority of the enemy is highlighted, with over 100,000 warriors mentioned in Judges 8:10. Second, the comparison to locusts (Judges 6:5) evokes imagery of complete devastation and unstoppable natural force. Third, the introduction of camel-mounted warfare represents a technological innovation that provided the Midianites with unprecedented mobility and tactical advantage.

The Divine Initiative: Theophany and Calling

The appearance of the Angel of the LORD to Gideon constitutes a theophany, a visible manifestation of the divine presence. This theological concept, prevalent throughout the Old Testament narrative, represents God's direct intervention in human affairs. The Angel of the LORD functions not merely as a messenger but as a divine representative possessing the authority to commission and empower human agents for specific purposes.

The location of this encounter—beneath an oak tree in Ophrah—carries symbolic significance within the broader biblical narrative, as sacred trees often serve as sites of divine revelation and covenant establishment. The casual nature of the Angel's appearance, sitting rather than standing in a position of proclamation, suggests divine accessibility and the ordinariness through which God often chooses to work.

The Angel's initial address to Gideon, "The LORD is with you, you mighty warrior (Judges 6:12), establishes the central theological tension of the narrative. This greeting presents a stark contradiction to Gideon's observable circumstances: he is hiding in a winepress, threshing wheat in fear of discovery by the Midianites, hardly the behavior expected of a "mighty warrior."

This apparent incongruity reveals a fundamental principle of divine calling: God's assessment of human potential operates independently of present circumstances or social perception. The designation "mighty warrior" functions prophetically, declaring not what Gideon is, but what he shall become through divine empowerment. This concept of divine election based on potential rather than performance recurs throughout biblical narrative, from David's selection as king to the apostolic calling of fishermen.

Human Response to Divine Calling

Gideon's response to the Angel reveals both sophistication and human limitation. His question, "if the LORD is with us, why then has all this happened to us?" (Judges 6:13), demonstrates familiarity with covenant theology while revealing an incomplete understanding of the relationship between divine presence and historical circumstances. Gideon's complaint that "the LORD has abandoned us" (Judges 6:13 NIV) reflects a common biblical theme: the human tendency to interpret difficult circumstances as evidence of divine abandonment rather than divine discipline.

The Angel's response redirects focus from speculation to practical obedience: "Go in the strength you have and save Israel out of Midian's hand. Am I not sending you?" (Judges 6:14). This commissioning follows the pattern of biblical calling narratives, emphasizing divine authorization rather than human qualification.

Gideon's protestations of inadequacy, citing his clan's weakness within Manasseh and his position as the youngest in his family, reflect what might be termed a motif of self-deprecation common in biblical calling narratives. These objections parallel Moses' reluctance at the burning bush (Exod 3–4) and Isaiah's cry of unworthiness (Isaiah 6:5), suggesting a literary and theological pattern in accounts of divine calling.

However, these expressions of inadequacy serve a dual function: they demonstrate human humility while highlighting divine sovereignty. God's selection of the least qualified emphasizes that success depends entirely on divine empowerment rather than human ability, thereby ensuring that glory accrues to God rather than human achievement.

Divine Assurance and Identity Transformation

God's response to Gideon's reluctance centers on two foundational promises. The first, "I will be with you" (Judg 6:16) echoes the divine promise given to Moses (Exodus 3:12) and later to Joshua (Joshua 1:5). This assurance of divine presence functions not merely as emotional comfort but as concrete reality: God's presence transforms the nature of the task itself, making victory certain despite overwhelming odds.

The second promise, "you will strike down the Midianites, every one of them" (Judges 6:16) provides specific assurance regarding the mission's outcome. The comprehensive nature of this promise ("every one of them") contrasts sharply with the overwhelming numerical disadvantage Gideon faces, emphasizing the supernatural character of the coming victory.

This prophetic assurance serves multiple theological purposes: it demonstrates God's sovereign control over historical events, provides psychological fortification for the human agent, and establishes the criterion by which divine faithfulness will be measured.

Divine Calling and Human Identity

The Gideon narrative illustrates the transformative power of divine calling on human identity. The designation "mighty warrior" given before any military action demonstrates that identity in the biblical context derives from divine declaration rather than human achievement or social recognition. This principle challenges contemporary assumptions about self-worth and capability, suggesting that human potential is ultimately determined by divine purpose rather than circumstances or qualifications.

Gideon's calling exemplifies God's consistent pattern of working through unlikely instruments to accomplish his purposes. This principle, evident throughout biblical narrative, serves multiple functions: it demonstrates divine sovereignty over human expectations, ensures that glory accrues to God rather than human achievement, and provides hope for those who consider themselves inadequate for divine service.

Conclusion

The opening portion of the Gideon narrative establishes foundational themes that will govern the subsequent account of Israel's deliverance from Midianite oppression. The tension between divine calling and human inadequacy, the promise of divine presence in the face of overwhelming odds, and the transformation of identity through divine designation create the theological framework within which Gideon's military victories must be understood.

The story's lasting importance lies not just in its historical account of military victory but also in its affirmation that divine calling exceeds human limits. Gideon's change from a fearful farmer to a mighty warrior shows the power of divine presence to overcome circumstances, inadequacy, and opposition. As the story unfolds, it raises the question of whether Gideon will accept the identity God has declared and trust his promises, offering a model for understanding divine calling and human response that goes well beyond its immediate historical setting.

The Gideon account thus serves as both a historical narrative and a theological paradigm, illustrating principles of divine election, human response to the call, and the relationship between divine presence and human achievement that remain relevant to contemporary understanding of divine-human interaction and the nature of faith itself.

The Old Testament Speaks to the Church

On June 9, 2019, my pastor, Jeff Griffin, Senior Pastor of Compass Church in Naperville, Illinois, delivered a powerful sermon on Judges 6:1–16 titled "Gideon: Against All Odds - Identity."

Jeff's sermon powerfully demonstrates how the Gideon narrative transcends its historical boundaries to address contemporary believers facing their own "winepress moments." Jeff's application reveals that the same God who transformed a fearful farmer into Israel's deliverer continues to work through unlikely instruments today, challenging believers to see themselves through divine rather than human perspective.

The central application principle emerges from the tension between human self-perception and divine declaration. Just as Gideon saw weakness where God declared strength, contemporary believers often focus on their limitations rather than their divine potential. Jeff's sermon illustrates that God's calling is not contingent on human qualifications but on divine purpose, suggesting that feelings of inadequacy may actually position individuals for greater dependence on divine strength.

Jeff's application extends beyond individual transformation to demonstrate the exponential impact of surrendered lives. His powerful conclusion —that God can use one person to impact thousands of lives worldwide —reflects the biblical principle of divine multiplication seen throughout Scripture. This concept challenges the contemporary tendency toward self-limiting beliefs by revealing that divine calling operates on scales far beyond human imagination or planning.

Gideon's story supports this idea: one hesitant farmer's obedience led to the freeing of an entire nation and forty years of peace (Judges 8:28). Likewise, modern believers who accept their divine identity may find that their faithful response to God's call causes ripple effects far beyond their immediate circle. This principle of multiplication works not through human plans but through divine sovereignty operating in and through lives submitted to it.

Three Foundational Principles for Contemporary Application

1. The Assurance of Divine Presence

Jeff's first application principle—recognizing God's continual presence—addresses the fundamental human fear of isolation in the face of overwhelming challenges. The promise "I will be with you" given to Gideon carries forward into the New Testament era through Christ's assurance: "I am with you always, to the end of the age" (Matthew 28:20). This divine presence transforms every challenge from human impossibility into a divine opportunity.

Contemporary believers facing their own "Midianite armies" — whether personal struggles, ministry challenges, or societal opposition —can draw courage from the same divine presence that empowered Gideon. This presence operates not merely as emotional comfort but as ontological reality: God's presence changes the fundamental nature of circumstances, making victory possible where defeat seemed inevitable.

2. *The Reality of Divine Transformation*

The second principle, believing that God can transform reluctant and inadequate people into mighty warriors, challenges contemporary assumptions about leadership and service. Jeff's application suggests that divine transformation operates independently of natural talent, educational background, or social position. This principle democratizes divine calling, making it accessible to anyone willing to surrender their limitations to divine power.

The transformation process often involves what could be called an internalization of divine perspective, learning to see oneself as God sees rather than as circumstances indicate. This shift from human self-assessment to divine declaration requires both intellectual agreement and experiential trust, as believers learn to behave from their divinely given status instead of their perceived limitations.

3. *The Necessity of Faith-Based Action*

Jeff's final principle, which is the belief that God can use us, shifts from theological understanding to practical action. This belief must lead to action because faith without corresponding behavior is incomplete (James 2:17). The Gideon story shows that divine calling needs a human response; God's power works through, not apart from, human obedience.

Contemporary application requires believers to move beyond passive agreement with divine promises to active engagement with divine purposes. This may involve stepping into roles or responsibilities that exceed perceived capabilities, trusting that divine empowerment will accompany divine calling.

Against All Odds: Knowing Your Identity in Christ

Jeff's concluding exhortation—"Against all odds, know who you are in Christ"—encapsulates the entire sermon's application. This identity knowledge operates on multiple levels:

Positional Identity: Understanding one's standing before God based on Christ's work rather than personal performance creates the foundation for confident service. This positional security enables believers to attempt great things for God without fear of divine rejection should they fail.

Functional Identity: Recognizing the roles and responsibilities God has assigned provides direction for service and ministry. Like Gideon's designation as "mighty warrior," contemporary believers possess divine callings that may not align with their self-perception but accurately reflect God's purposes.

Transformational Identity: Embracing the reality that God's calling includes God's empowerment enables believers to grow into their divine assignments. This process often involves moving from current limitations toward future potential through progressive surrender to divine working.

Jeff's application demonstrates that the Gideon narrative addresses persistent human challenges that transcend cultural and temporal boundaries. The fear of inadequacy, the temptation toward self-limiting beliefs, and the struggle to trust divine promises remain constant elements of human experience. The narrative's power lies not in its historical distance but in its contemporary relevance, offering hope and direction to believers facing their own impossible circumstances.

The sermon's conclusion challenges listeners to evaluate their response to divine calling in light of Gideon's example. Will contemporary believers allow perceived limitations to override divine declarations? Will they trust in God's presence and power enough to step into assignments that exceed their natural capabilities? The answers to these questions will determine whether they experience the transformation and impact that characterized Gideon's ministry.

Jeff's sermon application reveals that the God who called Gideon continues to call ordinary people to extraordinary service. The same divine presence that empowered ancient Israel's deliverer remains available to contemporary believers facing their own overwhelming challenges. The key lies not in achieving adequacy before responding to God's call, but in responding to God's call and discovering adequacy through divine empowerment.

Against all odds, believers can know who they are in Christ, not based on present circumstances or past failures, but on divine declaration and eternal purpose. This identity, rooted in God's character rather than human performance, provides the foundation for confident service and extraordinary impact. As Jeff powerfully concluded, God can indeed use any person today to accomplish work that brings glory to his name and blessing to countless lives worldwide.

CHAPTER 13

GIDEON: AGAINST ALL ODDS – IMPACT

The narrative of Gideon in the book of Judges represents a pivotal moment in Israel's cyclical pattern of apostasy, oppression, and deliverance. This chapter examines how Gideon's encounter with Yahweh catalyzed not only personal transformation but also initiated a broader religious renewal that expanded from individual commitment to national mobilization. The text demonstrates that effective spiritual leadership begins with a personal encounter with God and extends through concentric circles of influence, ultimately challenging the prevailing religious syncretism of the period.

Historical Context

Following the death of Deborah and Barak, who had secured forty years of peace after defeating Sisera and the Canaanite army (Judges 4:1–24), Israel once again fell into apostasy. The biblical text records that "the people did what was evil" and consequently "the LORD gave them into the hand of Midian seven years" (Judges 6:1). This period exemplifies the cycle of apostasy that characterizes the book of Judges: Israel's unfaithfulness leads to divine judgment through foreign oppression, which prompts the people to cry out for deliverance.

The Midianite oppression proved particularly devastating to Israel's agrarian economy. The systematic destruction of harvests and livestock by Midianite raiders reduced the Israelites to "utter misery" (Judges 6:6 TNK), creating both material and spiritual desperation. This economic warfare effectively undermined Israel's capacity for sustained resistance while reinforcing its dependence on divine intervention for deliverance.

Spiritual Causation of Political Crisis

In response to Israel's cry for help, Yahweh first sent an unnamed prophet to address the root cause of their suffering (Judges 6:7–10). The prophet's message reveals a crucial theological principle: political and military crises often stem from spiritual rebellion. While the people perceived their problem as primarily military, the oppression of the Midianites, the prophet identified the actual cause as covenant violation through Baal worship.

The prophetic indictment follows a classic pattern of covenant lawsuit, reminding the people of Yahweh's past deliverance from Egypt while highlighting their failure to observe the prohibition against worshiping "the gods of the Amorites" (Judges 6:10). Significantly, the prophet's message offers no immediate hope of deliverance, serving instead as a diagnostic tool that prepares the ground for the subsequent divine intervention through Gideon.

Gideon's Call and Commission

The theophany experienced by Gideon marks a turning point in the narrative. The appearance of the Angel of the LORD, who addresses Gideon as "a mighty warrior," reveals the divine perspective that transcends human perception. Gideon's self-perception as inadequate contrasts sharply with God's declaration of his potential, illustrating the transformative power of divine calling.

The commission given to Gideon, "Go in this might of yours and deliver Israel from the hand of Midian" (Judges 6:14), contains an apparent paradox. While Gideon protests his weakness, God attributes strength to him, suggesting that divine empowerment transforms human inadequacy into effective leadership. The assurance "I will be with you" (Judges 6:16) provides the theological foundation for Gideon's subsequent transformation.

The Sign of the Sacrifice

Gideon's request for a sign reflects both emerging faith and persistent doubt. His preparation of a meal for his divine visitor demonstrates the cultural importance of hospitality while simultaneously serving a deeper theological purpose. The Hebrew term *minḥâ* used for Gideon's "present" (Judges 6:18) carries both secular ("present") and religious ("offering") connotations, suggesting that what begins as hospitality transforms into worship.

The miraculous consumption of the offering by fire from the rock serves multiple functions. First, it confirms the divine identity of Gideon's visitor. Second, it transforms the meal into a legitimate sacrifice, establishing proper worship in contrast to the syncretistic practices prevalent in Israel. Third, it sanctifies the location, converting a place associated with Baal worship into a site dedicated to Yahweh.

Gideon's recognition that he had encountered "the angel of the LORD face to face" (Judges 6:22) represents a moment of spiritual awakening. His fear of death, followed by divine reassurance, leads to the establishment of an altar named "Yahweh Shalom" ("The LORD is Peace"), creating a permanent memorial to this transformative encounter (Judges 6:24).

The Challenge to Religious Syncretism

The divine command to destroy his father's altar to Baal and the associated Asherah pole marks Gideon's first specific act of obedience and religious reform. The act Gideon was about to undertake was one of defiance. He needed to destroy the altar of Baal, the Canaanite god worshiped by many in Israel. This altar to Baal belonged to Gideon's father. As Butler wrote, "Gideon must prove his commitment to Yahweh within his family before proving it in battle" (Butler 2009:205). This nighttime operation, carried out with ten servants, highlights both the controversial nature of the act and Gideon's ability to inspire others to join in religious change.

The symbolic significance of using two bulls—one representing Baal and another representing the seven years of oppression—suggests a deliberate theological statement. By offering the second bull as a burnt offering to Yahweh using wood from the destroyed Asherah pole, Gideon effectively desecrates the pagan symbols while simultaneously establishing legitimate worship.

The construction of Yahweh's altar "on top of the fortress" where Baal's temple was located represents a decisive act of religious reclamation. This geographical displacement of worship sites symbolizes the theological displacement of false gods by the true God of Israel.

Community Response and Paternal Support

The townspeople's reaction to the destruction reveals the depth of syncretistic commitment in Israel. Their demand for Gideon's death exposes the irony that they must defend Baal because the deity cannot defend himself. The Hebrew term *dāraš*, "enquire" (Judges 6:29), used to describe their investigation, carries connotations of divination, suggesting their continued reliance on pagan religious practices even in seeking justice.

Joash's defense of his son marks a crucial turning point in the narrative. His rhetorical question "Are you trying to save him [Baal]?" (Judges 6:31 NIV) exposes the logical absurdity of defending an allegedly powerful deity. Joash's challenge to "let Baal contend" with Gideon effectively calls Baal's bluff, demonstrating the father's gradual conversion from syncretism to personal faith in Yahweh.

The bestowal of the name "Jerubbaal" ("Let Baal contend with him") serves as both a challenge to the false god and a public declaration of Gideon's new religious identity. As Soggin notes, this naming represents Gideon's symbolic rebirth and new relationship with God. He wrote: "Gideon is as it were reborn, and his father gives him the name" (Soggin 1981:125).

The Expanding Circles of Influence

Gideon's transformation from farmer to religious reformer illustrates the progression from personal encounter to public ministry. The ten servants who assisted in destroying Baal's altar (Judges 6:27) represent the first circle of influence—those who work closely with transformed individuals and witness their commitment firsthand.

The mobilization of the Abiezrite clan following Gideon's trumpet call demonstrates how religious authenticity attracts followers. The same community members who initially sought Gideon's death for destroying Baal's altar subsequently joined his military campaign, illustrating the power of demonstrated commitment to effect attitudinal change.

Gideon's expansion from clan to tribe to intertribal coalition follows a logical progression of influence. The response of Manasseh, Asher, Zebulun, and Naphtali to his call represents a significant achievement in a period characterized by tribal fragmentation and individualism.

The selective response of only four out of twelve tribes reveals both the limitations of Gideon's influence and the pragmatic nature of ancient Israelite political alliances. Those tribes most directly threatened by Midianite oppression proved most willing to risk military engagement, suggesting that shared crisis creates opportunities for religious and political unity.

The Role of Courage in Religious Reform

The Gideon narrative establishes a paradigm for religious transformation that moves from divine encounter through personal commitment to public influence. This progression suggests that authentic spiritual leadership requires both personal experience with God and a willingness to challenge prevailing religious and social norms.

The text emphasizes that transformation begins with individuals but cannot remain individualistic. Gideon's impact extended through natural social networks—family, clan, tribe, and allied tribes—demonstrating that religious renewal spreads through existing relationships and shared interests.

Gideon's nocturnal destruction of Baal's altar illustrates the courage required for religious reform in hostile environments. His willingness to act despite fear, supported by a small group of committed followers, provides a model for minority reform movements facing majority opposition.

The narrative also demonstrates that religious reform requires both the destruction of false systems and the construction of true alternatives. Gideon's establishment of Yahweh's altar, where Baal's stood, symbolizes the replacement rather than mere elimination of religious practice.

The Old Testament Speaks to the Church

The transformative principles demonstrated in Gideon's story are clearly evident in everyday modern situations. My pastor, Jeff Griffin, Senior Pastor of The Compass Church in Naperville, Illinois, delivered a sermon on June 16, 2019, titled "Gideon: Against All Odds – Impact," which emphasized this connection through the inspiring testimony of a seventeen-year-old McDonald's employee whose strong Christian witness had a significant spiritual influence.

This modern comparison demonstrates that the Gideon paradigm functions regardless of social status, age, or vocational prominence. Just as Gideon was once an obscure farmer threshing wheat in a winepress, this teenager worked in what many would see as an ordinary service job. Yet both individuals discovered that faithful dedication to God, shown through genuine testimony in their immediate circles, could produce transformational impact far beyond their apparent limitations.

The teenager's story highlights the mathematical potential of faithful witness. Her dedication to Christ allowed her to influence one coworker—a humble start that echoes Gideon's initial work with his ten servants. Yet, this single conversion sparked a chain reaction that eventually included thirty-two people across four generations. This pattern of exponential growth mirrors the expanding circles of influence seen in Gideon's transition from personal change to tribal mobilization.

The four-generational impact shows the lasting power of genuine spiritual influence. While Gideon's immediate impact was on military victory and religious reform during his time, the teenager's witness left a legacy that went beyond his era. This multigenerational effect indicates that faithful testimony today can produce spiritual benefits for many years into the future.

Workplace Evangelism as Sacred Calling

The McDonald's setting provides a clear example of Gideon's principles in today's world. Modern workplaces, like ancient farming communities, are natural social networks where authentic relationships develop over time. The teen's ability to influence her coworker likely stemmed from daily interactions that demonstrated her faith through consistent character and genuine care.

This workplace witness challenges the artificial separation between sacred and secular areas. Just as Gideon's farming served as the setting for a divine encounter and subsequent ministry, the teenager's job became a place for spiritual influence. The story suggests that God can turn any occupation into a platform for kingdom work when individuals remain sincerely committed to Christ.

Both Gideon and the teenager started their transformative work within their close relationships. Gideon began with his servants before expanding to family, clan, and tribe. Similarly, the teenager focused on building an authentic relationship with one coworker rather than trying to evangelize the entire restaurant. This approach shows wisdom in understanding that lasting influence usually starts with depth rather than breadth.

The success of both approaches confirms the idea that genuine spiritual influence spreads through existing relationships rather than through impersonal mass communication. The teenager's coworker likely had his own network of relationships that served as the channel for further spiritual impact, forming a natural progression similar to Gideon's tribal expansion.

Both stories address the common objection that ordinary people cannot make a significant spiritual impact. Gideon's initial protest, "my clan is the weakest in Manasseh, and I am the least in my family" (Judges 6:15), echoes today in the idea that teenagers working at fast-food places cannot make a meaningful difference for eternity. However, both stories show that God's power can turn what seem like limitations into strategic advantages.

The teenager's age and workplace may have actually enhanced her credibility with peers who might have been suspicious of more formal religious approaches. Her authentic faith, demonstrated through consistent character in a demanding work environment, likely carried more persuasive power than professional ministry presentations. This principle suggests that contemporary Christians should view their ordinary circumstances as potential platforms for extraordinary impact rather than obstacles to spiritual influence.

Conclusion

The story of Gideon in Judges 6 offers a strong example of how religious transformation and leadership grow, going beyond history to give useful advice for modern Christian witness. Starting with a divine encounter and personal change, the story shows how influence spreads through layers of relationships and shared commitment. This pattern is clearly shown in Jeff's modern example of the teenage McDonald's worker.

Gideon's impact shows that true spiritual leadership comes from real encounters with God, requires courage to challenge established religious norms, and influences others through genuine commitment rather than just words. The modern example confirms that these principles work across different times and cultures, enabling ordinary people to make a powerful spiritual difference by being faithful witnesses in their immediate surroundings.

The theological significance of both stories transcends their respective contexts, offering insights into the processes by which religious renewal occurs in communities marked by spiritual decline. The progression from individual transformation to collective mobilization, whether in ancient Israel or contemporary America, suggests that lasting religious impact requires both personal authenticity and strategic engagement through existing social networks.

The teenager's story particularly illuminates how the Gideon paradigm operates in contemporary settings, demonstrating that neither age, social status, nor occupational prestige determines spiritual influence. Instead, committed faith expressed through authentic relationships in ordinary circumstances can generate an exponential impact that extends across generations.

Ultimately, both stories confirm that one person serving God can influence many lives. However, they also demonstrate that such influence requires divine help, sincere effort, and a patient, strategic approach over time to build relationships. The story of Gideon transforming from a fearful farmer into a mighty warrior, along with the teen's rise as an effective witness at her workplace, serves as both a historical example and a modern model of how divine encounters can inspire individual and community change against all odds.

As Jeff emphasized in his sermon, these stories challenge contemporary Christians to recognize their ordinary circumstances as potential platforms for extraordinary impact, encouraging faithful witness within existing relationships while trusting divine empowerment to generate influence far beyond apparent human limitations. The multigenerational impact documented in both accounts suggests that present faithfulness can create spiritual legacies that extend far beyond immediate visibility, making every believer's commitment to authentic witness a matter of eternal significance.

CHAPTER 14

GIDEON AGAINST ALL ODDS – DEPENDENCE

The story of Gideon in Judges 6–8 provides a powerful insight into divine sovereignty and human reliance within the cycle of Israel's repeated sins and deliverance. This chapter explores how the text builds a theological framework in which human weakness serves to reveal divine power, examining the struggle between faith and doubt through Gideon's character growth and God's gracious responses to human vulnerability.

Within this framework, the Gideon narrative (Judges 6–8) serves as a prime example of how Yahweh works through unlikely human agents to fulfill divine purposes. The story demonstrates a core theological principle: divine strength is most clearly shown through human weakness, and victory ultimately belongs to God rather than human military skill or strategic brilliance.

The historical context describes Israel's seven-year oppression by the Midianites and their allies as a result of the nation turning away from Yahweh and toward Canaanite gods. In this setting of national apostasy and foreign domination, the Angel of Yahweh appears to Gideon—a man threshing wheat in a winepress to hide from Midianite raiders—to call him as Israel's savior. This opening scene emphasizes the central conflict of the story: the contrast between divine calling and human weakness.

The Fleece: Faith, Doubt, and Divine Accommodation

Despite receiving multiple divine assurances—the Angel's declaration that "the LORD is with you" (Judges 6:12) and Yahweh's direct promise "I will be with you" (Judges 6:16)—Gideon seeks additional confirmation through the famous fleece test. This request reveals the complex psychology of faith under pressure and raises important questions about the relationship between divine patience and human doubt.

Block's observation that "the request for signs is not a sign of faith but of unbelief" (Block 1999: 272–273) provides a crucial interpretive lens for understanding Gideon's actions. The fleece incident represents not spiritual maturity but rather the persistent human tendency to demand tangible proof of divine promises. Gideon's words, "To see whether you will deliver Israel by my hand, as you have said" (Judges 6:36–37), betray his fundamental uncertainty about God's faithfulness to his word.

The Implications of the Fleece Test

Beck's analysis of the fleece story within the larger context of the Yahweh-Baal conflict provides important insight into the theological aspects of Gideon's request (Beck 2008:36) . The use of dew—usually linked to divine blessing and fertility—acts as a public display of Yahweh's dominance over Baal, the Canaanite storm god believed to control crops and prosperity. From this view, Gideon's test is not just about personal reassurance but also serves as religious argument, affirming Yahweh's exclusive right to Israel's loyalty.

The specific nature of Gideon's requests—first for dew on the fleece alone while the ground remains dry, then for the reverse condition—suggests deliberate design to eliminate natural explanations. Gideon's request for dew reflects the struggle with the religion of Baal since Baal was a storm God who provided "the dew of heaven." Gideon needed to show the people that it was Yahweh and not Baal who was sending him. Beck wrote, "Gideon selected the manipulation of dew as the way in which the Lord might assert and proclaim His sole right to the affections of Israel" (Beck 2008:37).

The second test, in particular, counters any argument that the fleece retained moisture longer than the surrounding earth. This systematic approach to divine verification reveals both Gideon's methodical skepticism and his deep need for certainty in the face of overwhelming odds.

Divine Grace and Human Weakness

God's response to Gideon's requests shows great patience and understanding. Even after giving multiple assurances, Yahweh agrees to both tests without criticism or anger. This divine patience underscores a crucial truth: God's grace extends even to those whose faith wavers under pressure. The story suggests that divine election does not require perfect faith, but instead accepts human weakness within the framework of complete dependence on God.

Gideon's acknowledgment, "Do not be angry with me if I speak just once more" (Judges 6:39), shows his awareness that his repeated requests might reasonably upset divine patience. However, the text records no divine anger, only patient tolerance of human needs. This pattern creates a model of divine-human relationship marked by grace rather than performance-based acceptance.

The Reduction of Gideon's Army

The most striking part of the Gideon story happens when Yahweh says that Israel's army of 32,000 soldiers is "too many" to fight against the Midianites, who number 135,000. This seemingly illogical military choice serves a key theological goal: ensuring that the victory is seen as the result of divine help rather than human strength or tactics.

The divine rationale is explicitly stated: "In order that Israel may not boast against me that her own strength has saved her" (Judges 7:2). This concern with proper attribution reveals the narrative's central theological preoccupation with the source of deliverance. The reduction of Israel's forces from 32,000 to 300 creates such overwhelming odds (450:1) that only divine intervention can account for victory.

The two-stage reduction of Gideon's army follows established biblical and ancient Near Eastern precedents while supporting the narrative's theological purpose. The first reduction, which allows fearful soldiers to go home, aligns with Deuteronomic military law (Deuteronomy 20:5–8) and results in the loss of 22,000 men—

two-thirds of the original force. This significant reduction emphasizes the level of fear among Israel's troops and underscores the need for divine rather than human strength.

The second test, which involves the method by which soldiers drink water, has generated considerable scholarly debate over its significance. Susan Niditch suggests "that those who lap like dogs will fight like wild creatures" (Niditch 2008: 197). According to Soggin (1981: 137), "the Jewish historian Josephus said that this test shows 'a sign of fear,' and commented how God chooses inadequate men so that all may redound to his glory." Soggin concludes, "It is probably more reasonable not to think in terms of any particular meaning; we are dealing here with a test, a kind of ordeal by which God selects his own men."

While some interpreters see the 300 "lappers" as either more or less militarily capable than their counterparts, Soggin's assessment that this represents a test by which God selects his men appears most consistent with the narrative's theological emphasis. The arbitrary nature of the selection criteria reinforces the theme that divine choice, rather than human qualification, determines participation in God's work.

The final army composition, with 300 Israelites against 135,000 Midianites, creates a scenario where traditional military wisdom would predict certain defeat. This huge numerical gap serves several purposes in the story. First, it dismisses the idea that victory depends on numbers or traditional military tactics. Second, it shows a situation where divine intervention seems to be the only realistic explanation for success. Third, it proves that God's power works independently of human resources or skills.

The narrative's focus on these overwhelming odds highlights broader biblical themes of divine sovereignty and human dependence. Throughout Scripture, God often works through unlikely situations and imperfect human agents to fulfill divine purposes, emphasizing the supremacy of divine power over human limitations.

The Nature of Gideon's Dependence

Despite his repeated requests for divine confirmation and his initial reluctance to accept his commission, Gideon's relationship with God illustrates healthy spiritual dependence rather than mere human weakness. His acknowledgment of inadequacy, although sometimes excessive, reflects an accurate assessment of the task's magnitude and his own limitations. This recognition of dependence becomes the foundation for divine empowerment instead of an obstacle to effective service.

The narrative structure highlights Gideon's reliance as both vital and supportive. His repeated requests for divine reassurance, while showing imperfect faith, also reflect an understanding that the success of the mission depends entirely on divine help. This lesson—that effective ministry requires total dependence on God—remains important across various historical and cultural settings.

God's Response to Human Weakness

The divine response to Gideon's weaknesses highlights key aspects of God's character that shape our understanding of divine-human relationships. Throughout the story, God shows patience with human flaws, accommodates human needs for reassurance, and remains committed to fulfilling divine purposes despite human shortcomings.

God's willingness to work through an insecure, doubt-prone leader like Gideon shows that divine election does not rely on human perfection. Instead of requiring perfect faith or complete confidence, God's call is extended to those who recognize their dependence on divine strength. This pattern indicates that weakness, when embraced and surrendered to divine control, can serve as a reflection of God's power rather than a hindrance to divine service.

The Fleece Tradition in Christian Practice

Murphy's analysis of how "laying out a fleece" has been interpreted within Christian tradition raises important questions about appropriate methods for seeking divine guidance. In his article, "Laying Out the Fleece: Reading Gideon's Requests with Reception History," Kelly J. Murphy writes, "Within certain Christian traditions, the phrase 'lay out a fleece' denotes a practice of petitioning God to provide a sign to an individual so that the person can make a decision according to God's will" (Murphy (2017: 241). Murphy says that Gideon's "appeal for divine assurance is likely an unquestionably recognizable character trait for many. Who among us hasn't, if we are being honest, wished for (more) guidance and assurance in the face of uncertainty?" (Murphy (2017: 242).

The narrative's emphasis on God's gracious acceptance of human weakness should not be interpreted as divine approval of sign-seeking as a common spiritual practice. Instead, it highlights God's patience with human frailty while guiding us toward the ultimate goal of trusting divine promises without needing extra signs.

Lessons in Leadership and Dependence

The Gideon story provides valuable insights into effective leadership in religious and wider settings. Gideon's initial hesitation and ongoing need for reassurance highlight common leadership challenges, especially when facing daunting obstacles or duties. The story suggests that strong leadership often comes not from self-confidence but from recognizing one's reliance on resources beyond human ability. From beginning to end, Gideon was dependent on God's help and God's power to defeat the Midianites. As Butler wrote, "Gideon fights for honor that rightly belongs to Yahweh" (Butler 2009:211).

The text's depiction of divine accommodation of human weakness offers comfort to those who face doubt or feelings of inadequacy in their calling. Instead of disqualifying people from service, these struggles can serve as opportunities to showcase divine grace and power when surrendered to God's control.

The Old Testament Speaks to the Church

The theological insights from the Gideon story find meaningful modern expression in pastoral practice. My pastor, Jeff Griffin, Senior Pastor of The Compass Church in Naperville, Illinois, delivered a sermon on June 23, 2019, covering Judges 6:36–7:8a, titled "Gideon: Against All Odds – Dependence." Jeff's preaching highlights the text's ongoing relevance by emphasizing pride as a core human issue that the Gideon story directly addresses.

Jeff's pastoral insight views pride as a common human tendency that distorts how we perceive success and achievement. This aligns with the biblical emphasis on giving proper credit for victory. Just as God reduced Gideon's army to prevent Israel from claiming "that her own strength has saved her" (Judges 7:2), modern believers face the same temptation to take credit for accomplishments that ultimately come from divine blessing and power.

Jeff's application expands the narrative's theological framework to explore modern questions of success, achievement, and recognition. His statement that "God is behind our success in life" and "God is the one who gives us the ability to be successful" directly parallels the biblical emphasis on divine agency in human accomplishment. This pastoral interpretation recognizes that the principle underlying God's reduction of Gideon's army, ensuring proper attribution of victory, applies equally to contemporary experiences of success and achievement.

The statement that "all that we are and all that we have are gifts from God" reflects a comprehensive theological view rooted in the doctrine of divine sovereignty. This perspective challenges the secular idea of self-made success and individual achievement that dominates modern culture. Just as the Gideon story shows that military victory belongs to God rather than human strategy or strength, Jeff's application suggests that professional, personal, and spiritual accomplishments should be seen as divine gifts rather than human achievements.

Jeff's use of C. S. Lewis's biographical material on pride demonstrates sophisticated homiletical methodology by linking biblical exegesis with literary and philosophical insight. Lewis's well-documented struggles with pride and his eventual theological understanding of humility offer a compelling bridge between ancient texts and modern application.

Lewis's view on pride, as mentioned in Jeff's sermon, illustrates how pride functions as a comparative sin, one that elevates people above others instead of acknowledging our shared dependence on divine grace. This idea aligns with the Gideon story's emphasis on avoiding boasting and ensuring that the credit for victory goes to God, not human pride. The connection between Lewis's personal struggle with intellectual pride and Gideon's need for divine reassurance creates a powerful parallel that spans centuries and cultures.

The biographical approach to Lewis's views on pride also shows how theological insight often comes from personal struggle rather than abstract thinking. Just as Gideon's weaknesses provided the setting to show divine strength, Lewis's journey from atheism to faith, shaped by ongoing struggles with pride, demonstrates how human flaws can serve as the stage for divine grace.

Jeff's application of the Gideon narrative to the problem of pride offers several practical implications for contemporary Christian discipleship:

Recognition of Divine Agency: Jeff's sermon challenges believers to reflect on their attribution of success, encouraging acknowledgment that abilities, opportunities, and achievements ultimately stem from divine blessing rather than personal merit. This perspective shifts gratitude from occasional acknowledgment to a core aspect of life.

Humility in Achievement: Just as God reduced Gideon's army to prevent boasting, believers are encouraged to stay humble in success, acknowledging that accomplishments serve divine purposes rather than personal pride. This perspective shifts how we view professional success, academic achievements, and ministry effectiveness, seeing them as stewardship roles rather than ownership.

143

Community over Competition: Lewis's insight that pride is a comparative sin, highlighted in Jeff's application, suggests that healthy spiritual growth involves moving beyond competitive relationships toward mutual dependence and a shared recognition of divine grace. This view challenges individualistic ideas about faith and success.

Dependence as Strength: Jeff's focus on dependence as a positive spiritual quality, rather than a weakness to overcome, offers counter-cultural wisdom for modern believers facing pressure to show self-sufficiency and independence.

The pastoral wisdom evident in Jeff's application lies in his recognition that the Gideon narrative addresses not merely historical events but enduring patterns of human behavior and divine response. By focusing on pride as a universal human tendency, Jeff's sermon connects the specific circumstances of ancient Israel's military crisis with the ongoing spiritual challenges faced by contemporary believers.

Conclusion

The Gideon narrative in Judges 6–8 constructs a sophisticated theological framework that explores the relationship between divine sovereignty and human dependence. Through the interplay of Gideon's weakness and God's strength, the text demonstrates that divine power is most clearly manifested when human inadequacy is acknowledged and surrendered to divine control.

Jeff's pastoral application, enriched by insights from C. S. Lewis's biographical struggle with pride, demonstrates the narrative's continued relevance for addressing contemporary spiritual challenges. The story's emphasis on overwhelming odds—both in Gideon's personal struggles with doubt and in the military disadvantage faced by Israel's reduced army—highlights the exclusive role of divine intervention in achieving victory while challenging modern assumptions about self-made success and individual achievement.

Gideon emerges from this narrative not as a superhero but as a representative human figure whose weaknesses become the stage for divine demonstration of power. His story suggests that God's calling extends to the inadequate, the fearful, and the doubtful, transforming human weakness into vehicles for divine glory. In going "against all odds," Gideon discovers that victory ultimately belongs to God rather than to human strength, strategy, or courage, a lesson that Jeff's contemporary application shows remains as relevant today as it was in ancient Israel.

Gideon's story's enduring significance lies in its realistic portrayal of human struggle within the context of divine calling and its demonstration that God's grace accommodates human frailty while fulfilling divine purposes. For contemporary readers, guided by pastoral insights like Jeff's, Gideon's story offers both comfort to those who wrestle with doubt and a challenge to those who rely on human resources rather than divine power to fulfill their calling. Most importantly, it provides a framework for understanding success, achievement, and recognition that counters cultural narratives of self-sufficiency while affirming the dignity of human participation in divine purposes.

CHAPTER 15

GIDEON: AGAINST ALL ODDS – COURAGE

Crisis management and leadership under pressure remain key issues in both ancient and modern times. The biblical story of Gideon serves as a classic example of how individuals face overwhelming challenges and how divine intervention can turn human weakness into strength. During the time of the Judges, Israel endured harsh oppression from the Midianites, who had continually weakened the nation through repeated invasions (Judges 6:6). In this crisis, Gideon appears as a figure whose change from a fearful man to a victorious leader provides deep insights into the nature of courage and divine power.

The Context of Crisis and Divine Calling

The historical setting of Gideon's calling reflects a time of intense national crisis. The Midianite oppression had left Israel in severe poverty, causing the people to take refuge in caves and forts (Judges 6:2). The invaders came "on droves of camels too numerous to count" (Judges 6:5), creating a sense of helplessness and despair among the Israelites.

Gideon's divine mission to confront this overwhelming threat drives the main tension of the story. Called to lead a military campaign against forces that vastly outnumber Israel, Gideon illustrates the paradox of divine choice: God often selects unlikely individuals to carry out extraordinary tasks. The message of this story suggests that divine power operates best through human weakness, ensuring that the ultimate credit goes to the divine rather than human effort.

Divine Assurance in the Face of Fear

The divine command to reduce Gideon's army from 32,000 to 300 warriors is a crucial test of faith and a source of renewed anxiety. This significant reduction resulted in odds of roughly 450 to 1 against the Israelite forces, considering the Midianite army of 135,000 men (Judges 8:10). Although this strategic reduction might seem counterintuitive from a military standpoint, it serves important theological purposes: it guarantees that victory is not attributed to human strength or numerical advantage.

Webb observes that "fearfulness, for most people, is not a weakness that can be conquered once and for all, but something that must be resisted and overcome repeatedly" (Webb 2012: 244). This insight highlights Gideon's ongoing struggle with fear, despite previous divine assurances. The text explicitly acknowledges this psychological reality when God states, "But if you fear to attack, go down to the camp with your servant Purah" (Judges 7:10). The conditional phrase "if you fear" demonstrates divine understanding of human frailty and provides accommodation for Gideon's emotional state.

The Strategic Use of Reconnaissance

God's instruction for Gideon to conduct reconnaissance of the enemy camp serves multiple purposes beyond mere intelligence gathering. First, it provides a constructive outlet for Gideon's anxiety, channeling his fear into purposeful action. Second, it creates an opportunity for divine intervention through natural means: the overheard conversation about the dream. Third, it demonstrates the principle that faith often requires action despite fear, rather than the absence of fear.

The selection of Purah as Gideon's companion reflects careful divine planning (Judges 7:1011). The Hebrew term *na'ar*, translated as "servant," can denote various roles, including the role of armor-bearer or shield-bearer in military contexts. Purah's presence serves both practical and psychological functions: he provides witness to the events Gideon will observe and offers companionship during a moment of vulnerability. This detail highlights the importance of supportive relationships in leadership and crisis management.

The Dream and Its Interpretation

The dream described by the Midianite soldier (Judges 7:13) uses powerful symbolic images that need careful interpretation. The "cake of barley bread" that rolls into the camp and destroys a tent contains multiple meanings. Barley bread, seen as the food of the poor in ancient Near Eastern cultures, represents Israel's perceived insignificance and low status. Josephus noted that the Midianites called the people of Israel "eaters of barley bread." He explained that barley was often fed to animals, so the Midianites viewed the Israelites as a repulsive and loathsome group (Josephus 1987: 5:6.4).

However, the dream's imagery subverts these associations. The humble barley loaf becomes an instrument of destruction, overturning and collapsing the tent that represents the entire Midianite camp. This reversal motif reflects a common biblical theme: the elevation of the lowly and the humbling of the mighty. The small and seemingly insignificant proves capable of overwhelming the large and apparently powerful.

The interpretation of the dream by the Midianite's companion reveals the psychological state of the enemy forces: "This can be nothing other than the sword of Gideon, son of Joash, the Israelite. God has given the Midianites and the whole camp into his hands" (Judges 7:14). This interpretation demonstrates that fear had already begun to undermine Midianite morale before any actual combat occurred.

Soggin describes this phenomenon as "the psychology of imminent defeat which produces this kind of dream: the enemy is beaten before the battle proper has been lost" (Soggin 1981:142). The dream functions as what he terms a "nightmare" that reflects the Midianites' unconscious recognition of their vulnerable position.

Pedersen's analysis further elaborates this psychological dimension of the dream: "With the dream the matter is settled. The Midianites lack the strength of victory; their soul is inferior, a soul of defeat, and therefore it must create dreams of defeat, whereas victory is created in the soul of Gideon. The outcome of the succeeding battle is simply the consequence of all this. The dream of defeat and the defeat itself are only two different manifestations of the same idea: that the Midianites were weak souls which could create nothing but defeat" (Petersen 1991: 138).

The Transformation of Fear into Courage

Block highlights the key idea that Gideon's new courage "would not come through any external alteration in Israel's desperate circumstances" (Block 1999:279). Instead, the change happens through divine intervention that affects Gideon's inner state.

Gideon's new courage came from God. God used six different ways to encourage Gideon.

Familiarity. Gideon's previous experiences of divine faithfulness provide a foundation for renewed trust. His history of answered prayers and divine intervention creates a precedent for expecting continued divine support.

Friendship: The provision of Purah as a companion acknowledges the human need for support and witness during times of crisis. Leadership does not require complete independence; instead, effective leaders recognize the importance of trusted assistants and advisors.

Divine Sovereignty. The exact timing of Gideon's arrival at the enemy camp, just as the dream was being discussed, shows divine control over events. This sovereignty offers confidence that events are not random but guided toward a preplanned outcome.

Sympathy. God's acknowledgment of Gideon's fear without condemnation reflects divine empathy for human weakness. Rather than rebuking Gideon for his continued anxiety, God provides additional support tailored to his emotional needs.

Perspective: The revelation that the Midianites fear Gideon more than he fears them fundamentally alters his understanding of the situation. This shift in perspective transforms his approach to the coming battle.

Promise: The reiteration of divine commitment to victory provides concrete assurance upon which Gideon can base his actions. The promise "I will be with you, and you shall strike down the Midianites, every one of them" (Judges 6:16) offers specific and measurable expectations.

The Response of Worship and Action

Gideon's response to the overheard conversation demonstrates the effectiveness of divine encouragement. The text states that "when Gideon heard the telling of the dream and its interpretation, he worshiped" (Judges 7:15). The Hebrew expression, which indicates that "he bowed low," suggests a profound act of reverence and gratitude. This worship response represents the transformation of fear into faith, acknowledging divine sovereignty over the situation.

The immediate translation of this spiritual experience into decisive action illustrates the practical nature of genuine faith. Gideon returns to his camp with a completely altered demeanor, confidently declaring to his troops: "Get up; for the LORD has given the army of Midian into your hand" (Judges 7:15). The shift from tentative fear to bold proclamation demonstrates the thoroughness of his transformation.

The Strategy and Victory

Gideon's battle strategy reflects both practical wisdom and spiritual dependence. The distribution of trumpets, torches, and empty jars to his 300 warriors represents a radical departure from conventional military equipment. These items serve psychological rather than physical purposes, designed to create maximum confusion and fear among the enemy forces.

The timing of the attack, at midnight during the changing of the guard (Judges 7:19), shows tactical skill. This moment of transition, when outgoing sentries are tired and incoming guards are not fully alert yet, offers an ideal chance for surprise. The mix of sudden light, loud noise, and war cries creates sensory overload that causes panic and disorientation.

The battle's outcome illustrates the complex relationship between divine intervention and human action. While God causes the Midianites to turn on each other (Judges 7:22), this intervention occurs within the context of Gideon's strategic planning and execution. The narrative suggests that divine power operates through rather than instead of human effort, requiring both faith and practical wisdom.

The description of the Israelite warriors standing at their positions as they watch the enemy's self-destruction (Judges 7:21) emphasizes that ultimate victory belongs to divine rather than human agency. However, this divine victory requires human obedience, courage, and strategic thinking as preconditions for its manifestation.

The Nature of Divine Empowerment

The Gideon narrative highlights key principles about divine empowerment of human leaders. First, God often selects unlikely candidates for important tasks, showing that divine power works regardless of human qualifications or resources. Second, divine calling does not remove human emotion or weakness but offers resources to overcome these limits. Third, divine reassurance often comes through natural means rather than supernatural ones, requiring spiritual insight to recognize God's guidance.

Gideon's experience offers practical insights for contemporary leadership challenges. The narrative demonstrates that effective leadership does not require the absence of fear but rather the willingness to act despite fear. Additionally, it emphasizes the importance of seeking divine guidance, maintaining supportive relationships, and developing strategies that acknowledge both human limitations and divine resources.

The victory over the Midianites resulted in forty years of peace for Israel (Judges 8:28), demonstrating that courageous actions can have a lasting influence across generations. The story indicates that personal change, when aligned with divine purpose, can bring benefits that extend far beyond the immediate challenge.

151

Gideon's transformation from a fearful person to a victorious leader offers a strong example of how divine assurance works in human life. The story shows that courage is not the absence of fear but the willingness to act with divine guidance despite emotional and practical challenges.

The complex psychological aspects of this account highlight the biblical view of human nature as diverse and layered. Fear and faith can coexist within the same person, and divine accommodation for human weakness does not imply divine disapproval but rather divine understanding and compassion.

For modern readers, the Gideon story provides both spiritual insight and practical advice. It shows that significant challenges, while they might seem overwhelming from a human view, can become chances for divine help and personal growth. The main point is not to eliminate fear or doubt but to stay obedient to divine guidance despite these natural human feelings.

The testimony of Hebrews 11:32–34 provides an appropriate summary of Gideon's significance: "And what more can I say? Time is too short for me to tell about Gideon who by faith . . . gained strength after being weak, became mighty in battle, and put foreign armies to flight." This assessment emphasizes that Gideon's greatness lay not in his natural abilities but in his willingness to allow divine power to operate through his weakness, transforming both his circumstances and his character in the process.

The Old Testament Speaks to the Church

On June 30, 2019, my pastor, Jeff Griffin, Senior Pastor of The Compass Church in Naperville, Illinois, delivered a powerful sermon on Judges 7:8b–25 entitled "Gideon: Against All Odds – Courage." Jeff's message explored one of Scripture's most compelling narratives about divine empowerment in the face of overwhelming circumstances.

Jeff began his sermon with a compelling modern example of courage that immediately grabbed the congregation's attention. He shared the inspiring story of an 85-year-old man who showed extraordinary bravery when faced with three armed robbers. Despite being vastly outnumbered and physically at a disadvantage because of his age, this elderly man stood his ground with firm resolve. Instead of becoming a victim, he fearlessly confronted the would-be criminals, making them run away empty-handed and ensuring no one was hurt.

This opening illustration served as a powerful parallel to Gideon's story, demonstrating that courage is not dependent on physical strength, numbers, or conventional advantages. Instead, it springs from an inner resolve that can manifest at any age and in any circumstance.

Jeff's sermon focused on the pivotal moment in Judges 7:8b–25, where Gideon, following God's specific instructions, reduced his army from 32,000 men to merely 300. This dramatic reduction seemed counterintuitive from a military perspective, yet it set the stage for one of the Bible's most remarkable victories. Jeff emphasized how God often works through what appears to be weakness to demonstrate His strength and glory.

The passage reveals several key principles about divine courage:

God's Unconventional Methods: Just as the 85-year-old man's victory defied traditional expectations, God's strategy for Gideon challenged typical military wisdom. The reduction of forces from thousands to hundreds showed that God's ways go beyond human logic.

Courage Through Divine Assurance: Gideon's transformation from a fearful man hiding in a winepress to a confident leader demonstrates how God's presence can fundamentally change our perspective on seemingly impossible situations.

Victory Against Overwhelming Odds: The Midianite army was described as being "like locusts in abundance," yet 300 men with trumpets, torches, and empty jars achieved complete victory through God's intervention.

Jeff's concluding emphasis carried profound implications for modern believers facing their own "impossible" circumstances. He drew clear parallels between Gideon's experience and the challenges people encounter today, whether they involve:

- Personal struggles such as addiction, depression, or chronic illness
- Relational conflicts, including marriage difficulties, family tensions, or workplace disputes
- Financial hardships that seem insurmountable
- Career challenges or educational obstacles
- Spiritual battles against doubt, fear, or feelings of inadequacy

The sermon's central message revolved around God's consistent character as an encourager and deliverer. Jeff emphasized that the same God who encouraged Gideon in his moment of crisis continues to offer hope and strength to believers today.

Jeff's sermon's enduring relevance lies in its reminder that God specializes in impossible situations. Whether facing personal giants like the Midianites or confronting modern-day "robbers" that threaten our peace, security, or faith, we can draw courage from Gideon's example and the elderly man's bravery.

The message ultimately points to a God who not only encourages his people but actively participates in their victories, transforming ordinary individuals into vessels of extraordinary courage when they trust in his power rather than their own limitations.

PART 3

SAMUEL

INTRODUCTION

SAMUEL: LESSONS FROM A REMARKABLE CHILD – LIVING UPSTREAM

The narrative of Samuel's childhood in 1 Samuel 1–3 presents one of the most compelling accounts of divine calling and human faithfulness in the Old Testament. From his miraculous birth to his first prophetic encounter, Samuel's early years establish patterns of dedication, discernment, and devotion that would characterize his entire ministry as Israel's last judge and first prophet of the monarchical period.

The Context of Samuel's Birth and Dedication

Samuel's story begins not with the child himself, but with his mother Hannah's profound anguish over her barrenness. In the ancient Near Eastern context, a woman's inability to bear children was viewed not merely as personal misfortune but as a sign of divine disfavor. Hannah's rival, Peninnah, exploited this cultural understanding to torment her co-wife, creating a household dynamic that drove Hannah to desperate prayer at the sanctuary in Shiloh.

The narrative portrays Hannah's vow as both profoundly personal and theologically significant. Her promise to dedicate her yet-unconceived son to Yahweh "all the days of his life" (1 Samuel 1:11) represents more than maternal devotion; it constitutes a Nazirite-like commitment that would set Samuel apart for divine service from birth. This dedication prefigures the child's future role as one who would stand between the old order represented by Eli's corrupt priesthood and the new era of monarchical Israel.

Samuel's Early Years at Shiloh

Following his weaning, probably around age three or four, according to ancient practice, Samuel was brought to Shiloh to fulfill Hannah's vow. The text emphasizes the child's youth—he is described as a "little boy" who ministers before Yahweh while wearing a linen ephod, the garment of priestly service. This detail suggests Samuel's integration into the sanctuary's religious life despite his tender age.

The annual visits from his parents, particularly the bringing of a new robe each year, highlight the ongoing parental bond while underscoring Samuel's permanent residence at the sanctuary. These visits also provide narrative opportunities to contrast Samuel's faithful service with the corruption of Eli's sons, Hophni and Phinehas, whose abuse of their priestly office stands in stark opposition to the child's pure devotion.

Character Formation in a Corrupt Environment

One of the most remarkable aspects of Samuel's childhood is his moral and spiritual development despite the corrupt religious environment at Shiloh. While Eli's sons were "worthless men" who "did not know Yahweh" (1 Samuel 2:12), Samuel "continued to grow both in stature and in favor with Yahweh and with people" (1 Samuel 2:26). This description, echoing later language about the young Jesus, presents Samuel as an exemplar of righteous development.

The text suggests that Samuel's character was formed through faithful service in small matters. His regular duties included opening the doors of the house of Yahweh each morning, maintaining the sanctuary lamp, and serving alongside the aging priest Eli. These mundane responsibilities provided the foundation for the greater calling that would soon be revealed.

The Divine Calling

The climactic moment of Samuel's childhood comes in his nighttime encounter with Yahweh (1 Samuel 3:1–21). The narrative emphasizes the rarity of divine communication in that era: "The word of Yahweh was rare in those days; visions were not widespread." This context makes Samuel's calling all the more significant: God chooses to break the prophetic silence through a child.

The threefold calling scene illustrates both divine persistence and human learning. Samuel's initial confusion, thinking Eli was calling him, reflects his youth and inexperience with divine communication. Eli's eventual recognition of the divine origin of the call shows both his spiritual discernment and his role in guiding Samuel's prophetic growth.

Samuel's first prophetic message, which predicts judgment against Eli's house, puts the child in a very tough situation. He has to speak words of condemnation about the man who has acted as his surrogate father and spiritual mentor. Samuel's initial hesitance to share the vision shows his human sensitivity, while his eventual obedience shows his dedication to telling the truth prophetically, no matter what personal cost it brings.

Conclusion

Samuel's childhood represents a foundational period that shaped not only his personal character but also the future of Israel's religious and political institutions. His early experiences of dedication, service, and divine calling prepared him for the complex challenges he would face as an adult leader during Israel's transition from the period of judges to the monarchy. The narrative presents Samuel's childhood as proof that faithful service in small matters, combined with openness to divine communication, can prepare even the youngest person for significant roles in God's redemptive purposes.

My pastor, Jeff Griffin, Senior pastor of The Compass Church in Naperville, Illinois, preached a series of sermons on Samuel's childhood. The following four chapters are based on Jeff's sermons.

Jeff Griffin's Sermon Series: "Samuel: Lessons From a Remarkable Child – Living Upstream"

1. Samuel: Lessons From A Remarkable Child – Broken Dreams

Jeff's opening sermon focuses on Hannah's struggle with infertility and the deep emotional pain of unfulfilled maternal desires. Jeff explores how God can use our greatest disappointments and broken dreams as the foundation for his greater purposes. Hannah's barrenness becomes the catalyst for Samuel's birth and eventual ministry, demonstrating how God can transform our deepest wounds into sources of blessing not only for ourselves but for entire nations. The sermon addresses how believers today can maintain faith and hope even when their most cherished dreams seem permanently shattered.

2. Samuel: Lessons From A Remarkable Child – Dedication

The second message examines Hannah's faithful fulfillment of her vow to dedicate Samuel to God's service at the sanctuary in Shiloh. Jeff emphasizes the radical nature of Hannah's commitment—giving up her long-awaited son to serve God permanently. Jeff's sermon challenges parents and individuals to consider what it means to truly dedicate their lives and their children to God's purposes, moving beyond mere religious ritual to authentic surrender. The message explores how genuine dedication requires sacrifice but ultimately leads to God's greater blessing and to the fulfillment of God's purpose.

3. Samuel: Lessons From A Remarkable Child – Living Upstream

This central sermon, sharing its title with the overall series, focuses on Samuel's decision to live differently from the corrupt example set by Eli's sons, Hophni and Phinehas. Jeff uses this message to challenge believers to resist the moral currents of their culture and choose righteousness even when surrounded by compromise and corruption. The "upstream" metaphor emphasizes how living for God often means going against the flow of popular opinion and cultural trends, requiring courage and conviction that can only come through a close relationship with God.

4. Samuel: Lessons From A Remarkable Child – Hearing God

The final sermon in the series focuses on Samuel's first prophetic experience when God calls to him during the night at Shiloh. Jeff discusses what it means to develop spiritual sensitivity and recognize God's voice in our lives. The message highlights the importance of spiritual mentorship, as illustrated by Eli's guidance to Samuel, and stresses that God wants to communicate with his people today just as he did with young Samuel. The sermon ends with practical advice on cultivating the spiritual disciplines and attitudes needed to hear and respond to God's guidance in our daily lives.

Jeff and I hope that this series of studies on Samuel's early life will enrich your understanding and inspire you to embrace Hannah's unwavering commitment to God and her devoted love for Samuel.

CHAPTER 16

SAMUEL: LESSONS FROM A REMARKABLE CHILD – BROKEN DREAMS

Samuel stands as one of the most pivotal figures in Israel's history, serving simultaneously as priest, judge, and prophet during the nation's most critical period. His ministry bridged the chaotic era of the judges with the establishment of the monarchy, guiding Israel through existential threats from the Philistines and ultimately anointing its first king, Saul.

Yet Samuel's remarkable story begins not with his own achievements, but with his mother's broken dreams. Hannah's journey from barrenness to blessing offers profound lessons about navigating life's deepest disappointments while maintaining faith in God's goodness.

The Reality of Broken Dreams

Mother's Day brings joy to many, but for some mothers, it is a day shadowed by loss: remembering children who have died, grieving over children who have walked away from faith, or mourning unfulfilled dreams and unrealized potential. Hannah understood this pain intimately.

Hannah's story unfolds in the hill country of Ephraim, in a small city called Ramathaim ("the two Ramahs"). She was, by worldly standards, insignificant, a rural woman with no social standing. Yet God chose her to give birth and raise the child who would reshape Israel's destiny. This reflects a consistent biblical pattern: God often selects the overlooked and ordinary for extraordinary purposes.

A Family Marked by Pain

Hannah's husband, Elkanah, was a Levite from the family of Kohath. Though the Bible does not explicitly condemn polygamy, it consistently shows its destructive effects. Hannah was Elkanah's first wife, but her inability to bear children led him to take a second wife, Peninnah, who bore him several children.

In ancient agricultural societies, a woman's identity was primarily defined by her role as a mother. Hannah's barrenness was not just a personal disappointment—it was a social stigma that left her feeling incomplete and rejected. The situation worsened as Peninnah, described as Hannah's "rival" (1 Samuel 1:6), regularly provoked and taunted her about her childlessness.

The emotional toll was devastating. Hannah wept frequently and lost her appetite. The text says that "the Lord had closed her womb" (1 Samuel 1:6), raising difficult questions about God's role in human suffering. While we cannot know the specific medical reasons for Hannah's infertility, the narrative emphasizes that God ultimately has the power to open and close the womb.

Pathways Through Brokenness

Hannah's response to her broken dreams provides a blueprint for anyone facing life's crushing disappointments:

Despite her anguish, Hannah remained committed to worship. Each year, she accompanied Elkanah to Shiloh, where the Tabernacle stood, to offer sacrifices and seek God's face. Elkanah showed his love by giving Hannah a double portion of the sacrificial meal, yet even this kindness could not heal her deepest wound.

Hannah's consistent worship reveals a crucial truth: authentic faith does not require the absence of pain. She brought her broken heart to God's house, knowing that he "will not despise a broken and contrite heart" (Psalm 51:17). Worship became her anchor in the storm, not because it guaranteed answers, but because it connected her to the One who understands all suffering.

Though childless, Hannah had received genuine blessings from God—most notably, a loving husband. When Elkanah saw her distress, he gently asked, "Hannah, why do you weep? Why do you not eat? Why is your heart sad? Am I not more to you than ten sons?" (1 Samuel 1:8).

While Elkanah's question might seem insensitive, it reflected his deep love and desire to comfort his wife. Hannah's ability to appreciate this blessing, even while grieving her childlessness, demonstrates emotional maturity. When overwhelmed by what we lack, we can lose sight of what we have. Gratitude does not minimize our pain, but it provides perspective and hope.

Hannah's prayer at Shiloh was raw and desperate. She "wept bitterly" and poured out her soul to God, making a vow that if he gave her a son, she would dedicate the child to lifelong service in the temple. This was not superficial religious talk; it was the cry of a broken heart seeking the God of all comfort.

Her prayer was so intense that Eli the priest mistook her for a drunk woman. When confronted, Hannah respectfully corrected him: "Not so, my lord . . . I am a woman who is deeply troubled. I have not been drinking wine or beer; I was pouring out my soul to the LORD" (1 Samuel 1:15).

Hannah's example teaches us that God welcomes our honest emotions. We do not need to sanitize our prayers or hide our desperation. The God who knows our hearts before we speak invites us to bring our deepest longings and fears to Him.

After receiving Eli's blessing, "Go in peace, and may the God of Israel grant you what you have asked of him," Hannah left the temple transformed. She ate, and her face was no longer downcast. Nothing had changed on the outside, but inside, she had found peace through trust.

This was not naive optimism or wishful thinking. Hannah's trust was grounded in her understanding of God's character. She believed that the God who had called her to prayer could also answer that prayer. As the psalmist wrote, "My heart trusted in him, and he helped me" (Psalm 28:7).

The Miracle and the Sacrifice

163

God honored Hannah's faith. In due time, she conceived and bore a son whom she named Samuel, meaning "heard of God." But Hannah's greatest act of faith was yet to come. True to her vow, she brought young Samuel to the temple at Shiloh and gave him to Eli for lifelong service.

Imagine the emotional cost of this decision. After years of longing for a child, Hannah had to surrender him while he was still very young. Yet she did so with joy, declaring in her famous song of praise: "My heart rejoices in the LORD; in the LORD my horn is lifted high" (1 Samuel 2:1).

God's generosity exceeded Hannah's request. After Samuel's dedication, she bore three more sons and two daughters. Her willingness to honor her vow, even at significant personal cost, positioned her to receive even greater blessings.

When Prayers Are Not Answered

Hannah's story has a happy ending, but not all stories of faith do, at least not in this life. The three Hebrew young men thrown into Nebuchadnezzar's furnace showed mature faith when they said, "The God we serve is able to deliver us . . . but even if he does not, we want you to know, Your Majesty, that we will not serve your gods" (Daniel 3:17–18).

Sometimes God says yes to our prayers; sometimes he says no; sometimes he says wait. Faith is not measured by the answers we receive but by our willingness to trust God regardless of the outcome. Hannah teaches us that we can bring our broken dreams to God with confidence, knowing that he hears every prayer and works all things together for the good of those who love him.

The Old Testament Speaks to the Church

On May 9, 2021, my pastor, Jeff Griffin, Senior Pastor of The Compass Church in Naperville, Illinois, preached a sermon on Samuel 1:1–20 titled "Samuel: Lessons From a Remarkable Child – Broken Dreams." The power of Hannah's story becomes even more profound when we see how it intersects with our own experiences of loss and disappointment. Jeff understood this intersection deeply through his own family's journey with broken dreams.

When Dreams Go Up in Smoke

Jeff began his sermon with a story that brought Hannah's pain into sharp focus. He described the devastating fire that consumed his parents' dream home, a house where they had lived for over 27 years, a place that held decades of family celebrations, memories, and hopes for the future. In one terrible night, flames reduced their carefully built life to ashes and rubble.

As Jeff watched his parents grieve the loss of their dream home, he witnessed something profound: the raw, honest sorrow that comes when the things we have worked for, planned for, and loved are suddenly taken away. His parents did not just lose a house; they lost the physical container of their memories, the place where grandchildren had played, where holidays had been celebrated, where life had been lived fully.

Yet in their grief, Jeff observed the same principles that Hannah had demonstrated thousands of years earlier. His parents continued to worship, finding their foundation not in the physical structure they had lost but in the God who remained constant through the devastation. They expressed gratitude for their safety and for the years they had been blessed to live in that home. They prayed through their pain, bringing their sorrow to the God of all comfort. And they trusted that God would provide a path forward, even when the future seemed unclear.

The Ache of Empty Arms

Jeff's application became more personal as he shared his family's struggle with infertility. He and his wife experienced the same monthly disappointment that many couples face—the hope that grows, the careful planning, and the crushing realization that once again, their arms would remain empty. Month after month, year after year, they endured the same heartbreak that Hannah had gone through.

Like Hannah, Jeff and his wife brought their longing to God in prayer. They worshiped through their pain, even when worship felt hollow. They tried to appreciate the blessings they had while grieving the blessings they lacked. They attempted to trust God's timing while battling the fear that their prayers might never be answered.

The journey guided them towards adoption, a choice many couples with unfulfilled dreams of biological children make. They started readying their hearts and home for a child who would come to them through different means than they initially hoped for. In this process, they discovered that God's plans often differ from ours, but his love for us stays the same.

Then came the moment that mirrored Hannah's story: the unexpected news that Jeff's wife was pregnant. After years of disappointment, God had quietly been working behind the scenes, preparing to answer their prayers in his perfect timing. The joy was overwhelming—not just because their dream was being fulfilled, but because they had learned to trust God's character even when his timeline seemed uncertain.

The Four Keys to Healing

Through both his parents' experience and his own journey, Jeff witnessed the four pathways through brokenness that Hannah had modeled:

Worship as an Anchor. Even when dreams crumble, worship provides stability. It is not about feeling good or having all the answers; it is about remembering who God is when our circumstances seem to suggest he has forgotten us. Jeff's parents worshiped through their loss, and Jeff and his wife worshiped through their waiting, because they understood that God's worthiness is not dependent on their circumstances.

Appreciation as Perspective. In the midst of grief, gratitude does not minimize our pain, but it does provide a necessary perspective. Jeff's parents could mourn their lost home while still thanking God for their safety and years of blessing. Jeff and his wife could grieve their infertility while appreciating their strong marriage and the love they shared. Appreciation does not erase broken dreams, but it prevents them from eclipsing every blessing.

Prayer as Connection. Honest prayer became the lifeline that connected both families to God's heart. They did not offer sanitized, polite prayers, but poured out their confusion, fear, and pain. They discovered that God welcomes our raw emotions and desperate pleas. Prayer was not about changing God's mind, but about aligning their hearts with his will and finding peace in his presence.

Trust as Foundation. Perhaps most importantly, both families learned that trust in God's character provides the foundation for navigating broken dreams. They trusted not because they understood God's plan, but because they understood God's heart. Trust allowed them to rest in his sovereignty even when his ways seemed mysterious.

The Ministry of Broken Dreams

Jeff's sermon revealed a crucial truth: our broken dreams often become the foundation for our most significant ministry. His parents' experience with loss equipped them to comfort others facing devastating circumstances. Jeff and his wife's journey through infertility positioned them to support other couples walking the same difficult path.

Hannah's barrenness was not just a personal trial; it was preparation for raising a child who would change the trajectory of an entire nation. The pain that broke her heart also broke it open, making room for greater compassion, deeper faith, and more complete dependence on God.

God's Surprising Generosity

In both stories, Hannah's and Jeff's, God's response went beyond what was asked. Hannah requested one son and was given Samuel along with three more sons and two daughters. Jeff and his wife prayed for a child and ultimately received not only biological children but also a deeper, more mature faith built through suffering.

This reflects God's character: he does not just give us what we ask for; he gives us what we need to become who he has called us to be. Sometimes that includes the fulfillment of our dreams, but it always includes the transformation of our hearts.

The God of Broken Dreams

Hannah's ancient story and Jeff's contemporary application remind us that broken dreams are not the end of our story—they are often the beginning of a deeper chapter. When dreams shatter, we discover whether our foundation is built on our circumstances or on the unchanging character of God.

The four pathways Hannah modeled—worship, appreciation, prayer, and trust—are not just coping mechanisms; they are keys that unlock the door to God's healing presence in our broken hearts. They do not guarantee that our dreams will be restored exactly as we envision them, but they do guarantee that we will discover God's faithfulness in the midst of our pain.

For those currently walking through the ashes of broken dreams, take courage from Hannah's example and Jeff's testimony. The God who sees your tears, knows your longings, and understands your pain is the same God who specializes in bringing beauty from ashes, joy from mourning, and purpose from pain.

Your broken dreams might seem like an ending, but in God's hands, they often become the start of something more beautiful than you imagined. Trust him with the pieces, and see him create a masterpiece that glorifies his name and heals your heart.

CHAPTER 17

SAMUEL: LESSONS FROM A REMARKABLE CHILD – DEDICATION

The story of Samuel's birth stands as one of the most profound testimonies in Scripture to God's faithfulness in answering prayer. It is a narrative that weaves together themes of desperate longing, unwavering faith, divine intervention, and ultimate surrender. Hannah's journey from barrenness to motherhood, and from motherhood to sacrificial dedication, offers timeless lessons about trust, commitment, and the true nature of stewardship.

Samuel's story begins not with his birth, but with his mother's tears. Hannah's barrenness was not merely a personal disappointment; in ancient Israel, childlessness was often viewed as a sign of divine disfavor. Yet through her prolonged struggle, Hannah would learn that God's timing is perfect, and his purposes extend far beyond our immediate understanding.

The Burden of Barrenness: Hannah's Long Journey

Hannah's infertility was a source of profound anguish that extended over many years. The biblical text reveals that Peninnah, her husband's second wife, had "sons and daughters" (1 Samuel 1:4), indicating that Hannah's struggle with conception had persisted long enough for another woman to bear multiple children. This detail underscores the depth of Hannah's pain and the length of her waiting.

In the cultural context of ancient Israel, a woman's worth was often measured by her ability to produce children, particularly sons who would carry on the family name and inheritance. Hannah lived daily with the weight of this societal expectation, compounded by the cruel taunts of Peninnah, who "kept provoking her in order to irritate her" (1 Samuel 1:6). The Hebrew word used here suggests continuous, relentless antagonism, a daily reminder of Hannah's perceived failure.

Yet Hannah's response to her circumstances reveals remarkable spiritual maturity. Rather than becoming bitter toward God or abandoning her faith, she channeled her pain into prayer. Year after year, she accompanied her family to Shiloh for the annual sacrifice, never losing hope that God would remember her plight. Her persistence in prayer, despite years of apparent silence from heaven, demonstrates the kind of faith that refuses to surrender to circumstances.

The theological significance of Hannah's barrenness extends beyond personal suffering. Throughout Scripture, God often works through barren women—Sarah, Rebekah, Rachel, and later Elizabeth—to accomplish his purposes. These stories remind us that God's most significant works often emerge from situations that appear hopeless by human standards. Hannah's barrenness was not a punishment but a preparation for something greater than she could imagine.

A Vow Born of Desperation and Faith

Hannah's vow to God represents one of the most dramatic moments in the narrative. In her anguish, she went beyond mere petition to make a binding commitment: "O LORD Almighty, if you will only look upon your servant's misery and remember me, and not forget your servant but give her a son, then I will give him to the LORD for all the days of his life, and no razor will ever be used on his head" (1 Samuel 1:11).

This vow reveals several profound truths about Hannah's character and faith. First, her language demonstrates a profound understanding of God's nature. She addresses him as "LORD Almighty" ("Yahweh Sabaoth"), acknowledging his supreme power and authority. Her plea for God to "remember" her reflects understanding that God's remembrance is not about divine forgetfulness but about his timing and purposes.

Second, the nature of her vow shows remarkable spiritual insight. Hannah promised to dedicate her son as a Nazirite, set apart for God's service from birth. The Nazirite vow typically involved abstaining from wine, avoiding contact with the dead, and leaving

170

the hair uncut as a sign of consecration. By making this vow for her unborn son, Hannah was essentially promising to give up the very thing she most desired: a child to raise and enjoy.

The radical nature of Hannah's vow cannot be overstated. She was willing to trade temporary motherhood for the privilege of bearing a child dedicated to God's service. This represents a profound understanding of stewardship, recognizing that all children ultimately belong to God and are entrusted to parents as his representatives.

The Miracle of Remembrance

The phrase "the LORD remembered her" (1 Samuel 1:19) marks the turning point in Hannah's story. In Hebrew thought, divine remembrance is not about God recalling forgotten information but about his decisive action on behalf of his people. When God "remembers," he intervenes in human affairs to accomplish his purposes.

Hannah's conception and Samuel's birth demonstrate God's perfect timing. After years of waiting, God opened her womb at precisely the right moment in Israel's history. Samuel would be born into a nation in spiritual decline, with corrupt priests and absent spiritual leadership. His birth represented God's provision for Israel's future, though this broader purpose may not have been immediately apparent to Hannah.

The name Samuel, meaning "asked of God" or "God has heard," serves as a permanent reminder of God's faithfulness. Every time Hannah spoke her son's name, she was declaring that God answers prayer. The name also carries prophetic significance—Samuel would become the one through whom God would speak to Israel, establishing him as a prophet and judge.

Hannah's pregnancy and Samuel's birth highlight the idea that God's gifts have a purpose. Samuel was not just the answer to a mother's prayer but also God's chosen instrument during an important time in Israel's history. This shows us that every child comes with a divine purpose, and parents act as stewards of God's gifts.

The Struggle of Surrender

The period between Samuel's birth and his presentation at the temple shows Hannah's very human struggle with her vow. Despite her earlier commitment, she was reluctant to part with the child she had prayed for so long. This reluctance is clear from her choice not to join her family in going to Shiloh for at least three years, supposedly to nurse Samuel but maybe also to delay the unavoidable separation.

Hannah's extended nursing period, though common in ancient times, may have served as a way to delay fulfilling her vow. Archaeological evidence and historical sources show that weaning could occur anywhere from two to three years old, or even longer, depending on the situation. Hannah's decision to nurse Samuel for such a long time gave her valuable years with her son, but also revealed her internal struggle.

This struggle makes Hannah's story more relatable to modern readers. Her experience demonstrates that even people of great faith can wrestle with difficult decisions. The fact that she eventually followed through on her commitment, despite her natural reluctance, makes her sacrifice all the more meaningful. It shows that true dedication often requires acting against our immediate desires in favor of our higher commitments.

Elkanah's response to Hannah's hesitation reveals remarkable wisdom and love. Rather than invoking his legal right to nullify her vow, he supported her decision-making process. His words, "Whatever you think is best. Stay here for now, and may the LORD help you keep your promise" (1 Samuel 1:23 NLT), show both respect for his wife's spiritual autonomy and confidence in her character.

The Moment of Truth: Dedication at Shiloh

When Hannah finally brought Samuel to Shiloh, her words to Eli reveal the depth of her spiritual transformation. "I am the woman who stood here beside you praying to the LORD. I prayed for this child, and the LORD has granted me what I asked of him. So now I give him to the LORD. For his whole life he will be given over to the LORD" (1 Samuel 1:26–28).

This declaration represents one of the most profound acts of surrender in Scripture. Hannah was not merely fulfilling a reluctant obligation but making a conscious choice to honor God with her most precious possession. Her words demonstrate complete trust in God's ability to care for Samuel better than she could herself.

The physical act of leaving Samuel at the temple required tremendous courage. Hannah was entrusting her young son to Eli, whose own sons were corrupt and rebellious. From a human perspective, this decision might seem unwise. Yet Hannah's faith looked beyond immediate circumstances to God's ultimate purposes.

The presentation of Samuel also fulfilled symbolic and prophetic significance. By dedicating Samuel to temple service, Hannah was participating in God's plan to reform Israel's religious system. Samuel would grow up to become the bridge between the period of judges and the monarchy, anointing both Saul and David as kings.

Theological Implications and Modern Applications

Hannah's story offers several profound theological insights that remain relevant today. First, it demonstrates that God's timing is perfect, even when it differs from our expectations. Hannah's years of waiting were not wasted but were preparation for God's greater purposes.

Second, the story illustrates the principle of stewardship. Hannah's willingness to surrender Samuel reveals her understanding that children are gifts from God, entrusted to parents for a time but ultimately belonging to him. This perspective can transform how modern parents approach child-rearing, viewing themselves as stewards rather than owners. Third, Hannah's experience shows that true dedication often requires sacrifice. Her willingness to give up the son she had prayed for demonstrates that genuine commitment to God may cost us the things we value most. This principle challenges contemporary Christianity's emphasis on comfort and convenience.

Fourth, the story reveals God's heart for the marginalized and forgotten. Hannah's barrenness made her vulnerable in her society, yet God chose to work through her to accomplish His purposes. This pattern continues throughout Scripture and offers hope to those who feel overlooked or forgotten.

Israel's Spiritual Crisis

Samuel's dedication occurs at a crucial juncture in Israel's history. The nation was in spiritual decline, with corrupt priests and absent spiritual leadership. The judges were failing to provide consistent guidance, and the people were increasingly adopting pagan practices. Into this spiritual vacuum, God placed Samuel—a child dedicated from birth to serve him.

Samuel's upbringing in the temple under Eli's guidance, despite Eli's failures as a father, prepared him for his unique role in Israel's history. He would become the last judge, the first of the classical prophets, and the one who would anoint Israel's first two kings. His dedication as a child made possible his later service as an adult.

This broader context reminds us that individual acts of faith and dedication can have far-reaching consequences. Hannah's decision to honor her vow helped shape the entire future of Israel. Our own acts of faith and dedication, while they may seem small, can have impacts we never imagine.

Conclusion: The Legacy of Faithful Dedication

The story of Samuel's dedication stands as a testament to the power of faithful commitment. Hannah's journey from barrenness to motherhood to sacrificial surrender illustrates the transformative power of trusting God with our most precious possessions.

Her experience demonstrates that true worship often requires giving up what we most desire. Yet in her surrender, Hannah discovered that God's purposes were greater than her personal fulfillment. Samuel's service to God and Israel far exceeded what Hannah could have accomplished if she had kept him for herself.

Walter Brueggemann's observation captures the essence of Hannah's transformation: "In offering her thanksgiving, Hannah is aware of the amazing sequence by which her barrenness has eventuated in birth. The one whom she had 'asked' is now given back. Hannah is faithful; Yahweh is powerful. Hannah is appropriately grateful. In place of despair has come gratitude, resulting in submission and praise. The resolution is glad worship."

Hannah's story challenges modern believers to examine their own relationship with God's gifts. Are we willing to hold our blessings with open hands, recognizing that everything we have ultimately belongs to God? Are we prepared to make sacrifices for God's purposes, even when they conflict with our natural desires?

The legacy of Hannah's dedication extends far beyond her personal story. Through her sacrifice, she participated in God's plan to provide spiritual leadership for Israel. Her faithfulness in a private struggle contributed to public blessing for God's people. This reminds us that our personal decisions of faith and dedication can have impacts that extend far beyond our immediate circumstances.

Samuel's remarkable life—as judge, prophet, and kingmaker— stands as a monument to his mother's faithfulness. Her willingness to give up temporary pleasure for eternal purpose resulted in a legacy that continues to inspire believers thousands of years later. The story of Samuel's dedication remains a powerful reminder that God honors those who honor him, and that the most profound acts of worship often require the greatest sacrifices.

In our contemporary context, Hannah's example calls us to reconsider our priorities and commitments. It challenges us to move beyond convenient Christianity to costly discipleship. Most importantly, it reminds us that God's purposes are always greater than our personal preferences, and that true fulfillment comes not from holding onto our blessings but from surrendering them to God's service.

The story of Samuel's dedication ultimately points us to the greatest act of dedication in history—God's willingness to give his own Son for the redemption of humanity. Just as Hannah gave up her son for God's purposes, God gave up his Son for ours. In this light, Hannah's sacrifice becomes not just an example to follow but a reflection of God's own heart of love and sacrifice.

The Old Testament Speaks to the Church

My pastor, Jeff Griffin, Senior Pastor of The Compass Church in Naperville, Illinois preached a sermon on May 16, 2021 titled "Samuel: Lessons From a Remarkable Child – Dedication."

The timeless principles shown in Hannah's dedication of Samuel still change lives today, as seen in Jeff's personal testimony. His journey from aspiring doctor to faithful pastor offers a modern parallel to Hannah's ancient act of surrender, proving that God's call to dedication goes beyond time and culture.

During his senior year at Wheaton College, Jeff was firmly committed to pursuing a medical career. His academic preparation, personal interests, and carefully laid plans all pointed toward the healing profession. Like many young Christians, he saw medicine as a noble way to serve others while building a meaningful career. However, in what he describes as a "deep spiritual experience," Jeff encountered the unmistakable call of God to pastoral ministry.

This divine interruption came at the worst possible time from a human perspective, his senior year, when most students are finalizing their post-graduation plans. Yet the timing reflects a pattern we see throughout Scripture: God often calls people when they are already committed to other paths. Moses was shepherding when God appeared at the burning bush, the disciples were fishing when Jesus called them, and Paul was persecuting Christians when he encountered Christ on the Damascus road. Jeff's experience mirrors this biblical pattern, demonstrating that God's timing often conflicts with our human planning.

The internal struggle Jeff experienced was both understandable and profound. Medicine represented not just a career choice but a vision for meaningful service to humanity. Yet God's call to pastoral ministry required him to abandon these carefully laid plans, much like Hannah, who had to give up her long-awaited son. This surrender was not merely about changing career paths but about acknowledging a fundamental truth: his life belonged to God rather than to his own preferences and ambitions.

Jeff's decision to accept the call rested on the same theological foundation that empowered Hannah's dedication: the recognition that "his life was not his own; his life belonged to God." This understanding echoes Paul's teaching in 1 Corinthians 6:19–20: "You are not your own; you were bought at a price. Therefore honor God with your bodies." Just as Hannah recognized that Samuel ultimately belonged to God, Jeff acknowledged that his life, dreams, and future belonged to his Creator.

The phrase "all that he was and all that he had belonged to God" captures the comprehensive nature of Christian dedication. This includes not just our obvious spiritual gifts but our education, skills, relationships, and even our disappointments. Jeff's medical training and interests were not wasted but became part of his pastoral toolkit, enabling him to minister with unique compassion and understanding to those facing health challenges.

Jeff's personal testimony becomes more than an inspiring story; it serves as a bridge to challenge his congregation toward their own acts of dedication. His mention of church volunteers who serve because they know that as people of faith, people who belong to God, they should be involved in serving the Lord, demonstrates how individual acts of surrender can inspire and multiply in a faith community.

These volunteers represent the contemporary equivalent of Hannah's dedication. They may not be giving up children or changing careers, but they are surrendering their time, comfort, and personal preferences to serve God's purposes. Their service reflects the same theological understanding that motivated both Hannah and Jeff, that as people who belong to God, they are called to live for his purposes rather than their own.

The diversity of service opportunities in modern church life—from children's ministry to hospitality, from music to missions—provides multiple avenues for people to live out their dedication to God. Each act of service, regardless of its visibility or recognition, represents a choice to prioritize God's kingdom over personal convenience.

Jeff's conclusion that "all that we are and all that we have belongs to God" extends the challenge beyond vocational ministry to every aspect of Christian living. This principle applies to professional life, where Christians in any field are called to view their work as a service to God and as opportunities to advance his kingdom. It applies to family relationships, where Christian parents are called to view their children as gifts from God, raising them with the understanding that they ultimately belong to him. It encompasses financial resources, time, and talents, and major life decisions about education, career, relationships, and residence.

The practical implications of this understanding are far-reaching. Jeff's sermon challenges Christians to consider what dreams or plans God might be calling them to surrender for his purposes. Not everyone is called to vocational ministry, but everyone is called to serve God where they are. This includes examining what resources God has entrusted to us that could be used for his kingdom—not just obvious spiritual gifts but practical skills, relationships, and opportunities.

Jeff's story reminds us that dedication to God is not a one-time decision but an ongoing journey. His initial "yes" to the call to ministry was followed by years of theological education, pastoral preparation, and faithful service. Like Hannah, who continued to visit Samuel at the temple and support his ministry, Jeff's dedication required continued commitment and sacrifice. The pastoral ministry itself demands ongoing acts of surrender—giving up personal time for counseling sessions, prioritizing congregational needs over family preferences, and maintaining faithfulness even when ministry becomes difficult or discouraging.

Jeff's personal testimony illustrates that the principles demonstrated in Hannah's dedication of Samuel remain vibrant and transformative in contemporary life. His willingness to surrender his medical career for pastoral ministry demonstrates the same kind of faith that led Hannah to give up her son for God's service. The challenge he presents to the members of the church, to recognize that all we are and have belongs to God, extends the implications of dedication beyond dramatic life changes to the everyday choices that shape our character and impact.

Whether through vocational ministry, volunteer service, or faithful living in secular careers, we are all called to live out our dedication to God. The story of Samuel's dedication, illuminated by Jeff's personal experience, reminds us that God's purposes are always greater than our personal preferences. When we surrender our dreams to God's calling, we discover that his plans for our lives exceed our own imagination. Like Hannah, who saw her son become a great leader in Israel, and like Jeff, who found fulfillment in pastoral ministry, we can trust that God's purposes for our lives are good, even when they require us to give up what we thought we wanted most.

The call to dedication is not a call to misery, but to meaning, not to sacrifice for its own sake, but to participate in God's great work of redemption and restoration. As we follow the examples of Hannah, we discover that true fulfillment comes not from pursuing our own dreams but from surrendering them to the One who loves us most and knows us best. In this surrender, we find not loss but life abundant, not emptiness but purpose, not regret but the deep satisfaction that comes from aligning our lives with God's eternal purposes.

CHAPTER 18

SAMUEL: LESSONS FROM A REMARKABLE CHILD – LIVING UPSTREAM

The narrative of Samuel's early life and ministry presents a compelling case study in moral development within a corrupted religious environment. Following Hannah's dedication of her son to divine service, Samuel was placed under the tutelage of Eli the priest at Shiloh, where he would encounter both exemplary and deplorable models of religious leadership. This chapter examines how Samuel's formative years, spent in close proximity to the corrupt practices of Eli's sons, shaped his character and led him to deliberately choose to "live upstream" against the prevailing moral current of his time.

The biblical account repeatedly emphasizes Samuel's ministerial role, noting three times that he served the Lord under Eli's guidance (1 Samuel 2:11, 18; 3:1). However, this apprenticeship occurred within a context of significant moral compromise, as Eli's sons Hophni and Phinehas had corrupted their priestly office through greed, abuse of power, and sexual impropriety. Samuel's response to this environment provides valuable insights into the development of moral character and the possibility of ethical leadership despite adverse circumstances.

Eli's Sons as Negative Models

When Samuel arrived at Shiloh, Eli was an elderly priest of ninety-eight years who had delegated active priestly duties to his sons Hophni and Phinehas. The Hebrew designation of these men as "sons of Belial" (1 Samuel 2:12) carries significant theological weight, as this term typically denotes individuals whose actions threaten social and religious order (Lewis 1992:1:654–656). The irony of Eli's earlier accusation that Hannah was a "daughter of Belial" (1 Samuel 1:16) becomes apparent when contrasted with his sons' actual behavior, which truly merited such condemnation.

The statement that Eli's sons "had no regard for the LORD" employs the Hebrew concept of not "knowing" God, which in Old Testament usage signifies the absence of a personal relationship with the divine. This theological observation underscores the paradox of religious leaders who, despite their official positions as mediators between God and people, lacked authentic spiritual connection with the God they ostensibly served.

Manifestations of Corruption

The first area of corruption involved the violation of sacrificial procedures established in Levitical law (Leviticus 7:29–34). Hophni and Phinehas demonstrated insatiable greed by demanding portions of sacrificial meat beyond their legitimate allocation and by claiming their share before the required burning of fat upon the altar (1 Samuel 2:15). This behavior reflected not merely personal avarice but a fundamental disregard for the sacred nature of worship and the established order of sacrifice.

The economic dimension of their corruption is significant, as meat was a valuable form of compensation in an agricultural society. Their excessive demands revealed an attitude that prioritized personal gain over religious duty, transforming sacred service into a vehicle for material enrichment.

The second manifestation of corruption involved the systematic abuse of priestly authority. Hophni and Phinehas exploited their positions to coerce worshippers through threats of violence, instructing their servants to demand raw meat from sacrifice and to use force if necessary to obtain compliance (1 Samuel 2:16). This behavior represented a fundamental perversion of religious authority, transforming spiritual leadership into a mechanism of exploitation.

The community's recognition of this abuse is reflected in the biblical assessment: "This sin of the young men was very great in the LORD's sight, for they were treating the LORD's offering with contempt" (1 Samuel 2:17). Their actions not only violated divine law but also corrupted the worship experience for the people they were meant to serve.

The third area of corruption involved sexual impropriety with women who served at the tabernacle entrance (1 Samuel 2:22). While the specific duties of these women remain unclear, the Hebrew terminology suggests their involvement in legitimate Levitical service, possibly including musical ministry (Numbers 4:23). The sexual exploitation of these women represented a profound violation of sacred space and religious responsibility.

This behavior became widely known within the community and eventually reached Eli's attention. Despite paternal rebuke, Hophni and Phinehas persisted in their misconduct, demonstrating their fundamental rejection of accountability and correction (1 Samuel 2:25).

Samuel's Counter-Cultural Response

Samuel's response to this corrupted environment represents a remarkable example of moral autonomy and character development. Despite his youth and the powerful influence of his immediate environment, Samuel deliberately chose to reject the behavioral patterns modeled by his adoptive brothers. This decision to "live upstream" against the prevailing moral current required significant personal courage and commitment to transcendent values.

The concept of counter-cultural living involves the conscious rejection of dominant cultural norms in favor of alternative value systems. Samuel's choice becomes more significant when viewed in light of the potential social benefits of conformity: acceptance by Eli's sons and participation in their privileged lifestyle. Instead, Samuel chose the more difficult path of moral integrity, demonstrating what would later be confirmed in the divine principle: "Those who honor me I will honor" (1 Samuel 2:30).

Comparative Analysis: Four Contrasts

The biblical narrator employs a deliberate literary strategy, presenting four specific contrasts between Samuel's character and the behavior of Eli's sons. These comparisons illuminate the fundamental differences in their approaches to religious service and personal conduct.

Submission versus Rebellion

The first contrast centers on their respective relationships with divine authority:

Eli's sons: "They had no regard for the LORD" (1   Samuel 2:12).

Samuel: "The boy ministered before the LORD" (1 Samuel 2:11).

This comparison reveals a fundamental theological distinction. While Eli's sons lived in rebellion against divine authority, Samuel chose submission and reverence. His service demonstrated what Scripture calls "the fear of the LORD"—not terror, but the appropriate awe and respect that leads to obedience and worship.

Selflessness versus Selfishness

The second contrast addresses their treatment of others and their approach to service:

Eli's sons: "They were treating the LORD's offering with contempt" (1 Samuel 2:17–18).

Samuel: "Samuel was ministering before the LORD" (1 Samuel 2:18).

Samuel's selflessness manifested in his commitment to serve rather than to be served. This orientation toward others' welfare rather than personal gain marked a fundamental difference in character. The validation of this approach appears later in Samuel's career when he could challenge Israel: "Whom have I cheated? Whom have I oppressed? From whose hand have I accepted a bribe?" (1 Samuel 12:3). The people's affirmative response confirmed his lifelong integrity.

The third contrast examines their respective sources of fulfillment:

Eli's sons: "They slept with the women who served at the entrance to the Tent of Meeting" (1 Samuel 2:22).

Samuel: "Samuel grew up in the presence of the LORD" (1 Samuel 2:21).

While Eli's sons sought satisfaction through material excess and sexual gratification, Samuel found fulfillment in spiritual service and divine presence. This difference reflects the biblical principle that "whoever loves wealth is never satisfied with his income" (Ecclesiastes 5:10), contrasted with the satisfaction found in spiritual communion with God.

Honor versus Dishonor

The fourth contrast addresses their ultimate relationship with God and the consequences of their choices:

Eli's sons: Recipients of divine judgment and rejection from priestly service.

Samuel: Recipient of divine honor and appointment as faithful priest.

The divine pronouncement through the unnamed prophet encapsulates this contrast: "Those who despise me will be disgraced... those who honor me I will honor" (1 Samuel 2:30). Samuel's choice to honor God through faithful service resulted in divine blessing and recognition, while Eli's sons' contempt led to judgment and removal from office.

Theological and Practical Implications

Samuel's development demonstrates that moral character can flourish even in corrupted environments. His example challenges deterministic views of moral development that suggest individuals inevitably reproduce the patterns of their immediate context. Instead, Samuel's life illustrates the possibility of moral autonomy and the power of personal choice in character formation.

The concept of "living upstream" represents more than individual moral choice; it embodies a prophetic stance that challenges existing systems and points toward alternative possibilities. Samuel's counter-cultural position prepared him for his later role as a reformer and leader in Israel's transition from theocracy to monarchy.

Samuel's character provides a model for authentic religious leadership characterized by submission to divine authority, selfless service, spiritual satisfaction, and commitment to honor God rather than personal advancement. These qualities contrast sharply with the self-serving leadership exemplified by Eli's sons and offer timeless principles for religious service.

The narrative suggests that true religious authority derives not from position or heredity but from character and divine calling. Samuel's eventual appointment as a "faithful priest" (1 Samuel 2:35) confirms that God's selection criteria emphasize moral integrity and spiritual authenticity over conventional qualifications.

The contrasting fates of Samuel and Eli's sons demonstrate the long-term consequences of moral choices. While immediate benefits might appear to favor compromise and conformity, the narrative reveals that integrity and faithfulness ultimately receive divine vindication. This principle provides both warning and encouragement for those facing similar moral challenges.

The Old Testament Speaks to the Church

My pastor, Jeff Griffin, Senior Pastor of The Compass Church in Naperville, Illinois, delivered a compelling sermon on May 23, 2021, based on 1 Samuel 2:11–35, titled "Samuel: Lessons From a Remarkable Child – Living Upstream." Jeff's message resonates powerfully with contemporary Christians facing the challenge of maintaining biblical values in an increasingly secular culture.

185

Jeff's opening metaphor of kayaking provides a vivid illustration of the spiritual principle at stake. He observes that kayaking naturally involves going downstream, following the current, and moving with the flow of the water. This represents the path of least resistance, requiring minimal effort and struggle. However, Jeff notes that going upstream, while possible, demands significant effort, strength, and determination. This kayaking metaphor brilliantly captures the spiritual dynamic that Samuel faced and that contemporary Christians continue to encounter.

The downstream life represents conformity to cultural norms, social expectations, and the prevailing moral climate. It is the natural human tendency to follow the crowd, adopt popular opinions, and avoid the discomfort of standing against the majority opinion. Jeff's insight reveals that most people naturally choose this path because it appears easier and more socially acceptable.

The Upstream Choice: Biblical Worldview in Secular Culture

Jeff's exposition of Samuel's upstream choice speaks directly to the challenges facing twenty-first-century Christians. In Samuel's era, the corruption of religious leadership created a downstream current of moral compromise, financial impropriety, and sexual misconduct. Today's Christians face similar downstream currents in various forms: materialistic values, relativistic morality, sexual permissiveness, and the pursuit of personal success at any cost.

The concept of living with a biblical worldview in contemporary society requires the same upstream effort that Samuel demonstrated. This involves several key areas where Christians must choose to go against the cultural flow:

Ethical Integrity in Professional Life

Modern Christians often encounter workplace situations that mirror the corruption Samuel witnessed. Like Eli's sons, who exploited their positions for personal gain, contemporary professionals may face pressure to compromise ethical standards for career advancement, financial benefit, or social acceptance. The upstream choice involves maintaining honesty in business dealings, refusing to participate in corrupt practices, and prioritizing integrity over profit—even when such decisions may result in professional disadvantage.

Sexual Purity in a Permissive Culture

The sexual misconduct of Eli's sons finds a parallel in contemporary culture's casual approach to sexuality. Christians choosing to live upstream must navigate a cultural landscape that promotes sexual freedom without moral boundaries. This upstream choice involves maintaining biblical standards of sexual purity, supporting the sanctity of marriage, and refusing to participate in or celebrate sexual practices that contradict Scripture—despite facing accusations of being judgmental or outdated.

Financial Stewardship versus Materialism

Eli's sons' greed and excessive demands for material goods reflect the materialistic obsession of contemporary culture. Christians living upstream must resist the cultural emphasis on accumulating wealth, status symbols, and material possessions. This involves practicing biblical stewardship, generous giving, and contentment with God's provision—choices that often appear foolish to a culture that measures success primarily through material accumulation.

Truth versus Relativism

The fundamental issue underlying Eli's sons' corruption was their rejection of absolute truth and divine authority. Similarly, contemporary Christians must choose between biblical truth and cultural relativism. Living upstream requires affirming biblical principles even when they conflict with popular opinion, defending objective truth in a post-truth culture, and maintaining conviction in the face of social pressure to compromise or remain silent.

The Source of Upstream Power: Divine Enablement

Jeff's sermon emphasizes a crucial theological point: Christians cannot live upstream lives through human strength alone. The power to resist cultural currents and maintain biblical conviction comes through divine enablement, specifically through the sanctifying work of the Holy Spirit (2 Thessalonians 2:13; 1 Peter 1:2). This acknowledgment addresses a common misconception that upstream living depends primarily on human willpower or moral effort.

The Holy Spirit's sanctifying work provides several essential elements for upstream living:

Transformation of Desires

The Spirit works to align Christian desires with God's will, making upstream choices feel increasingly natural rather than forced. This gradual transformation enables believers to find satisfaction in spiritual rather than material pursuits, echoing Samuel's contentment in serving God rather than pursuing personal gain.

Strength for Resistance

The Spirit provides supernatural strength to resist cultural pressure and maintain biblical convictions. This strength enables Christians to stand firm when facing ridicule, rejection, or persecution for their faith, just as Samuel maintained his integrity despite the negative example of his adoptive brothers.

Wisdom for Navigation

The Spirit grants wisdom to discern between cultural practices that are merely different and those that are fundamentally opposed to biblical truth. This wisdom helps Christians engage appropriately with culture while maintaining their distinctive Christian identity.

Community for Support

The Spirit works through the church community to provide encouragement, accountability, and support for believers choosing upstream living. This communal dimension addresses the isolation that often accompanies counter-cultural choices.

Historical Precedent: Dietrich Bonhoeffer's Upstream Life

Jeff's conclusion, referencing Dietrich Bonhoeffer's opposition to Hitler, provides a powerful historical example of upstream living in extreme circumstances. Bonhoeffer's life demonstrates that the principles Samuel exemplified remain relevant and necessary in every generation.

Bonhoeffer faced a cultural and political current that demanded conformity to Nazi ideology, compromise with evil, and silence in the face of injustice. His upstream choice involved several elements that parallel Samuel's example:

Submission to Divine Authority

Like Samuel, Bonhoeffer maintained submission to God's authority rather than human power structures. His famous declaration that "when Christ calls a man, he bids him come and die" reflects the same sacrificial commitment that characterized Samuel's service.

Prophetic Voice

Bonhoeffer's opposition to Hitler represented a prophetic stance that challenged existing systems and called for a return to biblical values. Samuel's life similarly served as a prophetic witness that pointed Israel toward authentic worship and righteous leadership.

Personal Cost

Bonhoeffer's ultimate martyrdom demonstrates that upstream living may require significant personal sacrifice. While not all Christians face such extreme circumstances, the principle remains that upstream choices often involve real costs—social, professional, or personal.

Transformative Impact

Bonhoeffer's legacy continues to inspire Christians worldwide, demonstrating that upstream living can have far-reaching influence beyond immediate circumstances. Samuel's impact on Israel's history similarly shows that individual choices for righteousness can effect broader spiritual and social transformation.

Conclusion

Samuel's early life presents a compelling case study in moral development and leadership formation. His decision to "live upstream" against the corrupted practices of his environment demonstrates the possibility of character development that transcends immediate circumstances. Through four specific contrasts—submission versus rebellion, selflessness versus selfishness, satisfaction versus covetousness, and honor versus dishonor—the biblical narrative illustrates the fundamental differences between authentic and corrupt religious leadership.

Jeff's contemporary application of Samuel's story provides essential guidance for Christians navigating the moral complexities of modern culture. His kayaking metaphor effectively illustrates the spiritual principle that following God's will often requires going against cultural currents, while his emphasis on divine enablement through the Holy Spirit offers hope and practical direction for upstream living.

Jeff's reference to Dietrich Bonhoeffer provides a bridge between ancient biblical narrative and contemporary Christian living, demonstrating that the principles Samuel exemplified remain relevant and necessary in every generation. Bonhoeffer's upstream life in Nazi Germany illustrates both the cost and the significance of choosing biblical faithfulness over cultural conformity.

The lesson of living upstream remains powerfully relevant for contemporary religious and moral contexts, challenging individuals to rise above environmental pressures and embrace the higher calling of integrity, service, and divine honor. Through the sanctifying work of the Holy Spirit, Christians can find both the strength and the satisfaction necessary for upstream living, knowing that their faithful choices contribute to God's redemptive purposes in the world.

Samuel's legacy continues to inspire those who choose the challenging but rewarding path of counter-cultural faithfulness, reminding contemporary Christians that living upstream is not merely possible but essential for authentic Christian discipleship in any generation.

CHAPTER 19

SAMUEL: LESSONS FROM A
REMARKABLE CHILD –
HEARING GOD

The story of Samuel's early life provides a clear example of divine communication and spiritual growth within ancient Israel's religious traditions. Samuel's journey from a devoted temple helper to a recognized prophet across the nation took place in a difficult environment, Eli's troubled priestly household, yet his spiritual path stayed true. This chapter looks at the theological and practical lessons from Samuel's first encounter with God's message, treating the biblical account as both a historical record and a guide for understanding prophetic calling and spiritual insight.

Historical and Religious Context

The period during which Samuel's calling occurred marks a profound low point in Israel's spiritual history. The biblical text explicitly states that "the word of the LORD was rare; there were not many visions" (1 Samuel 3:1 NIV). This scarcity of divine communication characterized the era of the judges, a time marked by political instability, moral decay, and religious apostasy. The author of Judges captures this period succinctly: "In those days there was no king in Israel; everyone did what was right in their own eyes" (Judges 21:25 ESV).

Within this broader context of spiritual decline, the house of Eli exemplified the corruption that had infected Israel's religious leadership. Eli's sons, Hophni and Phinehas, demonstrated flagrant disregard for sacred duties and engaged in behavior that violated both religious law and moral standards (1 Samuel 2:12–17, 22). The prophet Amos later articulated the theological principle underlying God's silence during such periods: divine communication ceases when human rebellion reaches critical levels, resulting in "a famine of hearing the words of the LORD" (Amos 8:11 NIV).

The Divine Encounter

Samuel's first encounter with divine communication occurred while he was fulfilling his duties in the tabernacle at Shiloh. The biblical account emphasizes his proximity to the Ark of the Covenant, a detail that carries significant theological weight. The Ark represented God's presence among his people and served as the focal point for divine-human communication. Samuel's physical proximity to this sacred object symbolizes his spiritual access to divine revelation.

The narrative structure of God's repeated calling—four separate attempts to establish communication—demonstrates both divine persistence and human limitations in recognizing divine communication. The text explicitly states that "Samuel did not yet know the LORD, and the word of the LORD had not yet been revealed to him" (1 Samuel 3:7 ESV). This phrase indicates not moral ignorance but rather the absence of direct, personal revelation.

The Role of Spiritual Mentorship

Eli's function in facilitating Samuel's recognition of divine communication highlights the importance of spiritual mentorship in prophetic development. Despite his personal failures and those of his sons, Eli retained sufficient spiritual discernment to recognize the divine origin of Samuel's experience. His instruction to Samuel—"Speak, LORD, for your servant is listening" (1 Samuel 3:9 NIV)—provides a model for appropriate response to divine communication that emphasizes both receptivity and submission.

Content and Significance of the Revelation

The message Samuel received concerned divine judgment upon Eli's household, confirming earlier prophetic warnings (1 Samuel 2:27–36). This consistency between revelations demonstrates an important principle for validating divine communication: authentic divine messages align with previously established divine word. The severity of the judgment—permanent removal from priestly service—reflected the gravity of the family's offenses and God's commitment to holiness in religious leadership.

A Framework for Divine Communication

The Samuel narrative provides a comprehensive framework for understanding divine communication and spiritual discernment. This framework encompasses five essential elements that remain relevant for contemporary spiritual practice.

Positional Readiness

Samuel's encounter with God occurred in a context of dedicated service and physical proximity to sacred space. His presence in the temple, near the Ark of the Covenant, created conditions conducive to divine revelation. This suggests that spiritual positioning—both physical and symbolic—plays a crucial role in receptivity to divine communication.

Attentive Listening

The distinction between human and divine voices required careful attention and discernment. Samuel's initial confusion demonstrates the challenge of distinguishing between internal and external communication sources. The development of spiritual discernment requires intentional cultivation of listening skills to distinguish divine communication from human thoughts, emotions, and external influences.

Scriptural Precedent

Samuel's revelation aligned with previous divine communications, demonstrating the principle that authentic divine messages maintain consistency with established divine character and prior revelations. This principle provides a crucial test for evaluating claims of divine communication, as articulated in Jeremiah's appeal to "the prophets who lived before you and me" (Jeremiah 28:8 NIV).

Responsive Obedience

Samuel's declaration, "Speak, for your servant is listening" (1 Samuel 3:9), exemplifies the proper response to divine communication. The Hebrew term *šema*, translated as "listening," encompasses both cognitive understanding and behavioral compliance. Authentic reception of divine communication necessarily involves commitment to obedience.

Progressive Recognition

The narrative demonstrates divine patience in the process of human spiritual development. God's repeated attempts to communicate with Samuel reflect divine understanding of human limitations and commitment to successful communication despite initial human incomprehension.

Samuel's Discernment in Leadership

Samuel's early training in spiritual discernment proved essential for his later roles as judge and prophet. Two significant decisions in his career demonstrate the practical application of these principles.

The Anointing of Saul

When Israel's elders requested a king, Samuel's personal inclinations opposed monarchy. However, his ability to distinguish between his own preferences and divine will enabled him to fulfill God's command to anoint Saul, despite his personal reservations (1 Samuel 8:7). This episode illustrates the necessity of subordinating personal judgment to divine revelation.

The Selection of David

Samuel's choice of David over his older brothers required rejection of conventional wisdom and personal impressions. His initial attraction to Eliab's physical appearance contradicted the criteria for divine evaluation (1 Samuel 16:6–7). Samuel's willingness to override his initial impressions demonstrates mature spiritual discernment developed through years of practice in distinguishing divine communication from personal inclination.

Conclusion

The story of Samuel's calling offers both historical insight into ancient Israel's religious practices and universal principles for spiritual discernment. Samuel's growth from a young temple servant who could not recognize divine communication to a prophet known for his intercessory power (Jeremiah 15:1) shows the transformative power of a genuine encounter with God.

The narrative emphasizes that spiritual discernment is not innate but must be cultivated through practice, mentorship, and commitment to obedience. Samuel's ability to distinguish divine communication from personal inclination enabled him to serve effectively as Israel's spiritual leader during a crucial transitional period.

Furthermore, the account establishes that biblical prayer transcends monologue to encompass genuine dialogue between divine and human persons. Samuel's model of receptive listening, theological validation, and responsive obedience provides a framework for contemporary spiritual practice that honors both divine sovereignty and human responsibility in the communication process.

The enduring significance of Samuel's example lies not only in its historical value but also in demonstrating that true spiritual discernment remains accessible to those who, like Samuel, prepare themselves for a genuine encounter with God and dedicate themselves to responding faithfully to what God communicates.

The Old Testament Speaks to the Church

My pastor, Jeff Griffin, Senior Pastor of The Compass Church in Naperville, Illinois, delivered a compelling sermon on May 30, 2021, based on 1 Samuel 3:1–21, titled "Samuel: Lessons From a Remarkable Child – Hearing God."

Jeff's message shows how Samuel's encounter with God remains relevant for today's Christian life. Through his personal story and pastoral insights, Jeff connects the old story with modern spiritual practice, providing practical advice for believers trying to hear God's voice in their daily lives.

The Connection Metaphor: Prayer as Divine Communication

Jeff's opening illustration of the old telephone switchboard system provides a compelling metaphor for understanding prayer as divine communication. Just as international operators once facilitated connections between separated family members, prayer serves as the mechanism through which believers connect with their heavenly Father. This metaphor carries several significant implications for contemporary Christian practice.

The switchboard analogy challenges the common misconception of prayer as merely human petition or thanksgiving directed toward God. Instead, Jeff presents prayer as a two-way communication system where God actively speaks to his people through the Holy Spirit. This perspective transforms prayer from a religious duty into a dynamic relationship characterized by mutual communication and divine guidance.

The Role of Spiritual Discernment

Jeff's emphasis on learning to distinguish God's voice from "the voice of their own hearts" addresses one of the most significant challenges facing contemporary believers. In an era of information overload and competing voices, Christians must develop the spiritual maturity to differentiate between divine communication, personal desires, cultural influences, and potentially deceptive spiritual forces. This discernment requires the same intentional cultivation that Samuel demonstrated in his early encounter with God.

Personal Testimony: The Practical Application of Divine Guidance

Jeff's willingness to share his personal experiences of hearing God's voice provides concrete examples of how divine communication operates in contemporary Christian life. His testimony encompasses several critical life decisions that demonstrate the practical significance of spiritual discernment.

Jeff's account of how he became pastor of The Compass Church demonstrates that genuine Christian leadership comes from divine calling rather than human ambition or organizational appointment. His experience reflects the biblical pattern set by Samuel's calling, where God communicates to establish his chosen servants in spiritual authority. This testimony encourages modern believers to seek divine guidance in their career decisions and to trust God's direction even when it goes against conventional career plans.

Marriage and Family Formation

Jeff's testimony about divine guidance in marriage choices and adopting children shows that God's communication goes beyond church matters to include the most personal parts of life. This use of divine guidance urges believers to invite God's voice into all major life decisions, understanding that spiritual insight is relevant to family decisions, parenting, and relationships.

Ongoing Pastoral Ministry

Jeff's emphasis on hearing God's voice as central to his ministry approach reflects a commitment to Spirit-led leadership rather than programmatic or institutional ministry models. This perspective suggests that effective Christian ministry requires continuous divine communication, echoing Samuel's lifelong pattern of prophetic service guided by divine revelation.

Speaking to Modern Christians

Jeff's sermon addresses several critical issues facing contemporary Christians, offering biblical wisdom for navigating the complexities of modern spiritual life.

The Challenge of Spiritual Noise

Modern believers face unprecedented levels of distraction and competing voices that can interfere with their ability to hear God's communication. Social media, constant connectivity, entertainment culture, and the pace of contemporary life create spiritual noise that can drown out divine communication. Jeff's message calls Christians to cultivate the same intentional listening practices that Samuel developed, creating space for divine encounter through disciplined spiritual practices.

The Danger of Spiritual Passivity

Many contemporary Christians have relegated divine communication to professional clergy or historical biblical figures, failing to recognize that God continues to speak to all believers. Jeff's testimony challenges this passivity by demonstrating that ordinary believers can and should expect to hear God's voice in their daily lives. This democratization of divine communication empowers all Christians to seek an active relationship with God rather than passive religious observance.

The Importance of Spiritual Mentorship

Just as Eli guided Samuel in recognizing divine communication, Jeff's sermon implicitly highlights the importance of spiritual mentorship in modern Christian growth. Mature believers have a duty to help younger Christians develop discernment skills, and those seeking to hear God's voice should rely on spiritually mature mentors who can offer wisdom and accountability in the discernment process.

The Transformative Power of Divine Communication

Jeff's sermon ultimately presents divine communication as transformative rather than merely informational. His testimony demonstrates that hearing God's voice leads to significant life changes, meaningful relationships, and purposeful ministry. This transformative aspect of divine communication offers hope to contemporary believers who may feel disconnected from God or uncertain about their spiritual journey.

Jeff's focus on living "on the fringes of faith" recognizes that many Christians struggle with spiritual vitality and authentic divine encounters. His message provides practical hope that a true relationship with God—marked by two-way communication—can turn spiritual routines into a vibrant, life-changing connection.

Jeff's sermon speaks to contemporary Christians by demonstrating that the same God who called Samuel continues to communicate with his people today. This message challenges believers to cultivate the spiritual sensitivity, discernment skills, and responsive obedience necessary to hear and follow God's voice in their daily lives, thereby transforming both individual spiritual experiences and Christian community life through authentic divine encounters.

PART 4

DAVID

INTRODUCTION

DAVID: THE LIFE OF A KING

Israel's history is filled with stories of individuals whose lives have inspired people for thousands of years. Among these ancient heroes, King David is arguably the most recognizable figure of the Old Testament. David's victories as a warrior and his failures as a king shaped his life in such a way that he is remembered as the greatest king to rule Israel.

God had a special place in his heart for David. When Samuel announced to Saul that his kingdom would not continue, Samuel said that God had sought out a man after his own heart to replace him (1 Samuel 13:14). When David was chosen to be a king, he was just a young man, a humble shepherd who was destined to become the shepherd of God's people (2 Samuel 5:2) and Israel's greatest warrior.

The presence of David in the Bible reveals the kind of man David was. His name is mentioned 1118 times in the Bible. There are 62 chapters in the Old Testament detailing the life and activities of David. There are 73 psalms ascribed to David in the book of Psalms.

These references to David present him as the king of Israel, as a mighty warrior, as the commander of Israel's army, as a poet, as an instrumentalist, and as a composer of songs. David was called "Israel's beloved singer of songs" (2 Samuel 23:1).

The Old Testament presents David as a mighty king who established a prosperous kingdom in Israel. He strengthened Israel politically, economically, and socially. His accomplishments as a warrior helped Israel subdue its enemies and bring peace to his nation. Solomon's reign of peace and prosperity was the legacy David left to his son. Notwithstanding his lustful affair with Bathsheba, his many wives, and the many challenges he faced as a king, David became the agent God used to accomplish his work in the world.

Several months ago, my pastor, Jeff Griffin, the Senior Pastor of The Compass Church in Naperville, preached a series of sermons on David after he became king. That series of seven sermons titled "David: The Life of a King" focused on David's life after Saul anointed him and began to reign in Jerusalem. This series of sermons on David details the story and the drama of what happened in David's palace.

In introducing the series of sermons on the life of David as king, Jeff said, "The palace in ancient Jerusalem was filled with treachery, seduction, and murder. Surprisingly, God invites us to take a front row seat in watching the vile drama of King David's reign. We can learn from this royal mess and gain life-altering wisdom."

Sermon Series: David: The Life of a King

"David, The Lord's Anointed -- Growing a Heart that Loves God" - 1 Samuel 16:1–13

This opening sermon explores the foundational moment of David's calling, examining how God's choice of David over his older brothers reveals divine priorities that often contrast with human expectations. The message focuses on cultivating the kind of heart that attracts God's attention—one characterized by humility, faithfulness in small things, and genuine devotion rather than outward appearances or worldly qualifications.

David -- "Celebrating God Wholeheartedly" (Michal) -- 2 Samuel 6:1–23

Through the lens of David's exuberant worship as he brings the Ark to Jerusalem, this sermon contrasts authentic, passionate worship with his wife, Michal's, cynical disapproval. The message challenges believers to examine their own worship—whether it flows from genuine joy and gratitude or is constrained by concerns about dignity, tradition, or what others might think.

David -- "Loving the Overlooked" (Mephibosheth) -- 2 Samuel 9:1–13

This powerful sermon uses David's kindness toward Jonathan's disabled son, Mephibosheth, as a beautiful picture of grace in action. The message explores how David's covenant faithfulness to his deceased friend translates into practical care for someone society had forgotten, offering profound lessons about honoring commitments and extending compassion to the marginalized.

David -- "Facing the Truth" (Nathan's Rebuke) -- 2 Samuel 12:1–31

Perhaps the most convicting sermon in the series, this message examines David's response to Nathan's prophetic confrontation about his sin with Bathsheba. The sermon explores how self-deception can blind even godly leaders, the courage required for both giving and receiving brutal truths, and the pathway to genuine repentance and restoration.

David -- "Parenting Courageously" (Absalom) -- 2 Samuel 15:1–37

This deeply personal sermon explores one of David's most significant failures and heartaches—his strained relationship with his rebellious son Absalom. The message openly examines the effects of passive parenting, the struggle of balancing love and discipline, and how unresolved family dysfunction can lead to devastating outcomes for both families and leadership.

David -- "Forgiving Others" (Shimei) -- 2 Samuel 19:15–23

Drawing from David's merciful treatment of Shimei, who had cursed him during Absalom's rebellion, this sermon explores the difficult but essential practice of forgiveness. The message explores how choosing forgiveness over revenge reflects spiritual maturity and demonstrates trust in God's justice, even when the offender appears not to deserve mercy.

David -- "Joy in Giving" (Temple Preparation) -- 2 Samuel 24:18–25

The final sermon in the series highlights David's generous preparations for the temple that his son Solomon would build. This message examines how David's sacrificial giving stemmed from a heart of worship and a desire for God's glory, encouraging listeners to reflect on their own motivations and joy in giving, and how generous hearts can leave lasting legacies.

Conclusion

The following seven chapters are studies based on Jeff's sermons. Each chapter will be based on the ideas and concepts Jeff used in his sermons. The reason I write these studies on Jeff's sermons is that Jeff is a unique preacher. Preaching from the Old Testament is not easy. It requires much research, an in-depth analysis of the text, and some creativity.

These seven sermons on David's reign offer far more than historical narrative—they present a masterclass in authentic leadership, spiritual growth, and human vulnerability. Through David's triumphs and failures, we witness how God works through imperfect people to accomplish his perfect purposes. Each message reveals timeless principles that speak directly to contemporary challenges: the importance of authentic worship, the call to show grace to the forgotten, the necessity of accountability, the demands of courageous parenting, the freedom found in forgiveness, and the joy discovered in generous living.

David's story reminds us that being "a man after God's own heart" does not mean perfection—it means possessing a heart that remains tender toward God even in failure, quick to repent when confronted with truth, and committed to seeking God's will despite personal cost. In an age that often demands flawless leaders, David's complex legacy offers hope to all who struggle with the tension between calling and character, between public success and private failure.

Jeff and I hope you enjoy these studies on David. More importantly, our prayer is that these studies will help you better understand David as a king and learn essential truths from his life that you can apply to your own faith journey. May you, like David, grow in your pursuit of God's heart, finding both warning and encouragement in his story for the road ahead.

CHAPTER 20

DAVID: THE LORD'S ANOINTED

King David of Israel occupies a singular position in biblical narrative and theological tradition. His prominence is evidenced not only by the frequency of his mention—appearing 1118 times in the Old Testament, more than any other Israelite figure—but also by his multifaceted portrayal as shepherd, musician, warrior, and king. The narrative of David's anointing represents a pivotal moment in Israel's monarchical history, marking a theological shift from external qualifications to internal spiritual character. This chapter examines the divine selection of David as recorded in 1 Samuel 16, analyzing the theological implications of God's criterion for leadership and the concept of having "heart after God's own heart."

The Search for a New King

The selection of David as king must be understood within the broader context of Saul's rejection by Yahweh. Following Saul's disobedience to divine command, Samuel received a prophetic declaration: "The LORD has torn the kingdom of Israel from you this very day, and has given it to a neighbor of yours, who is better than you" (1 Samuel 15:28). This pronouncement established the theological foundation for the transition of kingship and introduced the concept of divine evaluation based on character rather than conventional qualifications.

The divine commission to Samuel represents a significant moment in Israel's political theology. While Samuel initially grieved over Saul's failure, Yahweh redirected his attention toward future leadership, commanding him to journey to Bethlehem to anoint Jesse's chosen son. Bethlehem's selection as the location carries symbolic weight, connecting David's narrative to the broader redemptive history through its associations with Ruth's settlement, the Davidic lineage, and the future birthplace of the Messiah (Luke 2:4; Matthew 1:1).

Samuel's hesitation to take on this mission underscores the political complexity of the situation. Anointing a new king while Saul was still in power could have been seen as treason. Yahweh's provision of a cover story—bringing a heifer for sacrifice—illustrates divine flexibility in accommodating human limits while still upholding the prophetic mission's integrity.

The Divine Selection Process

The anointing ceremony itself provides profound insight into the distinction between divine and human standards of evaluation. Samuel's initial assessment of Eliab reveals the persistence of conventional wisdom in leadership selection. Eliab's presumed stature and appearance led Samuel to conclude, "Surely the LORD's anointed stands here before the LORD" (1 Samuel 16:6). This assessment paralleled the criteria used in Saul's selection, where physical attributes—height, handsomeness, and imposing presence—were considered indicative of royal potential (1 Samuel 9:2).

However, Yahweh's rejection of Eliab introduced a revolutionary principle in leadership evaluation: "Do not consider his appearance or his height... The LORD doesn't see things the way you see them. People judge by outward appearance, but the LORD looks at the heart" (1 Samuel 16:7 TLT). This divine pronouncement establishes a fundamental theological principle that internal character supersedes external qualifications in God's economy of leadership.

The systematic rejection of Jesse's seven older sons emphasizes the thoroughness of divine selection. Each rejection reinforced the principle that human expectations and conventional wisdom fail to align with divine purposes. The fact that David was not initially summoned to the ceremony reflects his family's low estimation of his potential, despite his eventual divine selection.

The Anointing of David

David's eventual summons and anointing carry multiple layers of theological significance. The text's description of David as "ruddy, with a fine appearance and handsome features" (1 Samuel 16:12) presents an interesting paradox: while physical appearance was explicitly rejected as a criterion, David's attractiveness is nonetheless noted. This suggests that God's selection transcends rather than negates physical attributes—the heart remains paramount, but external qualities need not be absent.

The anointing ceremony itself represents a pivotal moment in Israel's theological development. The Hebrew term "messiah" (the anointed one) finds its most significant Old Testament application in David's selection, establishing a messianic tradition that would culminate in Christian theology. The immediate consequence of David's anointing, "from that day on the Spirit of the LORD came upon David in power" (1 Samuel 16:13), demonstrates the inseparable connection between divine selection and spiritual empowerment.

The Heart in Hebrew Anthropology

The divine criterion of judging "the heart" requires careful theological analysis within Hebrew anthropological concepts. In Hebrew psychology, the heart (*leb*) functions as the comprehensive center of human personality, encompassing emotional, moral, spiritual, and intellectual dimensions Wolff 1974: 51–55). Unlike modern Western thought, which often compartmentalizes these aspects, Hebrew understanding views the heart as the unified seat of human identity and decision-making capacity.

The prophetic literature consistently presents God as one who "searches the heart" (Jeremiah 17:10), establishing divine knowledge of human interiority as a foundational theological principle. Samuel's earlier declaration that "the LORD has sought out a man after his own heart and appointed him leader of his people" (1 Samuel 13:14) introduces the concept of divine-human heart alignment as the ultimate qualification for leadership.

The Meaning of "A Heart After God's Own Heart"

Paul's interpretation in Acts 13:22 provides crucial insight into the meaning of David's heart condition: "I have found David, son of

Jesse, to be a man after my heart, who will carry out all my wishes". This explanation suggests that having "a heart after God's own heart" primarily involves alignment of will and purpose rather than moral perfection. David's later moral failures, particularly the Bathsheba incident, demonstrate that this designation does not imply sinlessness but rather a fundamental orientation toward God's purposes.

Three dimensions of David's heart condition emerge from the biblical narrative:

Commitment to Divine Purposes

David's reign demonstrated consistent alignment with God's redemptive purposes for Israel. His establishment of Jerusalem as the political and religious center, his desire to build the temple, and his role in establishing the Davidic covenant (2 Samuel 7:13) reflect his participation in divine plans that extended beyond his immediate context.

Authentic Worship and Fellowship

David's passionate worship, exemplified in his dancing before the Ark of the Covenant despite royal dignity concerns (2 Samuel 6), reveals a heart genuinely devoted to divine fellowship. His psalmic expressions demonstrate profound longing for God's presence: "The one thing I ask of the LORD–the thing I seek most–is to live in the house of the LORD all the days of my life, delighting in the LORD's perfections and meditating in his Temple" (Psalm 27:4 NLT).

Responsive Relationship to Divine Correction

Throughout his reign, David consistently demonstrated responsiveness to prophetic correction and divine discipline. His repentance following Nathan's confrontation regarding Bathsheba illustrates a heart that, despite moral failure, remained fundamentally oriented toward God.

Contemporary Theological Implications

The principle established in David's selection carries significant implications for understanding divine evaluation and human leadership. The text suggests that God's assessment criteria fundamentally differ from human standards, prioritizing internal character development over external qualifications. This principle challenges contemporary emphasis on credentials, appearance, and conventional markers of success in favor of character, integrity, and spiritual alignment.

The ongoing divine search for committed hearts, as described in 2 Chronicles 16:9, "The LORD's eyes scan the whole world to find those whose hearts are committed to him," suggests that the principle established in David's selection remains active in divine economy. This implies that God continues to evaluate and select individuals based on heart condition rather than external qualifications.

The Old Testament Speaks to the Church

On February 20, 2022, my pastor, Jeff Griffin, Senior Pastor of the Compass Church, delivered a sermon titled "The Lord's Anointed: Growing a Heart that Loves God," based on 1 Samuel 16:1–13. Jeff's exposition offers profound implications for modern Christian discipleship and spiritual formation, with his central message: that God evaluates the heart rather than external appearances, speaking directly to contemporary Christians navigating a culture obsessed with image, achievement, and social media presentation.

In his sermon, Jeff emphasized that God is actively seeking people whose hearts are right. Specifically, God searches for people who have chosen to love with God's love; people who are willing to share God's way of life with others; people who have the same passion for a relationship with God; and people whose purpose is to build God's kingdom in the world. This fourfold emphasis provides a framework for understanding what constitutes a heart after God's own heart in contemporary Christian contexts.

Jeff's Fourfold Framework for Heart Transformation

Jeff's sermon identifies four essential characteristics that God seeks in contemporary believers, providing a practical framework for spiritual development:

Choosing to Love with God's Love

Jeff's emphasis on choosing to love with God's love addresses one of the most fundamental aspects of Christian discipleship. This principle challenges contemporary believers to move beyond natural human affection toward supernatural, divine love that transcends personal preferences and cultural boundaries. In a world marked by increasing polarization, tribalism, and conditional acceptance, Christians are called to embody the unconditional, sacrificial love that characterizes God's nature.

This divine love manifests in practical ways: loving those who disagree politically, extending grace to those who have caused personal harm, and demonstrating compassion to marginalized individuals whom society often overlooks. Jeff's insight suggests that possessing a heart after God's own heart requires the deliberate choice to love as God loves, even when such love contradicts natural inclinations or social expectations.

Sharing God's Way of Life with Others

Jeff's second characteristic—willingness to share God's way of life—speaks to the evangelical and discipleship dimensions of Christian faith. This goes beyond mere verbal proclamation to include the embodiment and demonstration of God's principles in daily living. Contemporary Christians are challenged to become living examples of divine values, allowing their transformed lives to serve as testimonies to God's transformative power.

In practical terms, this means Christians are called to demonstrate integrity in their business dealings, compassion in their relationships, forgiveness in conflicts, and justice in their social interactions. Jeff's sermon suggests that those with hearts after God's own heart naturally become conduits through which God's character and values are transmitted to others, creating ripple effects that extend God's kingdom influence throughout society.

The third characteristic Jeff identifies, having the same passion for a relationship with God, addresses the contemplative and devotional aspects of Christian spirituality. This passion transcends mere religious duty or cultural conformity, embracing genuine spiritual hunger and an authentic encounter with God.

In contemporary contexts marked by digital distraction and superficial connections, Jeff's emphasis on passionate divine relationship challenges Christians to prioritize practices that foster genuine spiritual intimacy. This includes contemplative prayer, meditative engagement with Scripture, worship that engages both emotion and intellect, and lifestyle choices that reflect a love for God rather than social pressure or personal convenience.

Jeff's insight suggests that a passionate relationship with God should become the organizing principle around which all other aspects of life are arranged. This passion provides motivation for obedience, strength for moral courage, and joy that transcends circumstances.

Committing to Building God's Kingdom

Jeff's final characteristic, having as one's purpose the building of God's kingdom, addresses the missional and transformational aspects of Christian calling. This purpose orientation challenges contemporary believers to align their life goals, career choices, and daily decisions with God's redemptive purposes in the world.

Building God's kingdom involves both personal transformation and social engagement, as well as individual sanctification and community involvement. Jeff's sermon suggests that those with hearts after God's own heart naturally seek opportunities to participate in God's work of restoration, reconciliation, and renewal in both personal and societal contexts.

Jeff's emphasis on God's heart-focused evaluation confronts the modern Christian's tendency to measure spiritual worth through external metrics. In an era dominated by social media platforms where curated images often mask internal realities, the narrative of David's selection serves as a countercultural reminder that divine evaluation transcends public perception. Christians today are challenged to prioritize heart transformation over reputation management, authentic spiritual growth over performative religiosity.

Jeff's insight that "God has more assignments than he has people whose hearts are committed to him" particularly resonates in contemporary Christian contexts. This principle suggests that God's kingdom work remains constrained not by divine limitations but by human availability and heart condition. Modern Christians are thus challenged to examine whether their hearts genuinely desire God's purposes or merely God's blessings.

Implications for Christian Leadership

The sermon's insights regarding divine selection criteria have profound implications for contemporary Christian leadership development. Rather than prioritizing charisma, educational credentials, or organizational skills, the narrative suggests that spiritual leadership should emerge from character development and heart alignment with God's purposes.

This principle questions both how Christian leaders are selected and prepared. Churches and Christian organizations should evaluate potential leaders based on spiritual maturity, integrity, and authentic love for God rather than solely relying on traditional qualifications. At the same time, aspiring leaders are encouraged to focus on character development and spiritual growth rather than merely acquiring skills and building a reputation.

Growing a Heart That Loves God: Jeff's Central Message

The ultimate application of Jeff's sermon centers on cultivating genuine love for God through the practical embodiment of his fourfold framework. The narrative suggests that David's selection was not based on his abilities or potential, but on his authentic affection for God and desire for divine fellowship. Contemporary

Christians are thus challenged to examine their motivations for spiritual engagement through Jeff's practical lens.

Jeff's sermon suggests that many Christians might participate in religious activities without cultivating true love for God. This love shows in loving with divine love, sharing God's way of life, pursuing a passionate relationship with God, and committing to kingdom building. Genuine spiritual growth requires moving from obligation-based religion to relationship-based devotion, which naturally leads to these four qualities.

This transformation involves cultivating practices that foster an authentic encounter with God and practical engagement with Jeff's framework: contemplative prayer that deepens a passionate relationship with God; meditative Scripture reading that reveals God's way of life; worship that engages both emotion and intellect in divine love; and service that flows from kingdom-building purpose rather than mere duty.

Conclusion

The story of David's anointing, as shared in Jeff's sermon, marks a key moment in understanding divine choice and what qualifies someone for leadership, resonating deeply with today's Christian experience. By rejecting traditional standards and focusing on the heart, the text sets forth principles that directly address the struggles modern believers face.

Jeff's sermon shows that the lasting importance of David's choice is not just in its historical role but in revealing divine values and priorities that stay constant across time and cultures. In a time marked by superficiality, performance anxiety, and seeking external validation, the message that "the LORD looks at the heart" offers both comfort and a challenge to modern Christians.

The comfort comes from understanding that divine judgment goes beyond human standards, giving hope to those who feel inadequate by worldly measures. The challenge is a call to true heart transformation, moving past superficial religiosity toward real spiritual depth and dedication to God's plans.

Jeff's sermon shows that the lasting importance of David's choice is not just about history but about revealing divine values and priorities that remain the same across time and cultures. In today's world, marked by superficiality, performance anxiety, and a quest for external validation, Jeff's message that "the LORD looks at the heart" offers both comfort and a challenge to modern Christians.

The comfort is found in understanding that divine judgment surpasses human evaluation, offering hope to those who feel inadequate by worldly standards. The challenge involves Jeff's call to genuine heart transformation through his fourfold framework: choosing to love with God's love, willingness to share God's way of life, cultivating a passionate relationship with God, and committing to building God's kingdom.

Jeff's exposition shows that David's example continues to guide our understanding of divine evaluation and human spiritual growth in today's world. The heart becomes the key battleground where divine and human goals either come together or differ, through the practical application of Jeff's four characteristics. David's model shows that such alignment, even if it does not guarantee moral perfection, lays the groundwork for meaningful involvement in divine purposes and genuine spiritual leadership.

For Christians today, Jeff's sermon application is clear: God continues to seek individuals whose hearts embody these four characteristics—not for their perfection but for their genuine desire to know him, serve his purposes, and love him authentically through practical obedience. In a world that often values appearance over substance, performance over character, and achievement over relationship, the story of David's anointing, as explained by Jeff, reminds believers that spiritual transformation begins in the heart and flows outward into genuine Christian living through love, witness, relationship, and kingdom service.

The core message for today's Christians, as Jeff highlighted, is both deep and practical: cultivating a heart that loves God through these four areas remains the highest calling and the most certain way to participate in God's ongoing work in the world actively. As Jeff's sermon shows, God's kingdom work is not about having more talent, but about having more hearts genuinely dedicated to his purposes and eager for his presence—demonstrated through divine love, kingdom witness, spiritual intimacy, and missional engagement.

CHAPTER 21

DAVID: "CELEBRATING GOD WHOLEHEARTEDLY" – MICHAL

The transition from Saul's monarchy to David's reign represents a pivotal moment in Israel's political and religious history. This transformation was not merely a change in leadership but reflected divine election and the establishment of Jerusalem as both political capital and religious center. The narrative of David bringing the Ark of the Covenant to Jerusalem provides crucial insights into the intersection of political legitimacy, religious devotion, and the tension between royal dignity and authentic worship in ancient Israel.

The Divine Rejection of Saul and Election of David

The biblical narrative presents Saul's downfall as rooted in his failure to maintain covenant obedience to Yahweh's commands. The decisive moment occurred during the campaign against the Amalekites, where Saul's incomplete execution of the divine mandate led to his rejection as king (1 Samuel 15:1-2). Samuel's prophetic declaration to Saul crystallizes this divine decision: "The LORD has torn the kingdom of Israel from you this very day, and has given it to a neighbor of yours, who is better than you" (1 Samuel 15:28).

This "neighbor" was David, whom the text identifies as "a man after God's own heart" (1 Samuel 13:14). The biblical account emphasizes that David's selection was not based on human criteria but represented divine election. Following Saul's death at Mount Gilboa (1 Samuel 31:1–13), David's rise to power occurred in stages, beginning with his coronation as king over Judah, followed seven years later by his acceptance as king over all Israel (2 Samuel 5:1–3).

The theological significance of David's election becomes particularly evident in Solomon's retrospective declaration: "I have chosen Jerusalem in order that my name may be there, and I have chosen David to be over my people Israel" (2 Chronicles 6:4–6). The Hebrew term *bāḥar* ("chosen") employed here carries the weight of divine election, establishing both David's legitimacy as ruler and Jerusalem's status as the chosen city for Yahweh's dwelling place.

Jerusalem as the New Capital and Religious Center

David's selection of Jerusalem as his capital represented a strategically and theologically significant decision. Unlike Saul's capital at Gibeah, which was situated within Benjaminite territory, Jerusalem occupied neutral ground on the border between Judah and Benjamin. This geographical positioning facilitated David's goal of uniting the northern and southern tribes under a single monarchy while avoiding favoritism toward any particular tribal territory.

The conquest of Jerusalem from the Jebusites and its subsequent designation as "the city of David" (2 Samuel 5:9) established both political and religious precedent. Jerusalem's elevation from Jebusite stronghold to Israel's capital city represented more than military victory; it symbolized the divine election of both king and city for Yahweh's purposes.

The Transportation of the Ark: Failure and Success

David's decision to relocate the Ark of the Covenant to Jerusalem served multiple purposes: religious centralization, political legitimization, and the establishment of Jerusalem as Israel's spiritual center. The Ark, representing Yahweh's throne and presence among his people (1 Samuel 4:4; Psalm 29:10), constituted Israel's most sacred religious symbol. Its presence in David's capital would provide divine sanction for the united monarchy.

The initial attempt to transport the Ark reveals the tension between pragmatic expediency and ritual propriety. David's adoption of Philistine transportation methods, placing the Ark on a new cart pulled by oxen (2 Samuel 6:3), demonstrated either ignorance of or disregard for Mosaic instructions regarding the Ark's proper handling (Exodus 25:12–14). The tragic death of Uzzah, who touched the Ark when the oxen stumbled, served as a stark reminder that divine holiness cannot be approached casually or improperly.

Walter Brueggemann's analysis captures the theological lesson inherent in this episode: "the ark must not be presumed upon, taken for granted, or treated with familiarity. The holiness of God is indeed present in the ark, but that holiness is not readily available. To touch the ark is to impinge on God's holiness, to draw too close and presume too much" (Brueggemann 1990:261).

The three-month sojourn of the Ark in the house of Obed-edom, a non-Israelite who nonetheless received divine blessing through its presence (2 Samuel 6:12), prepared David for a second, successful attempt. This time, David ensured proper Levitical handling: "the Levites carried the ark of God on their shoulders with the poles, as Moses had commanded according to the word of the LORD" (1 Chronicles 15:15).

David's Worship and Royal Identity

The triumphant procession bringing the Ark to Jerusalem was marked by David's exuberant worship, characterized by dancing "before the LORD with all his might" while wearing a linen ephod (2 Samuel 6:14). The ephod, typically worn by priests, signified the ritualistic nature of the occasion and David's role as both king and worship leader. However, the garment's brevity created potential for exposure during vigorous movement, particularly during ecstatic dance.

David's uninhibited worship raises important questions about the relationship between royal dignity and authentic religious expression. His willingness to appear undignified in pursuit of wholehearted worship demonstrates a prioritization of divine approval over human opinion, a theme that resonates throughout his reign.

The Michal Incident: Royal Dignity versus Authentic Worship

The confrontation between David and Michal provides a window into competing perspectives on kingship, worship, and gender dynamics in ancient Israel. Michal's criticism, "How distinguished the king of Israel looked today, shamelessly exposing himself to the servant girls like any vulgar person might do" (2 Samuel 6:20), reflects her concern for royal propriety and dignity.

Several scholarly interpretations shed light on Michal's motivation. As Saul's daughter, she might have had different expectations for royal conduct, influenced by her father's more reserved approach to kingship. Moreover, her forced separation from her husband, Paltiel, and her subsequent return to David as a political symbol rather than as a beloved wife may have affected her emotional state (Sachs 2006:263).

Ellen White's feminist reading suggests that David's public exposure compromised Michal's status as queen, effectively sharing what should have been exclusively hers with common servant girls (White 2007:460). Similarly, David Clines argues that David's behavior constituted a form of sexual vulgarity that humiliated Michal and demonstrated his indifference to marital loyalty (Clines 1991:138).

David's response to Michal's criticism reveals his theological motivation: "It was before the LORD, who chose me in place of your father and all his household, to appoint me as prince over Israel, the people of the LORD, that I have danced before the LORD" (2 Samuel 6:21). His declaration emphasizes divine election over human approval and positions his worship as a response to God's choosing rather than concern for public opinion.

Furthermore, David's willingness to appear "even more foolish" and to be "humiliated in my own eyes" (2 Samuel 6:22, NLT) demonstrates his commitment to authentic worship regardless of social expectations. This attitude establishes a paradigm where divine approval supersedes human dignity and social propriety in matters of worship.

Conclusion

The story of David bringing the Ark to Jerusalem covers several theological and political themes: divine election, proper worship, the tension between sacred and secular authority, and the relationship between genuine spirituality and social expectations. David's journey from an unsuccessful first attempt to a successful second effort shows the importance of approaching divine holiness with proper reverence and following divine instruction.

The conflict with Michal highlights enduring questions about the nature of authentic worship and its relationship to social propriety. David's model suggests that wholehearted devotion to God may require the abandonment of human dignity and social expectations in favor of divine approval.

Ultimately, this episode establishes Jerusalem as both the political capital and religious center of the nation, while affirming David's reign through divine selection and proper worship. The story shows that effective leadership in God's kingdom requires not just political skill but also genuine spiritual devotion, even when that devotion conflicts with traditional ideas of royal dignity.

The Old Testament Speaks to the Church

The theological insights from David's narrative find profound contemporary relevance through the pastoral application presented by my pastor, Jeff Griffin, Senior Pastor of The Compass Church in Naperville, Illinois, in his sermon "David: Celebrating God Wholeheartedly," delivered on May 21, 2023, based on 2 Samuel 6:1–23. Jeff's treatment of this passage offers valuable insights for modern Christian worship and spiritual formation.

The Priority of Divine Approval over Human Opinion

Jeff's central emphasis that David danced because he was trying to please God rather than people resonates powerfully with contemporary worship challenges. In an era where church services are often evaluated through the lens of consumer satisfaction and social media appeal, David's model presents a counter-cultural approach to authentic worship. Modern Christians, like David, face the tension between maintaining social respectability and expressing genuine spiritual devotion.

The pastoral application challenges contemporary believers to examine their motivations in worship. Are our expressions of praise constrained by fear of judgment, cultural expectations, or the pursuit of social approval? David's willingness to appear foolish before others while maintaining his focus on divine pleasure provides a template for authentic Christian worship that transcends cultural barriers and personal inhibitions.

Celebrating God's Faithfulness Through Liturgical Memory

Jeff's focus on David's response in the song recorded in 1 Chronicles 16:34, proclaiming "O give thanks to the LORD, for he is good; for his steadfast love endures forever," emphasizes the significance of liturgical memory in Christian growth. David's celebration was not just emotional but also a theological statement rooted in God's covenant faithfulness.

This aspect of Jeff's sermon speaks directly to contemporary worship practices that sometimes prioritize emotional experience over theological content. David's model demonstrates that authentic worship combines passionate expression with doctrinal substance. Modern Christians are called to ground their celebrations in the concrete realities of God's character and actions rather than in subjective emotional states alone.

The integration of music, movement, and theological declaration in David's worship provides a holistic model for contemporary church practice. Jeff's emphasis suggests that Christian worship should engage the whole person—intellect, emotion, and body—in response to God's steadfast love.

Sustaining Worship Through Divine Mercy

Jeff's conclusion, drawing from Lamentations 3:22–23, "The steadfast love of the LORD never ceases, his mercies never come to an end; they are new every morning," connects David's historical celebration to the ongoing experience of divine mercy in Christian life. This application addresses the challenge of maintaining worship enthusiasm beyond momentary spiritual highs.

The pastoral insight recognizes that authentic worship must be sustained by more than emotional peaks or favorable circumstances. David's joy was rooted not in temporary success but in God's unchanging character and covenant commitment. Similarly, contemporary Christians are called to base their worship on the daily renewal of God's mercies rather than on fluctuating personal circumstances.

Conclusion

Jeff's application of David's wholehearted worship provides contemporary Christians with both challenge and encouragement. The challenge lies in the call to prioritize divine approval over social acceptance, to ground worship in theological truth rather than emotional manipulation, and to maintain authentic spiritual expression regardless of cultural pressures.

The encouragement comes through recognition that God's steadfast love provides both the motivation and sustenance for wholehearted worship. Like David, contemporary believers can celebrate not because of perfect circumstances but because of God's perfect character and unfailing covenant love.

Jeff's sermon ultimately calls the modern church to recover the integration of passionate expression and theological substance that characterized David's worship. This recovery requires both pastoral leadership willing to model vulnerability and congregational commitment to authentic spiritual engagement that transcends social conventions and personal inhibitions.

CHAPTER 22

DAVID: LOVING THE OVERLOOK - MEPHIBOSHETH

This chapter explores David's relationship with Mephibosheth as described in 2 Samuel 9, placing it within the larger framework of covenant theology and divine faithfulness in ancient Israel. The analysis shows how David's treatment of Jonathan's disabled son exemplifies the Hebrew idea of *hesed* (covenant loyalty) and highlights how divine grace works through human agents.

The Fall of Saul's Dynasty

The transition from Saul's monarchy to David's reign marks a crucial moment in Israel's political and spiritual growth. In this transition, the story of Mephibosheth, son of Jonathan and grandson of Saul, offers deep insights into covenant fidelity, divine grace, and the treatment of marginalized individuals in ancient Near Eastern societies. David's actions toward Mephibosheth show both personal loyalty and spiritual principles that echo throughout Hebrew scripture.

The demise of Saul's reign culminated in the catastrophic defeat at Mount Gilboa, where Israel's forces succumbed to Philistine military superiority (1 Samuel 31:1–13). Faced with imminent capture and potential torture, Saul chose suicide over humiliation, falling upon his own sword when his armor-bearer refused to kill him (1 Samuel 31:4). This decisive battle resulted in the deaths of three of Saul's sons, Jonathan, Abinadab, and Malchishua, while Ishbosheth alone survived, likely due to his absence from the battlefield.

The political fragmentation that followed Saul's death demonstrates the precarious nature of the early Israelite monarchy. Under Abner's orchestration, Ishbosheth assumed control over the northern tribes for a two-year period (2 Samuel 2:10). In contrast, the tribe of Judah anointed David as their regional king, a position he held for seven years and six months (2 Samuel 2:11).

This division illustrates the challenges of establishing unified monarchical authority in ancient Israel.

The David-Jonathan Covenant

The profound friendship between David and Jonathan transcended typical court relationships, establishing a covenant bond that would have lasting theological and practical implications. David's compositional response to Jonathan's death, "The Song of the Bow" (2 Samuel 1:17–27), reveals the depth of their relationship. Significantly, while three of Saul's sons perished in battle, David's lament focuses exclusively on Jonathan, underscoring their unique bond.

David's grief-stricken declaration, "I grieve for you, Jonathan, my brother. You were such a friend to me" (2 Samuel 1:26, CSB), reflects not merely personal loss but the breaking of a sacred covenant. The friendship's foundation rested upon Jonathan's request that David demonstrate "the faithful love (ḥesed) of the LORD" (1 Sam 20:14) in perpetuity, a commitment that would prove central to David's later actions.

The covenant's specific terms, as articulated by Jonathan, established David's obligation: "If I am still alive, show me the faithful love of the LORD; but if I die, never cut off your faithful love from my house" (1 Sam 20:13–15). This covenant invocation of divine ḥesed elevated their agreement beyond human friendship to participation in God's own covenant faithfulness.

Mephibosheth: The Vulnerable Heir

Mephibosheth, identified in Chronicles as originally named Merib-baal (1 Chronicles 8:34), represents a fascinating case study in ancient Near Eastern naming practices and theological sensitivities. The substitution of "*bosheth*" (shame) for "Baal" reflects later editorial concerns about associating Saul's lineage with Canaanite deities (Avioz 2011:12). This textual modification suggests ongoing theological refinement in Israel's understanding of appropriate religious expression.

The narrative of Mephibosheth's flight illustrates the vulnerability of royal families during dynastic transitions. Historical precedent, exemplified by Athaliah's systematic elimination of Judah's royal family following Ahaziah's death (2 Kings 11:1), provided ample justification for the nurse's fears regarding David's potential actions toward Saul's surviving descendants.

The tragic accident that left five-year-old Mephibosheth permanently disabled happened during a desperate journey to Lo-dabar, a Transjordanian city where Machir, son of Ammiel, offered sanctuary (2 Samuel 4:4). This disability would become significant in ancient Near Eastern society, where physical impairment often led to social marginalization and exclusion from community life.

David's own recorded attitudes toward the disabled offer a troubling context for understanding Mephibosheth's vulnerable position. During the conquest of Jerusalem, David's reference to "the lame and the blind, those whom David hates" (2 Samuel 5:8) indicates societal prejudices that may have shaped policy. Brueggemann argues this attitude led to "a programmatic expulsion of the blind and lame from the city, and perhaps later from the temple" (Brueggemann 1990:252).

Within this social framework, Mephibosheth's physical condition rendered him politically and socially powerless. As Rouse observes, "Mephibosheth in his weakened condition is not at all a threat; he is physically helpless and defenseless" (Rouse 2008:188). His disability thus becomes both a symbol of his vulnerability and a literary device emphasizing David's grace.

David's Initiative

The chronology of David's inquiry regarding Saul's surviving descendants presents analytical challenges. When Mephibosheth fled as a five-year-old, his eventual appearance before David, as the father of a young son named Mica (2 Samuel 9:12), suggests a fifteen- to twenty-year interval. This extended timeframe raises questions about David's motivations and the narrative's historical sequence.

The intervening period included significant events affecting Saul's lineage, particularly the execution of seven of Saul's sons to appease the Gibeonites and end a three-year famine attributed to Saul's bloodguilt (2 Samuel 21:1–7). Notably, David specifically protected Mephibosheth during this crisis "because of the oath of the LORD that was between them, between David and Jonathan son of Saul" (2 Sam 21:7).

David's inquiry, "Is there still anyone left of the house of Saul to whom I may show kindness for Jonathan's sake?" (2 Samuel 9:1), initiated through Saul's former steward Ziba, demonstrates David's intentional pursuit of covenant fulfillment. Ziba's identification of Mephibosheth as "crippled in his feet" (2 Samuel 9:3) emphasizes the heir's physical vulnerability while avoiding mention of his name, perhaps reflecting political caution.

The Concept of *Ḥesed*

The Hebrew term *ḥesed*, appearing three times in the David-Mephibosheth narrative (vv. 1, 3, 7), represents one of the Hebrew Bible's most significant theological concepts. Often translated as "steadfast love," "covenant loyalty," or "faithful love," *ḥesed* describes God's unwavering commitment to his covenant people. The term appears in foundational descriptions of divine character, notably in Exodus 34:6, where God is described as "abounding in steadfast love."

Ḥesed encompasses multiple dimensions: grace (unmerited favor), mercy (compassion toward the afflicted), and faithfulness (reliability in covenant relationships). When David commits to showing *ḥesed* to Jonathan's descendants, he assumes responsibility for manifesting divine attributes through human agency.

David's treatment of Mephibosheth exemplifies how humans can act as channels of divine grace. The king's actions go beyond political strategy or simple friendship loyalty, embodying theological principles that anticipate later biblical teachings on grace and restoration.

As Jeff observes, David's intentional assistance to Mephibosheth represents "David at his best, and an example of David living as a man after God's own heart" (Griffin 2018:171). This assessment recognizes David's actions as reflecting divine character rather than mere human virtue.

The Restoration: Grace in Action

When summoned before David, Mephibosheth's prostration and evident fear demonstrate his awareness of royal power's potential for both destruction and deliverance. His position as a disabled heir to a defeated dynasty left him entirely dependent upon David's disposition. The king's immediate reassurance, "Do not be afraid, for I will show you *ḥesed*" (2Samuel 9:7), transforms a potentially threatening encounter into a moment of grace.

David's restoration of Mephibosheth encompasses both material and social dimensions. The return of Saul's property addresses economic security, while the invitation to "eat at the king's table" (2 Samuel 9:7) grants social rehabilitation and political protection. This table fellowship, described as treating Mephibosheth "like one of the king's sons" (2 Samuel 9:11), represents complete social restoration.

Some scholars suggest hidden political motives, seeing David's actions as a form of surveillance over a possible rival. However, the narrative's focus on *ḥesed* and the thoroughness of Mephibosheth's restoration argue against purely political readings. The sincere nature of David's generosity comes through in his extreme kindness, going "above and beyond" normal expectations.

The David-Mephibosheth narrative offers multiple theological insights relevant to contemporary faith communities. First, it demonstrates covenant faithfulness as extending beyond the original parties to their descendants, suggesting intergenerational responsibility within covenant communities. Second, it illustrates how divine attributes can be manifested through human agents, providing a model for believers seeking to embody divine character.

Third, the narrative challenges contemporary attitudes toward disability and social marginalization. David's treatment of the disabled Mephibosheth contrasts sharply with typical ancient Near Eastern practices, suggesting that covenant loyalty transcends social prejudices and physical limitations.

The Old Testament Speaks to the Church

My pastor, Jeff Griffin, Senior Pastor of The Compass Church in Naperville, Illinois, on May 28, 2023, preached a sermon titled "David: Loving the Overlooked," based on 2 Samuel 9:1–13. In his sermon, Jeff articulated the profound contemporary relevance of David's actions toward Mephibosheth for Christian discipleship and community formation.

Jeff's interpretation of the text emphasizes the remarkable nature of David's commitment, showing God's kindness to a member of the family whose patriarch had repeatedly attempted his assassination. This paradoxical demonstration of grace, extending *hesed* to the son of one's former enemy, illustrates the radical nature of divine love operating through human agents. Jeff's approach recognizes that David's actions transcend mere political expediency or social courtesy, representing instead a theological commitment to embodying divine character.

Jeff's definition of *hesed* as "extraordinary love" provides crucial insight for contemporary Christian application. His characterization of *hesed* as "love that goes beyond that which is expected" captures the essential nature of divine grace: unmerited, sacrificial, and transformative. This understanding challenges contemporary Christians to move beyond conventional expressions of kindness toward radical demonstrations of divine love.

Jeff's emphasis on *hesed* as "undeserved love" and "sacrificial love" that "seeks to bless people who do not deserve love" directly confronts cultural tendencies toward transactional relationships and conditional acceptance. In Jeff's challenge to Christians today, he said that Christians are called to love not on the basis of merit, reciprocity, or social advantage, but as participants in God's own gracious character.

The Reciprocal Nature of Divine Grace

Jeff's theological insight that "Christians have received *ḥesed* from God" and therefore "should give *ḥesed* to others" establishes the foundation for Christian ethics rooted in divine grace. This reciprocal understanding moves beyond duty-based morality toward grace-motivated service. Christians are not merely commanded to show kindness; they are invited to participate in the divine nature through acts of radical love.

This principle addresses contemporary challenges faced by Christian communities as they grapple with issues of inclusion, social justice, and care for marginalized populations. Jeff's application suggests that Christian response to disability, poverty, racial difference, and social exclusion should be characterized by the same extraordinary love that God has demonstrated toward undeserving humanity.

Practical Framework for Contemporary Christians

Jeff's conclusion provides a practical framework for Christian discipleship through four essential questions that contemporary believers must continually address:

1. *"Whom can I love?"* This question challenges Christians to identify specific individuals or communities that contemporary society overlooks or marginalizes. Like David seeking out Mephibosheth, Christians are called to intentionally pursue relationships with those who exist on society's periphery: the disabled, the elderly, the economically disadvantaged, refugees, the grieving, and the socially isolated.

2. *"What can I give?"* This question moves beyond financial generosity toward comprehensive gift-giving that includes time, presence, skills, advocacy, and emotional support. David's restoration of Mephibosheth's property and provision of table

231

fellowship illustrate how Christian giving should address both material needs and social restoration.

3. *What can I say?* Communication becomes a means of *ḥesed* through words of affirmation, encouragement, restoring dignity, and truth-telling. David's reassuring words to Mephibosheth, "Do not be afraid," show how language can turn fear into hope and shame into dignity.

4. *"What can I do?"* This final question demands concrete action that embodies divine love through systemic change, personal sacrifice, and sustained commitment. David's ongoing provision for Mephibosheth illustrates how Christian discipleship requires not momentary charity but lifestyle transformation.

Jeff's application challenges contemporary Christians to examine their practices regarding inclusion, accessibility, and care for vulnerable populations. Churches must ask whether their physical spaces, programs, leadership structures, and community life reflect the radical inclusivity demonstrated in David's treatment of Mephibosheth.

Jeff's emphasis on seeking out the overlooked challenges Christians to actively identify and pursue relationships with marginalized communities rather than waiting for them to appear. This proactive approach reflects David's intentional inquiry about Saul's surviving descendants and suggests that Christian discipleship requires deliberate engagement with social justice issues.

Conclusion

David's care for Mephibosheth teaches more than history; it shows how divine grace and human duty work. By staying true to his promise with Jonathan, David shows how people can take part in God's *ḥesed*, giving kindness to those who are vulnerable and overlooked.

David's actions set a standard for covenant faithfulness that goes beyond personal relationships to include wider social responsibility. By treating Mephibosheth with respect and kindness despite his disability and political vulnerability, David demonstrates divine grace in human form, providing both inspiration and guidance for embodying covenant loyalty in their own lives.

Jeff's pastoral application transforms this ancient narrative into a contemporary call for Christian discipleship characterized by extraordinary love. His perspective on this story challenges modern believers to become "agents of God's kindness in a world that desperately needs to experience God's love." This calling requires Christians to move beyond conventional expressions of faith toward radical demonstrations of divine *ḥesed* that transform both giver and recipient.

The lasting significance of this narrative lies not merely in its historical detail but in its theological insight: divine *ḥesed* finds expression through human agents committed to faithfulness, compassion, and justice. Jeff's application of the text demonstrates how this ancient principle remains profoundly relevant for Christians seeking to manifest divine character through intentional love for the overlooked, marginalized, and forgotten members of society.

In a world marked by increasing social fragmentation, political polarization, and cultural division, the David-Mephibosheth story offers a transformative vision of community characterized by radical inclusion, sacrificial love, and restorative justice. Through Jeff's pastoral lens, contemporary Christians are challenged to ask not merely what they can receive from their faith communities, but whom they can love, what they can give, what they can say, and what they can do to extend the extraordinary *ḥesed* they have received from God to others who desperately need to experience divine love made manifest through human agents.

CHAPTER 23

DAVID: "FACING THE TRUTH" – NATHAN'S REBUKE

The story of David's affair with Bathsheba is one of the most complex and morally difficult episodes in the Hebrew Bible. This account, described in 2 Samuel 11–12, shows the connection between political power, moral failure, and divine justice in the Davidic monarchy. The story is not just a historical record but also a theological reflection on sin, accountability, and redemption within the covenant between God and Israel's leadership.

The biblical author's careful construction of this account reveals multiple layers of meaning that go beyond the immediate circumstances of adultery and murder. Through detailed analysis of the narrative structure, prophetic intervention, and penitential lament, this chapter explores how the David-Bathsheba episode serves as both a cautionary tale and a testament to the possibility of divine forgiveness, even in the face of serious moral transgression.

The Context of Transgression

The biblical narrator establishes the temporal and circumstantial framework for David's moral failure with deliberate precision: "In the spring of the year, the time when kings go out to battle . . . David remained at Jerusalem" (2 Samuel 11:1). This opening verse is laden with implicit criticism, suggesting that David's presence in Jerusalem during the traditional campaign season represents an abdication of royal responsibility that creates the conditions for subsequent moral compromise.

The phrase "David remained at Jerusalem" employs the Hebrew verb *yāšab*, which can denote both physical dwelling and a state of complacency or settling. This linguistic choice suggests that David's physical absence from the battlefield reflects a deeper spiritual and moral disengagement from his divinely appointed role as Israel's warrior-king.

The narrative's characterization of David as "a man after God's own heart" (1 Samuel 13:14) creates a deliberate tension with the events that follow, emphasizing that even those who enjoy special divine favor remain susceptible to moral failure when they abandon their proper sphere of responsibility and accountability.

The Sequence of Transgression

The biblical account depicts the initial encounter between David and Bathsheba with concise storytelling. While walking on his palace roof at dusk, David notices "a beautiful woman bathing" (2 Samuel 11:2). The emphasis on beauty immediately highlights the aesthetic aspect of temptation while also raising questions about voyeurism and the misuse of power, both literally and figuratively.

Upon inquiry, David learns the woman's identity: "Bathsheba, the wife of Uriah the Hittite" (2 Samuel 11:3). The narrator's inclusion of both Bathsheba's name and her marital status, along with specific identification of her husband as one of David's elite warriors (2 Samuel 23:39), emphasizes the multiple layers of betrayal inherent in David's subsequent actions.

The textual evidence regarding Bathsheba's agency remains ambiguous. While the New International Version suggests voluntary compliance ("she came to him"), the Hebrew text's use of the verb *lāqaḥ* ("took her") implies coercion, highlighting the power differential between monarch and subject that renders meaningful consent problematic.

The Escalation of Moral Compromise

Bathsheba's pregnancy (2 Samuel 11:5) transforms private indiscretion into public crisis, precipitating David's increasingly desperate attempts at concealment. The king's initial strategy involves recalling Uriah from the battlefield under the pretext of receiving military intelligence, then encouraging him to "go down to your house and wash your feet" (2 Samuel 11:8), a euphemistic expression for sexual intimacy.

Uriah's refusal to enjoy domestic pleasures while "the ark and Israel and Judah remain in booths, and my lord Joab and the servants of my lord are camping in the open field" (2 Samuel 11:11) creates dramatic irony. The Hittite convert demonstrates greater covenant fidelity than Israel's divinely appointed king, embodying the very principles of solidarity and sacrifice that David has abandoned.

When attempts at indirect manipulation fail, David resorts to premeditated murder, sending Uriah back to battle with sealed orders for his own death: "Set Uriah in the forefront of the hardest fighting, and then draw back from him, so that he may be struck down and die" (2 Samuel 11:15). This calculated elimination of the wronged husband represents the ultimate abuse of royal authority and military command structure.

Prophetic Confrontation and Divine Justice

Following Uriah's death and David's marriage to Bathsheba, the biblical narrative notes that "the thing that David had done displeased the LORD" (2 Samuel 11:27). This divine displeasure prompts the intervention of Nathan the prophet, whose confrontation with David exemplifies the Hebrew Bible's understanding of prophetic function as divine conscience to earthly power.

Nathan's approach employs a carefully constructed parable featuring "two men in a certain city, the one rich and the other poor" (2 Samuel 12:1–4). The story's central image, a wealthy man seizing a poor man's beloved ewe lamb to feed a guest, creates emotional distance that allows David to render moral judgment without immediate self-recognition.

The effectiveness of the parable lies in its symbolic meaning. The poor man's lamb, which "used to eat of his meager fare, and drink from his cup, and lie in his bosom, and it was like a daughter to him" (2 Samuel 12:3), symbolizes the close domestic relationship between Uriah and Bathsheba. The rich man's theft of the lamb mirrors David's taking of another man's wife, while preparing the lamb for a guest reflects the destruction of Uriah to fulfill David's desire.

David's immediate response, "As the LORD lives, the man who has done this deserves to die" (2 Samuel 12:5), demonstrates both his retained moral sensibility and his capacity for self-deception. Nathan's devastating reply, "You are the man," shatters this protective distance and forces David to confront the full magnitude of his actions.

The Catalog of Violations

Nathan's subsequent indictment systematically exposes David's multiple transgressions against divine law. The prophet's analysis reveals violations of four fundamental commandments from the Decalogue:

1.   *Coveting*: "You shall not covet your neighbor's wife" (Exodus 20:17)

2.   *Adultery*: "You shall not commit adultery" (Exodus 20:14)

3.   *Theft*: "You shall not steal" (Exodus 20:15). Nathan declares, "you have stolen his wife" (2 Samuel 12:9)

4.   *Murder*: "You shall not murder" (Exodus 20:13). Nathan declares, "You have killed Uriah the Hittite with the sword" (2 Samuel 12:9)

This comprehensive catalog demonstrates that David's actions constitute not isolated moral lapses but systematic violations of covenant law. Nathan's phrase "sin of high hand," indicates premeditated rebellion rather than momentary weakness, emphasizing the gravity of David's offense against divine authority.

The Response of Repentance

David's response to Nathan's confrontation is notably immediate and unequivocal: "I have sinned against the LORD" (2 Samuel 12:13). This confession, while brief, represents a fundamental shift from concealment to acknowledgment, from self-justification to acceptance of divine judgment.

The simplicity of David's initial confession contrasts sharply with the elaborate nature of his preceding deception, suggesting authentic recognition rather than calculated damage control. Nathan's immediate response, "The LORD also has put away your sin; you shall not die" (2 Samuel 12:13), indicates divine acceptance of genuine repentance even for high-handed transgression.

David's Repentance

The fuller development of David's repentance finds expression in Psalm 51, whose superscription explicitly connects it to the aftermath of the Bathsheba affair: "A Psalm of David, when Nathan the prophet came to him, after he had gone in to Bathsheba."

David's prayer demonstrates a sophisticated understanding of sin's theological dimensions. His declaration, "Against you, you only, have I sinned and done what is evil in your sight" (Psalm 51:4), does not minimize the horizontal damage caused by his actions but recognizes that all moral transgression ultimately constitutes rebellion against divine authority.

The Hebrew term *peša'*, translated as "transgression" or "rebellion," denotes willful violation of an established relationship rather than mere legal infraction. David's use of this terminology acknowledges that his actions represent a personal betrayal of the covenant bond with Yahweh.

Appeal to Divine Grace

Recognizing the inadequacy of traditional sacrificial atonement for high-handed sin, David appeals directly to divine *ḥesed* (steadfast

238

love): "Have mercy on me, O God, according to your steadfast love; according to your abundant mercy blot out my transgressions" (Psalm 51:1).

This appeal demonstrates theological sophistication in recognizing that forgiveness for deliberate covenant violation requires divine initiative rather than human merit. The Mosaic legislation explicitly states that "whoever acts high-handedly . . . shall be cut off from among the people" (Numbers 15:30–31), making David's situation apparently hopeless under strict legal interpretation.

Request for Transformation

David's prayer moves beyond mere forgiveness to request fundamental transformation: "Create in me a clean heart, O God, and renew a right spirit within me" (Psalm 51:10). The verb *bara'* ("create") is the same used for divine creation in Genesis 1:1, suggesting that David recognizes the need for nothing less than divine recreation of his moral nature.

This request for a "clean heart" and "right spirit" acknowledges that authentic repentance requires internal transformation rather than external conformity. David's recognition that "you will not delight in sacrifice" (Psalm 51:16) demonstrates understanding that ritual cannot substitute for genuine spiritual renewal.

Spiritual Lessons and Theological Takeaways

The David-Bathsheba narrative operates on multiple theological levels, offering insight into the nature of moral failure, prophetic accountability, and divine grace within the covenant relationship. Several key themes emerge from careful analysis of this episode:

The Universality of Moral Vulnerability

Although he is called "a man after God's own heart," David's remarkable moral failure shows that no person, no matter their spiritual status or divine favor, is immune to moral lapses. The story suggests that positions of power and privilege might actually make someone more vulnerable to temptation by removing usual restrictions on behavior.

The Function of Prophetic Witness

Nathan's confrontation with David illustrates the Old Testament's view of the prophetic role as divine conscience guiding human authority. The prophet's use of parable instead of direct accusation shows a sophisticated understanding of psychological dynamics, fostering self-awareness rather than defensive reactions.

The Possibility of Authentic Repentance

David's response to Nathan's confrontation, elaborated in Psalm 51, provides a paradigm for authentic repentance that moves beyond mere regret to genuine transformation. The narrative suggests that even the gravest moral failures need not result in permanent separation from divine favor when met with genuine acknowledgment and appeal to divine grace.

The Relationship Between Justice and Mercy

While David receives divine forgiveness, the narrative makes clear that forgiveness does not eliminate consequences. The prophet's declaration that "the sword shall never depart from your house" (2 Samuel 12:10) indicates that divine mercy operates within rather than apart from moral order. Grace provides restoration of the relationship but does not suspend the natural consequences of moral choice.

The David-Bathsheba episode serves both as a warning and a source of hope: warning about the destructive potential of moral compromise, especially among those in positions of authority, and offering hope that no sin can keep the truly repentant out of reach of divine grace. This dual message continues to resonate in Jewish and Christian traditions as both a cautionary tale and a testament to the transformative power of genuine repentance.

The Old Testament Speaks to the Church

The enduring relevance of David's experience with transgression, confrontation, and repentance finds powerful contemporary expression in the preaching ministry of my pastor, Jeff Griffin Senior Pastor of The Compass Church in Naperville, Illinois. In his sermon "David: Facing the Truth," delivered on June 11, 2023, and based on 2 Samuel 12:1–31, Jeff articulated the practical implications of David's journey for modern Christian discipleship, emphasizing themes that resonate deeply with contemporary believers struggling with moral failure and the challenging path of authentic repentance.

The Paradigm of Repentance

Jeff's central thesis, that "David's prayer is an example of the power of repentance," establishes David's response as paradigmatic rather than merely historical. This interpretive framework transforms the ancient narrative into a practical template for contemporary Christian experience. Jeff's emphasis on repentance as "powerful" suggests not weakness or defeat, but spiritual strength that emerges through honest confrontation with moral reality.

The paradigmatic function of David's repentance operates on multiple levels for contemporary Christians. First, it demonstrates that moral failure, however grievous, need not result in permanent spiritual exile. Second, it provides concrete language and structure for approaching God in the aftermath of sin. Third, it illustrates the progression from recognition through confession to transformation that characterizes authentic spiritual renewal.

Jeff's observation that "people who hide their sins have relationship problems which will have a great impact on their emotional lives" identifies a crucial dynamic that extends far beyond the biblical narrative into contemporary Christian experience. Jeff's insight recognizes that concealed sin functions as a relational toxin, poisoning not only one's relationship with God but also creating barriers in human relationships as well.

This principle is especially relevant in modern culture, where social media, professional networking, and carefully crafted public personas often promote the kind of concealment David practiced during his months after the affair. Jeff's teaching indicates that the emotional and relational damage caused by maintaining false appearances ultimately outweighs the temporary discomfort of honest acknowledgment.

The Paradox of Difficult Freedom

Jeff's acknowledgment that "the work of repentance is difficult, but in repentance, one encounters freedom" captures a key paradox of Christian spirituality that relates directly to modern struggles with accountability and personal growth. This insight acknowledges that the journey to spiritual freedom involves navigating the challenging process of honest self-reflection, confession, and the vulnerability that comes with seeking forgiveness.

The concept of repentance as "work" challenges current cultural trends leaning toward easy solutions and instant gratification. Jeff's teachings show that real spiritual growth requires continuous effort, intentional practices, and a willingness to face the uncomfortable process of confronting personal failures. This perspective offers both an honest view of the challenges of spiritual transformation and hope that such change remains achievable through persistent effort.

The "freedom" that Jeff sees as a result of repentance includes several aspects important to modern Christian life. This freedom involves releasing oneself from the mental burden of hidden guilt, forming genuine connections with others for relational freedom, and experiencing spiritual freedom through restored fellowship with God. For modern Christians dealing with perfectionism, shame, or fear of being vulnerable, Jeff's teaching offers hope that the temporary discomfort of confession ultimately leads to lasting freedom.

Learning the Art of Repentance

Jeff's recognition that "we have to learn how to repent" addresses a significant gap in contemporary Christian formation. Many believers, particularly those raised in traditions that emphasize forgiveness while minimizing the process of repentance, find themselves lacking practical skills for navigating moral failure. Jeff's emphasis on repentance as a learnable skill transforms what might seem like a natural response into a discipline that can be developed and strengthened over time.

The pedagogical role of David's example becomes especially important in this context. Psalm 51 functions not just as a historical record but also as instructional material, giving contemporary Christians the vocabulary and framework needed for genuine confession. Jeff's approach views David's prayer as a masterclass in repentance, providing specific language and ideas that modern believers can adapt to their own situations.

The Restoration of Relationships

Jeff's emphasis on repentance leading to "restoration of relationships with family, friends, and others" identifies one of the most tangible and motivating outcomes of authentic spiritual renewal. This insight recognizes that sin's damage extends beyond the individual perpetrator to encompass entire networks of relationships, while simultaneously affirming that genuine repentance can initiate healing processes that restore damaged connections.

The relational dimension of Jeff's application speaks directly to contemporary challenges in marriage, family life, friendship, and professional relationships. In an era characterized by increasing social fragmentation, political polarization, and the superficiality of digital communication, the promise of restored authentic relationships through repentance offers hope for deeper, more meaningful human connections.

Jeff's teaching suggests that the vulnerability required for authentic repentance actually strengthens rather than weakens relationships by creating foundations of honesty and mutual accountability. This perspective challenges contemporary cultural narratives that equate vulnerability with weakness, instead positioning openness about failure as evidence of relational maturity and commitment.

Conclusion

The enduring power of the David-Bathsheba narrative lies not merely in its historical significance but in its capacity to illuminate universal patterns of human moral failure and divine grace. Jeff's contemporary application of this ancient story demonstrates how biblical narrative continues to speak with relevance and power to contemporary Christian experience, offering both diagnostic insight into the nature of sin's damage and practical guidance for the journey toward restoration.

Jeff's focus on repentance as a key, challenging yet freeing process that involves intentional learning and leads to relational healing offers modern Christians both realistic expectations and true hope. His teaching acknowledges that moral failure is a universal human experience while affirming that such failure does not have to result in permanent spiritual exile or relational damage.

In an age marked by polarization, superficiality, and the fear of vulnerability, the message of David's repentance and God's forgiveness offers a hopeful counter-narrative. Jeff's sermon reminds modern believers that no failure can keep them beyond the reach of divine grace, no concealment provides lasting security, and no one must face the journey of repentance alone. The same God who confronted David through Nathan's prophecy and restored him through divine mercy still offers believers today both the challenge of honest self-examination and the promise of complete forgiveness.

The ultimate testimony of David's experience, as articulated through Jeff's contemporary application, is that authentic Christianity provides resources not for the avoidance of moral failure, an impossible goal for finite humans, but for the transformation of such failure into opportunities for deeper intimacy with God and more authentic relationships with others. In this transformation lies both the challenge and the hope of Christian discipleship, the difficulty and the freedom of authentic repentance, and the enduring relevance of ancient wisdom for contemporary spiritual formation.

CHAPTER 24

DAVID: "PARENTING COURAGEOUSLY" – ABSALOM

King David's legacy in biblical literature includes both his notable achievements as Israel's greatest king and his significant failures as a father. Although he is celebrated as "a man after God's own heart" (1 Samuel 13:14), David's personal life paints a complex picture of parental struggles that ultimately affected his family and his reign. This chapter explores the repeated failures in David's parenting, especially his relationships with his sons Amnon and Absalom, and shows how his weak paternal leadership led to a series of tragic events that marked the later part of his rule.

David's extensive family structure reflects the political marriages and household arrangements typical of ancient Near Eastern monarchs. Historical records show that David had eight wives and numerous concubines, resulting in at least nineteen sons and several daughters. His early marriages to Michal (Saul's daughter), Ahinoam of Jezreel, and Abigail (Nabal's widow) took place before his kingship, while later marriages, including his union with Maacah of Geshur, were mainly diplomatic. This complex family dynamic created natural tensions and rivalries that David, as the head of the family, failed to manage effectively.

Four Critical Parental Failures

David's insufficient parenting can be systematically examined through four core failures that together undermined his authority and eroded family cohesion. These failures, lack of close knowledge of his children, poor moral examples, absence of disciplinary measures, and refusal to seek reconciliation, produced an environment where harmful behaviors thrived unchecked.

First Failure: Inadequate Knowledge of His Children

David's main failure as a father is his shallow understanding of his children's characters and motivations. The story of Amnon's deception highlights this disconnect. When Amnon, following Jonadab's advice, pretended to be sick to manipulate his father, David easily approved his request without suspicion (2 Samuel 13:6–7). The text's point that Jonadab, a simple friend, had better insight into Amnon's character than David himself emphasizes this core failure.

This knowledge gap arises from David's focus on royal duties rather than his role as a father. The responsibilities of governance, military operations, and political strategies absorbed David's attention, leaving little time for real involvement with his children. As a result, David lacked awareness of his sons' moral growth, emotional states, and behavioral traits, a significant obstacle to effective parenting.

The consequences of this failure go beyond simple neglect. David's decision to allow Tamar to meet privately with Amnon shows how his lack of awareness of his son's nature created chances for moral disaster. A father who truly understood Amnon's lustful tendencies would have seen the danger in such a situation.

Second Failure: Deficient Moral Modeling

David's second major failure was his inability to provide consistent moral leadership for his children. The comparison between David's adultery with Bathsheba and Amnon's assault on Tamar highlights the tragic principle in Ezekiel 16:44: "like mother, like daughter," or in this case, like father, like son. David's breach of sexual boundaries with Bathsheba set a pattern that his son would later surpass through incestuous rape.

The Hebrew word *nebālâ*, used to describe Amnon's actions (2 Samuel 13:12), signifies not just sexual misconduct but deep moral corruption that breaches community standards. Tamar's protest, "Such a thing should not be done in Israel," highlights how Amnon's behavior went against accepted moral norms. Still, Amnon's actions can be seen as a severe extension of the patterns he observed in his father's behavior.

David's moral failures fostered a household environment where sexual transgression became common. His multiple wives and concubines, though politically advantageous and culturally accepted, created a context where sexual relationships were mainly transactional rather than based on vows. This modeling influenced his sons' flawed understanding of proper sexual boundaries and respect for women.

Third Failure: Absence of Disciplinary Action

Perhaps David's most consequential failure was his refusal to discipline Amnon following the rape of Tamar. The text explicitly states that despite David's anger upon learning of the assault, "he would not punish his son Amnon, because he loved him, for he was his firstborn" (2 Samuel 13:21). This response represents a fundamental misunderstanding of paternal love and responsibility.

The wisdom literature highlights the importance of discipline in raising children: "Discipline your children, and they will give you rest; they will give delight to your heart" (Proverbs 29:17). David's failure to enforce consequences for Amnon's criminal actions broke this rule and led to several negative results. First, it denied justice to Tamar, who remained "desolate" in Absalom's house (2 Samuel 13:20). Second, it sent a message to other family members that serious moral violations would be tolerated. Third, it forced the family to seek other forms of justice, which eventually resulted in Absalom's vigilante killing of Amnon.

David's inaction resulted from a mistaken mix of love and permissiveness. His favoritism toward his firstborn kept him from taking the tough but necessary step of holding Amnon accountable. This lack of resolve would prove disastrous for family unity and royal succession.

Fourth Failure: Refusal to Pursue Reconciliation

David's final critical failure was his inability to properly manage reconciliation with Absalom after Amnon's death. Although David initially brought Absalom back to Jerusalem through Joab's intervention, he then refused to see his son for two years (2 Samuel

247

14:24, 28). This extended separation showed a fundamental misunderstanding of the reconciliation process.

The story emphasizes David's internal conflict, loving his son while also maintaining distance. This conflicting feeling led to a harmful cycle where neither justice nor mercy was fully realized. Absalom's return to Jerusalem without access to his father's court created a charged atmosphere of waiting and alienation, where resentment grew in place of healing.

The wise woman of Tekoa's parable effectively pointed out David's inconsistency by showing his willingness to support reconciliation in theoretical cases while refusing to apply the same principles within his own family (2 Samuel 14:4–13). This hypocrisy ultimately weakened David's moral authority with Absalom and contributed to his son's later rebellion.

When reconciliation finally occurred, it was not enough to repair the damaged relationship. Absalom's submission and David's kiss (2 Samuel 14:33) served as symbolic gestures rather than real solutions to the underlying problems. The absence of honest dialogue about past issues and future hopes left core problems unresolved.

Consequences: The Unraveling of Royal Authority

The cumulative impact of David's parental failures manifested in Absalom's systematic rebellion against royal authority. Having lost respect for his father's moral leadership and judicial integrity, Absalom positioned himself as an alternative source of justice and governance. His strategy of intercepting petitioners at the city gates and criticizing royal administration (2 Samuel 15:2–6) directly exploited David's perceived weaknesses as a leader.

Absalom's rebellion succeeded in attracting broad popular support, forcing David to flee Jerusalem as a refugee from his own son. The irony of this reversal, in which the great warrior king is reduced to flight by his own son, demonstrates how domestic failures can undermine even the most successful public leadership.

David's inability to maintain order within his household ultimately compromised his capacity to govern the nation.

The rebellion also revealed the broader consequences of David's modeling failures. Absalom's public violation of his father's concubines (2 Samuel 16:21–22) represented both political calculation and personal revenge, demonstrating how patterns of sexual transgression continued to plague the royal family. The cycle of violence and sexual impropriety that began with David's adultery reached its culmination in his son's public humiliation of him.

David's parental failures provide lasting lessons for modern leadership, especially about the link between private character and public effectiveness. The story shows that personal integrity and family relationships cannot be separated from professional duties. Leaders who fail to demonstrate proper values within their own homes weaken their credibility and effectiveness in wider spheres of influence.

The text also highlights the importance of accountability and discipline in fostering healthy organizational cultures. David's hesitance to address serious misconduct within his family created an environment where harmful behaviors could grow. Modern leaders can learn from this example the importance of addressing issues quickly and decisively, regardless of personal relationships or emotional ties.

Finally, David's experience highlights the complex nature of reconciliation and conflict resolution. His failure to properly handle the reconciliation process with Absalom shows that symbolic gestures without meaningful dialogue and real accountability are not enough to heal broken relationships.

The Old Testament Speaks to the Church

The analysis presented in this chapter draws significantly from a sermon delivered by my pastor, Jeff Griffin, Senior Pastor of The Compass Church in Naperville, Illinois, on June 18, 2023, titled "David: Parenting Courageously," based on 2 Samuel 15:1–37.

Jeff's exposition of David's parental failures provides crucial insights for contemporary Christian families seeking to avoid the destructive patterns that plagued Israel's greatest king.

Jeff emphasized that David's core mistake was in not investing enough time to truly understand his children. This neglect created a relational gap that enabled harmful influences to impact his sons' growth. For modern Christian parents, this principle calls for intentional engagement with their children's interests, concerns, and developmental struggles.

Today's world presents unique challenges that demand even more parental vigilance than what David faced. Digital technology, social media, peer pressure, and cultural messaging form complex environments that can significantly shape children's worldview and moral development. Christian parents must actively "enter their children's world," as Jeff noted, to understand the forces influencing their children's thoughts and behavior.

This engagement requires more than superficial conversation or shared activities. It demands genuine curiosity about children's inner lives, their struggles with identity formation, their questions about faith and morality, and their navigation of contemporary social pressures. Parents who prioritize knowing their children create opportunities for meaningful guidance and support during critical developmental periods.

Jeff's emphasis on bonding reflects biblical principles of discipleship, where meaningful relationships form the foundation for spiritual and moral growth. Just as Jesus invested deeply in the lives of his disciples, Christian parents should prioritize relationship-building as the essential first step for providing practical guidance and instruction.

Modeling Faith and Integrity

Jeff's second major application highlights David's failure to model consistent moral behavior for his children. The comparison between David's adultery and Amnon's sexual assault shows how parental compromise can create permission structures for children's moral failures. This idea has important implications for modern Christian families.

Jeff noted that "children know how their parents live and they see what their parents do." This observation emphasizes that genuine Christian parenting involves living authentically, where private conduct matches public profession. Children have a keen ability to detect hypocrisy and inconsistency in their parents' behavior, and such realizations often lead to their rejection of parental values and faith commitments.

The modern challenge involves demonstrating faith and integrity across various aspects of everyday life. Christian parents need to show authenticity through their financial choices, entertainment preferences, relationship habits, work ethics, and handling of conflicts. This all-encompassing approach provides a framework for children to grasp practical Christianity rather than just theoretical faith.

Jeff's insight that "children adopt their parents' values, but they do not embrace their parents' boundaries" highlights an important aspect of modern family life. Children may understand and accept their parents' moral teachings on an intellectual level but reject the behavioral limits that come with those values. This situation requires parents to clarify the link between values and boundaries, helping children see that genuine faith involves both believing and adjusting how they behave.

Establishing Consequences and Accountability

The third point from Jeff's sermon discusses David's failure to discipline Amnon after his assault on Tamar. This neglect created a justice gap that eventually led to vigilante violence and family breakdown. Modern Christian parents need to understand that love involves giving appropriate consequences for harmful actions.

Modern parenting culture often struggles to balance grace and accountability, especially within Christian settings where forgiveness is strongly emphasized. However, Jeff's analysis of David's failure shows that true love requires parents to enforce consequences for harmful behavior. Without proper discipline, it suggests that moral violations lack real importance.

Christian parents must differentiate between punishment and discipline, recognizing that biblical discipline focuses on restoration rather than retribution. The aim is to help children see the link between their choices and consequences while preserving the relationship and working toward eventual restoration. This method requires consistency, wisdom, and a long-term dedication to shaping children's character.

In today's sociocultural climate, the pursuit of discipline and accountability faces unprecedented complexities. Cultural messaging that questions parental authority, legal restrictions on disciplinary methods, and societal emphasis on children's rights create complex environments for Christian parents seeking to implement biblical principles. However, the core principle remains constant: children need clear boundaries enforced through appropriate consequences.

Breaking Generational Patterns

Jeff's view of grace breaking cycles of harm is that "the curse of bad parenting can be broken by one's commitment to God" and that "godly parents can produce godly children." This idea offers strong encouragement to Christian parents who recognize harmful patterns in their own family histories.

Many Christian parents struggle with the fact that they experienced inadequate parenting themselves and lack positive role models for family leadership. The cycle of dysfunction that affected David's family still impacts today's families, leading to intergenerational patterns of relationship problems, moral issues, and spiritual confusion.

Jeff's emphasis on divine transformation provides hope that committed Christian parents can break these destructive cycles through intentional spiritual growth and practical behavior modification. This process requires honest acknowledgment of past failures, genuine repentance, and systematic development of healthy parenting practices grounded in biblical principles.

The modern church community plays a vital role in helping parents who want to break harmful generational cycles. Mentoring relationships, parenting classes, pastoral counseling, and accountability partnerships can offer resources and support for families dedicated to living out their Christian faith.

Conclusion

David's legacy as Israel's greatest king is deeply marked by his failures as a father, yet his story offers essential guidance for today's Christian families. Jeff's analysis of David's parenting mistakes, such as failing to know his children, poor moral example, lack of discipline, and ineffective reconciliation, gives specific advice for modern parents who want to avoid these damaging habits.

David's failure as a parent serves as both a warning and an encouragement for Christian families. It demonstrates that even individuals with special gifts and divine favor can be susceptible to parental mistakes, but it also highlights specific behaviors and attitudes that can help prevent family failure. Jeff's emphasis that "godly parents can produce godly children" offers hope that intentional Christian parenting can break cycles of dysfunction and establish healthy family legacies.

The story of David's family ultimately reminds contemporary Christians that parenting represents one of the most significant aspects of faithful discipleship. The children entrusted to Christian parents provide opportunities to demonstrate authentic faith, model biblical values, and participate in God's redemptive work across generations. Through commitment to knowing their children, modeling integrity, implementing appropriate discipline, and pursuing reconciliation when needed, Christian parents can avoid David's failures and create family environments that honor God and support healthy human development.

Jeff's sermon challenges contemporary Christians to view parenting as a sacred responsibility that requires intentional effort, genuine spiritual growth, and persistent hope in God's transformative power. By learning from David's failures and applying biblical principles within modern contexts, Christian parents can break destructive cycles and establish healthy patterns that will bless their children and grandchildren for generations to come.

CHAPTER 25

DAVID: "FORGIVING OTHERS" – SHIMEI

The story of King David's encounter with Shimei during Absalom's rebellion offers a compelling case study in the intricate dynamics of forgiveness, political reconciliation, and divine justice within the Hebrew biblical tradition. This episode, documented in 2 Samuel 16 and 19, highlights the tension between personal magnanimity and political pragmatism that marked David's reign. The event takes place against the backdrop of Absalom's revolt, which stems from David's failure to address the sexual violence committed by Amnon against Tamar, showing how unaddressed injustice can lead to wider societal upheaval.

Absalom's Rebellion

Absalom's rebellion against his father David marks a crucial moment in the Davidic kingdom, driven by David's moral shortcomings and their political effects. The spark for this uprising was David's inaction after Amnon assaulted his half-sister Tamar, an event that scholars compare to David's own sexual sin with Bathsheba. David's failure to deliver justice in this family matter damaged his moral authority and set the stage for Absalom's act of vigilante justice.

After Absalom orchestrated Amnon's death and fled to Geshur for three years, his return to Jerusalem marked the beginning of a calculated effort to weaken David's rule. The text notes that "Absalom lived two full years in Jerusalem, without coming into the king's presence" (2 Samuel 14:28), reflecting David's ongoing hesitance to face the consequences of his earlier failures. Absalom's strategy of stationing himself at the city gates, where he would intercept people seeking royal judgment and suggest that "the king was not concerned about their situation," demonstrates a sophisticated understanding of how to exploit public dissatisfaction with the current system.

The proclamation of Absalom as king in Hebron (2 Samuel 15:10) forced David into a tough choice between armed conflict and strategic retreat. David's decision to leave Jerusalem, even though the city's defenses made this questionable from a military standpoint, may have reflected deeper worries about legitimate authority and the costs of civil war. As Cartledge suggests, David may have aimed "to avoid a conflict that would leave obvious scars for the public to see in years to come" (Cartledge 2001: 567–568), showing a concern for the kingdom's long-term stability that went beyond immediate political gains.

David's Encounter with Shimei

David's departure from Jerusalem became a procession of grief, marked by weeping, covered heads, and barefoot walking, the traditional signs of mourning and humiliation. This public display of vulnerability made David particularly vulnerable to the kind of attack he faced from Shimei at Bahurim. Shimei's identification as "son of Gera" places him within the Benjaminite clan, linking him to tribal ties that remained loyal to the memory of Saul's house.

The specific accusations made by Shimei, calling David a "murderer" (2 Samue 16:7) and "man of blood" (2 Samuel 16:8), reflect deeper tribal grievances about David's rise to power and how he treated Saul's descendants. Although David was not directly responsible for the deaths of Abner or Ishbosheth, his approval of the Gibeonite execution of seven sons of Saul (2 Samuel 21:6) gave fuel to these accusations. Shimei's description of David as "a man of Belial" (2 Samuel 16:7 KJV) uses language that suggests moral corruption and divine opposition, implying that David's current trouble is a form of divine punishment for past wrongs.

David's response to Shimei's verbal attack shows impressive restraint and theological insight. When Abishai asked for permission to kill Shimei for his treacherous words, David's refusal was based on a deep understanding of divine sovereignty and human free will. David's statement, "If he is cursing because the LORD has said to him, 'Curse David,' who then shall say, 'Why have you done so?'" (2 Sam 16:10), shows his view that Shimei's actions might serve divine purposes, even if Shimei himself was unaware of this.

This theological framework helped David endure the humiliation without retaliation, seeing it as potential divine discipline linked to Nathan's earlier prophecy that "I will raise up trouble against you from within your own house" (2 Samuel 12:11). Brueggemann's comment that David was "prepared to let the cursing go unanswered, not as an admission of guilt but as an act of faith" (Brueggemann 1990:319) highlights the core dynamic in David's response, a willingness to submit to divine will while holding onto hope for eventual vindication.

Reconciliation and Forgiveness

The resolution of Absalom's rebellion and David's return to power created new circumstances for handling the Shimei incident. Shimei's approach to David at Gilgal, accompanied by a thousand Benjaminites and bearing signs of repentance, reflects both a calculated political move and a moral acknowledgment. His words, "May my lord not hold me guilty or remember how your servant did wrong," recognize both the seriousness of his earlier actions and his reliance on David's mercy for survival.

David's decision to forgive Shimei and assure his safety reflects several overlapping considerations. Politically, David's statement that "This is not a day for execution but for celebration!" (2 Samuel 19:22, NLT) shows his understanding that reconciliation, rather than revenge, was vital for national healing. The public act of forgiveness conveyed a strong message about the potential for restoration for those who had opposed his rule.

From a theological view, David's actions follow the Levitical command, "You shall not take vengeance or bear a grudge against any of your people, but you shall love your neighbor as yourself" (Leviticus 19:18). This idea of loving even your enemies shows a deep ethical standard that David demonstrated in this moment, despite the personal cost and political danger involved.

The Limits of Forgiveness: Solomon's Resolution

The complexity of David's relationship with forgiveness becomes clear in his deathbed instructions to Solomon about Shimei. David's words show that while he chose not to execute Shimei, he had not forgotten the insults or their impact on royal authority. His statement to Solomon, "But now, do not consider him innocent. You are a man of wisdom; you will know what to do to him" (1 Kings 2:9 NIV), implies that David saw his own oath as personally binding but not necessarily binding on his successor.

This development raises important questions about the nature and limits of political forgiveness. David's careful distinction between his own promise ("I will not put you to death with the sword") and the broader question of Shimei's ultimate accountability shows a nuanced understanding of how personal mercy relates to institutional justice. The fact that David's oath was understood as not binding on Solomon indicates the recognition that royal forgiveness, while powerful, functions within larger frameworks of political stability and deterrence.

Solomon's eventual execution of Shimei, following the violation of house arrest terms, demonstrates how forgiveness in the political sphere often involves conditional arrangements rather than unconditional absolution. The text's notation that "the LORD will repay you for your wrongdoing" (1 Kings 2:44 NIV) suggests that divine justice ultimately transcends human mercy, even when that mercy has been genuinely extended.

The Old Testament Speaks to the Church

The preceding analysis draws heavily from the insights of my pastor, Jeff Griffin, the Senior Pastor of The Compass Church in Naperville, Illinois, whose sermon "David: Forgiving Others," preached on June 25, 2023, provided the foundational framework for understanding this biblical narrative's contemporary relevance. Jeff's exposition of 2 Samuel 19:15–23 offers profound guidance for Christians navigating relationships with difficult and hurtful people in today's world.

The Challenge of Hurtful Relationships

Jeff's sermon addresses a universal human experience: encountering individuals who cause significant emotional, relational, or even spiritual harm. The David-Shimei narrative provides a biblical template for responding to such challenges with what Jeff identifies as the essential Christian virtues of "endurance, patience, love, and forgiveness." This approach stands in stark contrast to contemporary cultural responses that often emphasize self-protection, retaliation, or complete relational severance when faced with hurtful people.

The parallel Jeff draws between David's responses to both Absalom and Shimei illustrates how forgiveness must extend beyond familial relationships to include those who have no claim on our affection or loyalty. While forgiving a beloved but wayward son might seem natural, extending grace to a hostile stranger who publicly humiliates us during our most vulnerable moments requires a supernatural love that can only be sustained through faith.

Three Principles for Handling Mistreatment

Jeff's sermon articulates three fundamental principles that emerge from David's example, each offering practical guidance for contemporary Christian living:

First, enduring mistreatment heroically transforms suffering into worship. David's response to Shimei's verbal assault demonstrates how believers can honor God precisely in their moments of greatest vulnerability and pain. This principle challenges the modern tendency to view victimization as primarily about personal rights and demands for immediate vindication. Instead, Jeff suggests that faithful endurance becomes a form of worship, a recognition that God's sovereignty extends even over our suffering and that our response to mistreatment can serve as a testimony to divine grace.

This heroic endurance does not require passive acceptance of abuse or the abandonment of appropriate boundaries. Rather, it involves maintaining spiritual composure and Christ-like character even when others act destructively. Such endurance reflects the

259

deeper biblical truth that our ultimate identity and security rest not in human approval or fair treatment, but in our relationship with God.

Second, the Christian response to mistreatment involves loving one's enemies rather than seeking retribution. Jeff's emphasis on loving "those who act as their enemies" directly echoes Jesus's teaching in the Sermon on the Mount (Matthew 5:44) and is perhaps the most challenging aspect of Christian ethics. David's restraint of Abishai and his later forgiveness of Shimei demonstrate this principle in action, showing that loving your enemy is not just a lofty idea but a real possibility, even in politically charged and personally painful situations.

This principle requires Christians to reject the natural human impulse toward "getting even" and instead to pursue the more difficult path of seeking the good of those who have harmed them. Such love does not necessarily require immediate trust or the removal of all consequences, but it does demand the genuine desire for the other person's welfare and spiritual transformation.

Third, entrusting one's case to God recognizes divine justice while letting go of personal vengeance. Jeff's reference to Exodus 34:7, that God "does not leave the guilty unpunished," provides the theological basis for why Christians can safely relinquish their right to revenge. This principle acknowledges that although human justice systems are imperfect and often lacking, divine justice is both certain and perfect.

This dedication to divine justice frees believers from the exhausting burden of making sure wrongdoers face appropriate punishment. It enables Christians to focus on healing, growth, and positive actions rather than on checking whether offenders are receiving enough consequences for their actions.

The Wider Social Implications

Jeff's conclusion, inspired by Martin Luther King Jr.'s words about the importance of loving one's enemies, raises the discussion from personal spiritual growth to broader social change. King's warning about the "chain reaction of evil, hate begetting hate, wars producing more wars" directly addresses the rising polarization and hostility seen in today's social and political conversations.

Jeff's application shows that Christian forgiveness is not just a personal spiritual practice but also a public testimony with the power to break cycles of revenge that threaten to ruin communities and nations. When Christians respond to wrongs with grace instead of revenge, they provide a real alternative to the harmful patterns that define broken human relationships.

This social aspect of forgiveness becomes especially important in a time marked by political division, social media-driven conflicts, and growing cultural separation. The David-Shimei story shows that even when there are valid grievances and real injustices, the way forward is through forgiveness, not endless conflict.

Practical Implementation in Contemporary Contexts

The principles Jeff draws from the David-Shimei story have direct relevance to many modern situations. In workplace relationships, these principles guide how to handle difficult coworkers, unfair bosses, or organizational injustices without losing professionalism or personal integrity. In family settings, they offer a way to navigate complex interactions with relatives who may hold harmful views or behave destructively.

Perhaps most importantly, these principles address the challenge of political and ideological disagreement in today's society. Jeff's sermon indicates that Christians are called to demonstrate a different way of engaging with those whose political, theological, or cultural views they find offensive or harmful. Instead of demonizing opponents or seeking to destroy them, believers are called to preserve their humanity and seek their good, even while strongly disagreeing with their positions.

Jeff's sermon also addresses the particular challenge of social media culture, where public shaming and mob dynamics often mirror Shimei's behavior toward David. Jeff's principles suggest that Christians should resist both participating in such behavior and responding vengefully when they become its targets.

Conclusion

The Shimei incident, as shown through Jeff's pastoral application, provides a clear framework for understanding how forgiveness works within the broader biblical view of justice, mercy, and divine sovereignty. David's initial restraint and later forgiveness show that it is possible to respond to offense with grace, while the final resolution under Solomon highlights the complex balance between mercy and justice in human institutions.

Jeff's application of the text shows how this ancient story relates directly to the struggles Christians face in an increasingly divided and hostile world. The three principles he highlights—heroic endurance, enemy-love, and commitment to divine justice—offer practical guidance for maintaining Christian integrity while dealing with tough relationships and social conflicts.

Most significantly, Jeff's vision of forgiveness as a force for breaking cycles of hatred and preventing social annihilation elevates Christian ethics from personal spiritual formation to cosmic significance. In a world threatened by escalating conflict and mutual destruction, the Christian practice of forgiveness emerges not as weakness or naivety, but as a desperately needed source of healing and hope.

The David-Shimei narrative thus serves as both a historical account of ancient political dynamics and a prophetic vision of how transformed relationships might contribute to the transformation of human society. Jeff's sermon reminds contemporary Christians that their personal responses to mistreatment carry implications far beyond their individual spiritual development, contributing to either the perpetuation of destructive cycles or the emergence of redemptive possibilities in human relationships.

CHAPTER 26

DAVID: "JOY IN GIVING" – TEMPLE PREPARATION

After David became king of the United Monarchy, one of his first acts was to bring the Ark of the Covenant to Jerusalem. According to the Book of Chronicles, David gathered his officials, the leaders of the people, "including the priests and Levites" (1 Chronicles 13:2), and expressed his desire to bring the Ark of the Covenant to Jerusalem.

The first attempt to bring the Ark failed because Uzzah reached out to steady it after the oxen pulling it stumbled and caused it to fall from the cart. Since Uzzah was ritually unclean, he died there before God.

The second attempt to transport the Ark to Jerusalem succeeded. David brought the Ark from Obed-edom's house. With great celebration, including music and dancing, David and all the people brought the Ark of the Covenant "and set it in its place, inside the tent that David had pitched for it" (2 Samuel 6:17).

David's Desire to Build the Temple

David's biggest dream was to build a beautiful temple in Jerusalem for God. For centuries, God has been worshiped in the tabernacle. David's goal was to replace the tabernacle with a temple that would be worthy of the God of Israel.

David told the prophet Nathan, "See now, I am living in a house of cedar, but the ark of God stays in a tent" (2 Samuel 7:2). Nathan approved the king to build the temple. But Yahweh came to Nathan that night and revealed to him that David was not the one who would build the temple.

Nathan said to David, "the LORD declares to you that the LORD will make you a house. . . . Your house and your kingdom shall be made sure forever before me; your throne shall be established forever" (2 Samuel 7:11, 16). God's promise to David was that his house, that is, his kingdom would be established forever. However, it would be his son who would build the temple in Jerusalem.

God also made another promise to David. Nathan conveyed God's promise to David, "When your days are fulfilled and you lie down with your ancestors, I will raise up your offspring after you, who shall come forth from your body, and I will establish his kingdom. He shall build a house for my name, and I will establish the throne of his kingdom forever" (2 Samuel 7:12–13).

Solomon, David's son, was the one chosen by God to build the temple after David's death. In his last days, David gathered his officers and the leaders of Israel and said to them, "Hear me, my brothers and my people. I had planned to build a house of rest for the ark of the covenant of the LORD, for the footstool of our God; and I made preparations for building. But God said to me, 'You shall not build a house for my name, for you are a warrior and have shed blood'" (1 Chronicles 28:2–3).

David had been a man of war, "a warrior," all his adult life. He first began serving in the army of Saul after he killed Goliath, the Philistine warrior who was threatening Israel. Then David spent the early part of his reign fighting against Israel's enemies in order to bring peace to the his kingdom. As a man of war, David would not be allowed to build the temple of God. As Klein writes, "what was prohibited to David as a man of war is permitted to Solomon," the man of peace (Klein 2006: 520).

David Challenges the People to Give to God

Although David was unable to build the temple for God, David was instrumental in developing the design for the temple. According to the Book of Chronicles, before he died, David gave Solomon "the plan of the vestibule of the temple, and of its houses, its treasuries, its upper rooms, and its inner chambers, and of the room for the mercy seat" (1 Chronicles 28:11). In addition, David provided the gold, the silver, the iron, and the wood that were to be used in the construction of the temple (1 Chronicles 29:2).

After detailing his gifts to God, David challenged the people to give sacrificially to God. David asked the assembly which had gathered to hear about the construction of the temple. David said to them, "Now who is going to make a freewill offering and devote himself today to the LORD?" (1 Chronicles 29:5 TNK).

In response to David's challenge, the leaders of the families, the leaders of the tribes of Israel, the commanders of regiments and battalions, and the officials in charge of the king's work gave generously. In response to the generosity of the people, David prayed a prayer of thanksgiving in which he expressed his feeling of gratitude for the people who had given their money to God with a willing attitude.

David was moved by the generosity of the people. David set the example in giving and the people followed his example. David had been blessed by the Lord and now he blessed God for the generosity of the people, "Blessed are you, O LORD, the God of Israel our father, forever and ever" (1 Chronicle 29:10). David's prayer (1 Chronicles 29:10–19) and the response of the people to give their money for the construction of the temple, teaches six basic principles about giving to God.

Six Principles of Biblical Giving

David's prayer of thanksgiving (1 Chronicles 29:10–19) and the people's generous response reveal six fundamental principles that characterize biblical approaches to giving and stewardship.

1. *Giving as Stewardship*

David's prayer demonstrates a profound understanding of divine ownership: "But who am I, and who are my people, that we could give anything to you? Everything we have has come from you, and we give you only what you first gave us" (1 Chronicles 29:14). This perspective recognizes that all material wealth ultimately belongs to God, making human beings stewards rather than owners of their possessions.

David's understanding aligns with the broader biblical concept of stewardship, where people manage resources on behalf of the true owner. This idea is reflected in the Mosaic law's tithing system, which required sharing resources "with the Levites . . . as well as with the foreigners living among you, the orphans, and the widows" (Deuteronomy 14:29), fostering community welfare and divine blessing.

2. *Giving as Future Investment*

Recognizing human mortality, David observed: "We are here for only a moment, visitors and strangers in the land as our ancestors were before us. Our days on earth are like a passing shadow, gone so soon without a trace" (1 Chronicles 29:15). This perspective on time encourages investing in eternal values rather than temporary material possessions.

The contrast between human transience and divine eternality, God exists "from eternity to eternity" (1 Chronicles 29:10), highlights that contributions to God's purposes go beyond individual lifetimes, leaving a lasting impact that extends past the giver's earthly life.

3. *Giving as Worship*

David's statement that "even this material we have gathered to build a Temple to honor your holy name comes from you! It all belongs to you" (1 Chronicles 29:16) highlights the worshipful nature of giving. The temple project was intended to be a place where "the people of Israel could come and worship God," making the act of fundraising itself a form of worship.

This principle shows that generous giving is a form of worship in which people recognize God's sovereignty and show gratitude for divine provision. The act of giving becomes a real act of worship rather than just a financial exchange.

4. *Giving as Divine Pleasure*

David's assertion that God "examine[s] our hearts and rejoice[s] when you find integrity there" (1 Chronicles 29:17) indicates that divine evaluation focuses on the giver's heart condition rather than the gift's magnitude. The Hebrew term translated "rejoice" typically describes God's emotional satisfaction with his people's faithful responses.

This principle emphasizes that God's pleasure derives from observing sincere generosity and genuine devotion rather than from receiving material benefit. The divine response to giving reflects relational satisfaction rather than material need.

5. *Giving as Voluntary Expression*

David's testimony that he had "done all this with good motives" and had "watched your people offer their gifts willingly and joyously" (1 Chronicles 29:17) underscores the voluntary nature of biblical giving. David's own contribution emerged from "the uprightness of my heart" as he "freely offered all these things" (1 Chronicles 29:17).

The voluntary principle aligns with New Testament teaching, as Paul instructed: "You must each decide in your heart how much to give. And don't give reluctantly or in response to pressure. For God loves a person who gives cheerfully" (2 Corinthians 9:7). Coerced giving contradicts the spirit of biblical generosity.

6. *Giving as a Joyful Experience*

The observation that people gave "willingly and joyously" (1 Chronicles 29:17) identifies joy as both a motivation for and result of generous giving. The Hebrew term for joy reflects an individual's disposition when performing actions that please God, often associated with heart attitudes rather than external circumstances.

This principle suggests that generous giving produces internal satisfaction and delight, particularly when givers recognize their contributions' potential for positive impact on their community's spiritual life and future generations' welfare.

The Old Testament Speaks to the Church

My pastor, Jeff Griffin, Senior Pastor of The Compass Church in Naperville, Illinois, delivered a compelling sermon on July 2, 2023, titled "David: Joy in Giving," based on 2 Samuel 24:18–25, which provides the foundational insights for this chapter. Jeff's modern application of David's example shows both the timeless relevance of these biblical principles and the distinct challenges facing today's Christian communities in fostering generous stewardship.

Jeff's central point, that modern believers often fail to "celebrate giving" because they do not fully understand that their possessions and abilities are divine gifts, addresses a basic disconnect between biblical theology and current practice. This lack of recognition of divine ownership diminishes the joy that marked David and Israel's leaders, turning what should be joyful worship into reluctant obligation.

Obstacles to Generous Giving

Jeff identified a major modern challenge that was absent in David's situation: widespread skepticism about church financial management. The documented instances of financial misconduct and dishonesty among some Christian leaders have fueled real concerns among potential donors, who question whether their giving truly helps advance God's kingdom or merely benefits those who handle the money.

This situation creates a pastoral and theological tension. While the biblical principles of joyful, voluntary giving stay the same, church leaders must recognize that modern contexts require better transparency and accountability measures that were not needed in David's theocratic society. The challenge for today's church leadership is to rebuild trust that encourages joyful giving while upholding biblical standards of generous stewardship.

The Model of Transparent Stewardship

Jeff's conclusion, highlighting The Compass Church's commitment to transparent stewardship that benefits both church members and the broader community, exemplifies how contemporary churches can address modern obstacles while maintaining biblical principles. By clearly articulating how contributions support gospel advancement "here, near, and far," church leadership demonstrates the same heart integrity that characterized David's giving, a willingness to be examined and found faithful in stewardship responsibilities.

This approach recognizes that while the biblical principles remain constant, their application must address contemporary concerns. Modern church leaders, like David, must demonstrate through their actions that they view themselves as stewards rather than owners of the resources entrusted to their care.

Conclusion

David's approach to temple fundraising offers a comprehensive model for understanding biblical principles of giving and stewardship that remains highly relevant for modern Christian practice. His leadership showed how personal example, inspiring challenge, and theological insight can motivate generous responses from the community. The six principles derived from this historical account—stewardship, future investment, worship, divine pleasure, voluntary expression, and joyful experience—provide timeless guidance for applying biblical generosity today.

However, as Jeff's application demonstrates, these timeless principles must be adapted to suit modern circumstances that present unique challenges and opportunities. The success of David's fundraising campaign resulted not only from effective techniques but also from a theological foundation that recognized God's ultimate ownership, humanity's stewardship responsibility, and giving's role as both worship and an investment in eternal purposes.

Christians can restore the joy that marked David and Israel's giving by addressing genuine concerns about financial stewardship while staying committed to biblical principles. When church leadership shows the same integrity that pleased God in David's time—by managing resources transparently and faithfully—they foster environments where generous giving becomes a celebration rather than a duty.

This biblical model continues to provide relevant guidance for religious communities seeking to understand and practice faithful stewardship, offering hope that contemporary Christians can experience the same joy in giving that characterized God's people in David's era. The key lies in remembering that giving reflects not financial capacity but heart condition, and that God's pleasure derives from witnessing sincere generosity expressed through willing, joyful stewardship of his gifts.

PART 5

JOEL

JOEL – THE SWARM

The Book of Joel emerges from one of history's most devastating natural disasters, a catastrophic locust invasion that swept through the Judean countryside. In this ecological catastrophe, the prophet Joel discerned a profound theological message: a harbinger of the approaching Day of Yahweh and its accompanying divine judgment.

Joel, whose name means "Yahweh is God," was the son of Pethuel, though beyond this paternal reference, we know virtually nothing about his family background or personal history. His prophetic work comprises the second book among the Minor Prophets, and while the text provides no explicit geographical markers for his ministry, internal evidence strongly suggests he prophesied primarily in Judah, with Jerusalem as his likely center of activity (Mariottini 2009:164).

The precise dating of Joel's ministry remains one of the most contested issues in Old Testament scholarship. Without clear historical markers or references to contemporary rulers, scholars have proposed dates ranging from the ninth century BC to the post-exilic period, making Joel's chronological placement highly debated (Mariottini 1987:125–130).

The Ecological Catastrophe

Joel's prophetic ministry coincided with an unprecedented ecological disaster that devastated Judah. The nation faced a dual calamity: a severe locust invasion followed by an equally devastating drought. While such natural disasters were not uncommon in the ancient Near East, the severity and duration of these particular events convinced Joel that they represented divine intervention, a visitation from God upon the nation and its people.

The Locust Invasion

The prophet provides vivid testimony to the extraordinary nature of this locust plague, emphasizing two critical aspects that distinguished it from ordinary infestations.

Multiple Successive Swarms: Joel describes not just a single locust invasion but multiple waves of different locust species that systematically devoured everything in their path: "What the cutting locust left, the swarming locust has eaten. What the swarming locust left, the hopping locust has eaten, and what the hopping locust left, the destroying locust has eaten" (Joel 1:4). This sequence of different locust types caused complete ecological devastation that left nothing untouched.

Multi-Year Duration: The catastrophe extended far beyond a single season. Joel later mentions God's promise to "repay you for the years that the swarming locust has eaten, the hopper, the destroyer, and the cutter, my great army, which I sent against you" (Joel 2:25). The plural "years" indicates that this was not a brief calamity but a prolonged period of suffering that tested the endurance and faith of the entire nation.

Comprehensive Devastation

The locust invasion caused complete agricultural collapse. Joel describes the total destruction of Judah's farming economy: "The fields are devastated, the ground mourns; for the grain is destroyed, the wine dries up, the oil fails. Be dismayed, you farmers, wail, you vinedressers, over the wheat and the barley; for the crops of the field are ruined. The vine withers, the fig tree droops. Pomegranate, palm, and apple—all the trees of the field are dried up" (Joel 1:10–12).

This comprehensive agricultural failure created a cascading crisis that affected every aspect of society. The destruction encompassed not only annual crops such as grain but also perennial fruit trees and vineyards, indicating damage that would take years to restore.

Societal and Religious Impact

Human Suffering

The ecological disaster created widespread famine and social distress. Joel describes how "the people were deprived of food because the storehouses were destroyed, the barns were ruined, and the grain had dried up" (Joel 1:16–17). The collapse of food storage systems amplified the crisis beyond the immediate agricultural losses.

Animal Welfare

The catastrophe extended beyond human suffering to encompass the animal kingdom. Joel poignantly describes the plight of livestock: "The animals moan with hunger! The herds of cattle wander about confused, because they have no pasture. The flocks of sheep and goats bleat in misery" (Joel 1:18 NLT). This detail demonstrates the prophet's comprehensive awareness of creation's interconnectedness and suffering.

Religious Crisis

Perhaps most significantly for Joel's theological message, the disaster disrupted the nation's religious life. The agricultural collapse made it impossible to maintain the daily temple offerings: "For there is no grain or wine to offer at the Temple of the LORD. So the priests are in mourning. The ministers of the LORD are weeping" (Joel 1:9 NLT). This suspension of regular worship represented not merely a logistical problem but a spiritual crisis that severed the people's primary means of maintaining their covenant relationship with God.

Joel's Prophetic Response

As both a prophet and a watchman appointed by God, Joel recognized his calling to interpret these devastating events and guide the people's response. Rather than viewing the catastrophe as merely natural misfortune, Joel understood it as divine visitation, a call to national repentance and spiritual renewal.
Joel's unique contribution to biblical prophecy lies in his practical wisdom for responding to crisis and calamity. His message

transcends his historical moment, offering timeless principles for how God's people should respond to hardship and suffering.

Contemporary Relevance

Joel's instructive words and his call for the people of Judah to return to God continue to speak powerfully to the twenty-first-century church. His message resonates particularly with those facing hardship and suffering today, offering both theological understanding and practical guidance for navigating life's most challenging circumstances.

This timeless relevance has been powerfully demonstrated in contemporary preaching. The following chapters are based on a three-part sermon series by my pastor, Jeff Griffin, Senior Pastor of The Compass Church, which explores Joel's message for modern believers:

1. **Joel: The Treasure of Stories** - Examining how our narratives of hardship can become sources of wisdom and strength.

2. **Joel: Return To Me** - Exploring Joel's central call to repentance and spiritual renewal.

3. **Joel: A Light at the End of the Tunnel** - Discovering hope and restoration in God's promises.

These contemporary expositions demonstrate how Joel's ancient message continues to provide guidance and hope for believers navigating their own seasons of trial and testing.

Conclusion

The book of Joel stands as a powerful testament to God's sovereignty over both natural disasters and human history. Through the lens of ecological catastrophe, Joel reveals profound truths about divine judgment, human responsibility, and the path to restoration. His message challenges readers to recognize God's hand in life's difficulties and to respond with genuine repentance and renewed commitment to covenant faithfulness.

Joel's prophecy ultimately points beyond immediate crisis to eschatological hope, offering assurance that even the most devastating circumstances cannot separate God's people from his love and his ultimate purposes for their good.

CHAPTER 27

JOEL: THE TREASURE OF STORIES

The book of Joel begins with a simple yet profound statement: "The word of Yahweh came to Joel, the son of Pethuel" (Joel 1:1). The prophet's name itself carries deep significance: "Joel" means "Yahweh is God," a fitting name for someone called to declare divine truth during a national crisis. Aside from his lineage as Pethuel's son, Scripture provides little information about Joel's background, yet his message remains relevant across time.

Joel's prophetic ministry arose during one of Judah's darkest times. The nation faced an unprecedented natural disaster: a devastating locust invasion that stripped the land bare. Through this ecological disaster, Joel delivered a message that went beyond immediate circumstances, emphasizing that even in our darkest moments, hope can emerge from hardship.

The Catastrophe: A Plague Like No Other

The Relentless Devastation

Joel's vivid description of the locust plague resembles a military campaign of total destruction: "What the cutting locust left, the swarming locust has eaten. What the swarming locust left, the hopping locust has eaten, and what the hopping locust left, the destroying locust has eaten" (Joel 1:4). Each successive wave of insects consumed what remained from the previous attack, leading to a systematic annihilation of the land's resources.

Archaeological and historical evidence confirms that locust plagues were a recurring nightmare in the ancient Near East. In his article, "Joel's Locusts in the Light of Near Eastern Parallels," John A. Thompson mentions locust plagues in Mari, Assyria, and Egypt. Thompson writes, "Locusts as an agricultural plague are mentioned in an Egyptian text warning of the sorrows of a farmer's life. Egyptian artists depicted locusts attacking various plants, including the grape vine and the wheat" (Thompson 1955: 53–54).

The plague in Joel's time exceeded all past instances in its severity. The prophet depicts a landscape turned into wasteland: vines destroyed, fig trees stripped of bark, branches remaining skeletal against the sky (Joel 1:7). The very foundation of farming life collapsed as grain vanished, oil grew scarce, and new wine dried up (Joel 1:10).

This environmental collapse triggered a wave of suffering affecting every living creature. Food supplies were empty, barns fell into disuse, and hunger haunted the land. Joel's compassionate gaze captured not only human despair but also the suffering of animals: "The animals moan with hunger! The herds of cattle wander around confused, because they have no pasture. The flocks of sheep and goats bleat in misery" (Joel 1:18 NLT).

The prophet's message to the farmers emphasizes the full extent of the disaster: "Despair, all you farmers! Wail, all you vine growers! Weep, because the wheat and barley—all the crops of the field—are ruined. The grapevines have dried up, and the fig trees have withered. The pomegranate trees, palm trees, and apple trees—all the fruit trees—have dried up" (Joel 1:11–12 NLT). No part of agricultural life escaped destruction.

The Call to Remember

Faced with this overwhelming catastrophe, Joel issued a solemn call to the nation's leaders and citizens: "Hear this, you elders; listen, all who live in the land. Has anything like this ever happened in your days or in the days of your forefathers?" (Joel 1:2). The prophet's rhetorical question expected a clear 'no'—this disaster surpassed anything in living memory or recorded history.

Even the locust plague during Amos' ministry, which had devoured fig and olive trees (Amos 4:9), was minor compared to the total destruction Joel observed. The Hebrew text uses multiple terms for locusts, possibly indicating different species or stages of development, but their common goal is clear: to completely destroy all edible plants.

The Sacred Duty of Storytelling

In the midst of a crisis, Joel delivered one of Scripture's most important commands about intergenerational communication: "Tell it to your children, and let your children tell it to their children, and their children to the next generation" (Joel 1:3). This was not merely advice; it was a divine mandate for the community to become chroniclers of their own experience.

The stories Joel commanded them to preserve were not sanitized accounts of easy victories. Instead, they were honest testimonies of overwhelming challenges, of situations that pushed human resources beyond their limits, and of divine intervention when hope seemed lost. These narratives serve as bridges connecting future generations to the God who rescues his people in their darkest hours.

The Biblical Foundation of Remembrance

Joel's emphasis on storytelling highlights a key biblical concept: remembrance as an act of faith. Throughout Scripture, memory is more than mere recall; it becomes a powerful force that shapes present actions based on past revelation. As Deuteronomy states: "Remember the days of old, consider the years long past; ask your father, and he will inform you; your elders, and they will tell you" (Deuteronomy 32:7).

Biblical remembrance links the past to the present, allowing the historical experiences of God's faithfulness to influence current decisions and future hopes. This has been called "a theology of recital." In describing this theology, Blair wrote, "It has become clear in recent years that the Bible contains a theology of recital. In both Testaments, the theme is the mighty deeds of God. These are celebrated in story, sermon, and song. What God has done is regarded as offering conclusive understanding of what he is doing and what he will do" (Blair 1961:41).

The Purpose of Sacred Stories

The Psalms reveal the ultimate purpose behind this divine command to remember and retell: "For he issued his laws to Jacob; he gave his instructions to Israel. He commanded our ancestors to teach them to their children, so the next generation might know them—even the children not yet born—and they in turn will teach their own children. So each generation should set its hope anew on God, not forgetting his glorious miracles" (Psalm 78:5–7 NLT).

This passage reveals the deep logic of biblical storytelling: each generation must experience God's faithfulness again, not through abstract theological ideas but through real stories of divine intervention. The stories act as vessels that carry hope across generations, making sure faith stays lively and personal instead of just tradition.

The Exodus Paradigm: A Model for All Deliverance

Israel's fundamental experience of liberation from Egyptian slavery set the pattern for all future remembrance. The Exodus was more than just a historical event; it became a day of remembrance for the people: "Remember this day on which you came out of Egypt, out of the house of slavery" (Exodus 13:3). This remembrance was to be everlasting, "throughout your generations" (Exodus 12:14), with each family responsible for explaining God's saving acts to their children (Exodus 12:26).

Joel's locust plague and its aftermath followed the same pattern: crisis, divine intervention, and the command to remember and retell. Just as Israel's Egyptian experience became a model for understanding God's character, the locust plague would serve future generations as proof of divine faithfulness amid environmental and economic disasters.

The Treasure of Stories

Through Joel's prophecy, God essentially called His people to be storytellers — not just entertainers or simple historians, but witnesses to His divine character revealed through times of crisis and deliverance. These stories were not optional entertainment but vital testimonies that revealed core truths about God's nature, love, and faithfulness.

The stories from Joel's time would become part of the larger biblical tradition, standing alongside accounts of the flood, the Exodus, the wilderness wanderings, and many other examples of divine intervention. Each story had multiple purposes: as a historical record, a theological lesson, and an evangelistic message.

These sacred stories have unique qualities that set them apart from typical historical accounts. They are engaging, appealing to both imagination and intellect. They are memorable because they embed themselves in consciousness through vivid imagery and emotional impact. Most importantly, they are powerful, capable of transforming hearts and minds across different centuries and cultures.

Unlike abstract theological propositions, stories invite listeners into experiential encounters with divine truth. They demonstrate rather than merely describe God's saving acts, allowing each generation to participate vicariously in the great drama of redemption. Through narrative, the distant past becomes the immediate present, and ancient testimonies speak with contemporary relevance.

Joel's ancient command echoes with modern urgency. Each generation's God's people face their own versions of the locust plague personal crises, community disasters, national upheavals that threaten to strip life of hope and meaning. Like Joel's audience, today's believers are called to be storytellers, passing down testimonies of divine faithfulness to future generations.

These stories serve as "heralds of the good news to all peoples in the present and in the future," conveying the core message that no crisis surpasses God's power for redemption. They remind each new generation that apparent endings can become divine beginnings and that devastation can lay the groundwork for extraordinary renewal.

The Old Testament Speaks to the Church

On June 19, 2016, my pastor, Jeff Griffin, Senior Pastor of The Compass Church in Naperville, Illinois, brought Joel's ancient message into sharp modern focus through his sermon "Joel: The Treasure of Stories." His application of Joel 1:1–4 shows how this prophetic text speaks directly to today's believers, challenging them to live with faith-filled purpose despite their trials.

The Sacred Obligation of Testimony

Jeff emphasized that Joel's exhortation places a sacred duty on every believer: we must pass our stories to the next generation. This isn't just about sharing happy memories or religious clichés, but honest testimony about experiencing God's goodness and mercy during life's toughest times. When parents and spiritual mentors share their genuine experiences of divine faithfulness, they build a living bridge that connects future generations to the same God who supported those before them.

This storytelling obligation goes beyond formal religious instruction to include the everyday rhythm of family life and community interaction. Children and young adults need to hear not only biblical stories but also modern testimonies—accounts of how the same God who delivered Israel continues to work in today's world. These personal stories become compelling apologetics, showing that faith remains relevant and essential in contemporary life.

Embracing the Transformative Potential of Hardship

One of Jeff's most thought-provoking insights focuses on the importance of embracing, rather than simply enduring, difficult circumstances. While no one welcomes hardship, Jeff reminded the congregation that every life has seasons of trial and testing. The main difference lies in how believers approach these unavoidable challenges.

Instead of seeing problems as meaningless suffering or divine punishment, Joel's message encourages believers to view hardship as part of a future testimony. This view doesn't downplay pain or imply that difficulty is desirable. However, it recognizes that God has the power to turn even the most tragic situations into "remarkable stories to be told to future generations."

This transformative view of hardship requires a fundamental shift in perspective. Instead of asking "Why is this happening to me?" believers are challenged to consider, "How might God use this experience to demonstrate his faithfulness?" This reframing does not eliminate suffering, but it infuses it with purpose and hope, creating space for divine redemption within human crisis.

The Courage of Anticipatory Faith

Perhaps the most challenging part of Jeff's application involves the difficulty of taking risks based on God's character rather than visible circumstances. When Joel instructed the people to prepare their testimonies, the locust devastation remained at its height. No signs of deliverance appeared on the horizon, no rescue efforts were in progress, and no evidence indicated that relief was near.

Yet Joel urged the people to trust in God's promise of intervention. This reflects a deep form of spiritual risk-taking: celebrating victory before deliverance comes, proclaiming God's faithfulness even while surrounded by signs of disaster. Such faith demands believers to base their confidence not on current circumstances but on the unchanging nature of God.

This anticipatory faith is rooted in Joel's proclamation: "Do not fear, be glad and rejoice, for the Lord has done great things" (Joel 2:21). The verb tense is important — God "has done" great things, indicating divine action as an accomplished fact even while the community still awaits visible signs of that deliverance.

Living with Prophetic Confidence

Jeff's sermon urges contemporary believers to embrace what might be called "prophetic confidence": the ability to speak and act based on God's promises rather than immediate appearances. This requires developing a faith that can look beyond current circumstances to see divine purposes at work beneath the surface of visible events.

Such confidence does not stem from naive optimism or denying real challenges. Instead, it develops from a deep familiarity with God's character as shown in Scripture and personal experience. When believers understand that God specializes in impossible rescues and unexpected redemptions, they can keep hope alive even when human logic points to despair.

This prophetic confidence also empowers believers to start sharing their testimonies before their stories are fully finished. Like Joel's audience, modern Christians can talk about God's faithfulness while still waiting for complete deliverance, trusting that the same God who began a good work will definitely see it through.

The Ripple Effect of Faithful Testimony

Jeff's application recognizes that individual testimonies create expanding circles of influence that reach well beyond immediate family ties. When believers bravely share their stories of divine faithfulness during difficult times, they add to a community-wide store of hope that bolsters everyone's faith.

These testimonies serve several important functions within the faith community. They offer practical encouragement to others facing similar challenges, showing that survival and even thriving are possible in tough circumstances. They also build theological understanding by helping believers see divine patterns of intervention and redemption that might otherwise go unnoticed. Furthermore, genuine testimonies serve as evangelistic tools by revealing God's character to those who haven't yet personally experienced His faithfulness. When believers share sincere stories of how God turned their darkest seasons into sources of strength and wisdom, they provide powerful evidence of divine reality that surpasses simple intellectual argument.

Conclusion: The Eternal Treasure

Joel's message, as reflected in Jeff's modern application, goes beyond its historical background to address basic human needs: the assurance that our stories matter, that our struggles have significance, and that divine faithfulness spans every generation.

The "treasure of stories" is not just a collection of ancient texts but a living store of hope, constantly enriched by each generation's testimony to God's saving power.

When commanding his people to become storytellers, God revealed something profound about the nature of faith itself: it is inherently narrative, communal, and transgenerational. Faith exists not in isolated individual experience but in the shared testimony of communities that remember, retell, and trust in the God who transforms locusts of devastation into harvests of hope.

The call to "tell it to your children, and let your children tell it to their children" continues to resonate through the ages, inviting each generation to add their chapter to the everlasting story of divine faithfulness. Jeff's challenge reminds us that Joel's ancient words become our modern mission: to be faithful witnesses, careful rememberers, and generous storytellers of the God who consistently writes redemption into the narrative of human crises.

In this way, every believer becomes both a recipient and a contributor to the treasure of stories, gaining hope from previous generations while creating testimonies that will strengthen those who come after. The locust plagues of our time—whether personal, communal, or global—become opportunities to rediscover that God remains faithful to turn devastation into deliverance, and every ending into a new beginning.

CHAPTER 28

JOEL: RETURN TO ME

The book of Joel presents a compelling theological narrative centered on divine judgment, human suffering, and the redemptive call to repentance. Set against the backdrop of a devastating locust plague, Joel's prophecy examines the complex relationship between divine sovereignty and human responses to crisis. The text reveals how catastrophic events, though experienced as divine judgment, ultimately serve as instruments of grace designed to restore the covenant relationship between God and his people. This chapter examines Joel's theological framework for understanding suffering, the nature of divine discipline, and the transformative potential of genuine repentance.

The Theological Context of Devastation

Joel 2:1–11 presents a vivid apocalyptic description of the locust invasion that has befallen Judah. The prophet employs military imagery to depict these insects as "a great and powerful army" whose devastation is unprecedented in scope and intensity (Joel 2:2). The text explicitly identifies Yahweh as the commander of this destructive force: "The LORD utters his voice at the head of his army" (Joel 2:11). This divine leadership of natural catastrophe raises profound theological questions about the nature of God's involvement in human suffering.

The transformation of the land from "like the garden of Eden" to "a desolate wilderness" (Joel 2:3) serves as both a literal description and a theological metaphor. The reversal from Edenic paradise to barren wasteland suggests a cosmic undoing of creation's goodness, connecting the locust plague to the broader narrative of human fallenness and divine judgment. The prophet's imagery emphasizes not merely the physical devastation but the theological significance of God's active participation in bringing judgment upon his covenant people.

A Theological Framework for Understanding Suffering

Joel's narrative contributes to the broader biblical discourse on theodicy by identifying multiple sources of human suffering. The book implicitly recognizes three primary categories of suffering that affect the human condition, each requiring distinct theological consideration.

First, much human suffering stems from the fundamental reality of living in a fallen world. The Genesis account establishes that God's original creation was "very good" (Genesis 1:31), but human rebellion introduced corruption into the cosmic order. The subsequent curse upon the ground (Genesis 3:17) represents the systemic brokenness that affects all natural processes, making the earth itself a source of hardship through disease, natural disasters, and ecological instability. This foundational brokenness explains why suffering affects both the righteous and the wicked, as all humanity shares in the consequences of the fall.

Second, human suffering frequently results from the natural consequences of moral choices. The wisdom literature consistently affirms the principle of moral causation: "those who plow iniquity and sow trouble reap the same" (Job 4:8). This category of suffering serves a pedagogical function, teaching individuals and communities about the moral structure of reality while maintaining human moral agency and responsibility.

Third, Joel specifically addresses suffering that functions as divine discipline. The prophet presents the locust plague not as a random natural disaster or human miscalculation, but as purposeful divine action intended to restore the covenant relationship. This understanding aligns with the broader biblical perspective that "the LORD disciplines those he loves, as a father the son he delights in" (Proverbs 3:11–12). Divine discipline differs from mere punishment in that it serves redemptive rather than merely retributive purposes.

The Paradox of Divine Love in Judgment

The book of Joel presents a theological tension that runs throughout Scripture: the apparent contradiction between divine love and divine judgment. The same God who sends devastating locusts is described as "gracious and merciful, slow to anger, and abounding in steadfast love" (Joel 2:13). This paradox requires careful theological reflection to avoid either antinomianism (denying God's justice) or legalism (denying God's mercy).

The resolution of this tension lies in understanding divine discipline as an expression of covenant love rather than arbitrary punishment. God's judgment serves to awaken his people to their spiritual condition and to create the conditions necessary for authentic repentance and restoration. The devastation caused by the locusts serves as both a consequence and an opportunity: a consequence of covenant unfaithfulness, but an opportunity for a renewed relationship with God. This dual nature of divine discipline reveals the redemptive intent underlying even the most severe forms of divine judgment.

The prophet's appeal to God's character, as revealed to Moses (Exodus 34:6–7), demonstrates theological continuity in understanding the divine nature. God's mercy and justice are not competing attributes but complementary expressions of his covenant faithfulness. Divine discipline emerges from love, not wrath, and aims at restoration, not destruction.

The Call to Authentic Repentance

Joel 2:12–13 presents the divine invitation that transforms the narrative from judgment to hope. The call to "return to me with all your heart" establishes both the possibility and the requirements for restoration. The prophet emphasizes that genuine repentance must encompass both internal transformation ("rend your hearts and not your clothing") and external expression ("with fasting, with weeping, and with mourning").

This comprehensive understanding of repentance reflects the biblical recognition that human beings are embodied souls whose spiritual condition necessarily affects their physical and social existence. Authentic repentance cannot remain merely internal but must manifest in concrete actions that demonstrate a fundamental reorientation of life priorities and loyalties.

The phrase "rend your hearts and not your clothing" (Joel 2:13) explicitly addresses the tendency toward ritualistic religion that substitutes external observance for internal transformation. Joel insists that covenant restoration requires heartfelt contrition rather than mere ceremonial compliance. This emphasis on authenticity reflects the prophetic tradition's consistent critique of empty religiosity and its call for genuine spiritual transformation.

Divine Sovereignty and Human Response

Joel's concluding question, "Who knows? He may reconsider and change his plan and leave a blessing for you" (Joel 2:14), introduces a crucial element of theological uncertainty that preserves both divine sovereignty and human responsibility. The phrase "who knows" acknowledges that genuine repentance does not manipulate or obligate God but instead creates the conditions for divine mercy to be extended.

This theological formulation simultaneously upholds several key principles. It preserves divine freedom by recognizing that God's response cannot be predicted or manipulated by human actions. It maintains human moral responsibility by emphasizing that repentance remains significant and essential. It affirms God's character by expressing confidence that a gracious and merciful God will respond appropriately to genuine repentance.

The rhetorical question also reflects the inherent mystery in the divine-human relationship. While God's character provides the basis for hope, the specific timing and manner of divine response remain within God's sovereign prerogative. This uncertainty calls for faith rather than presumption, humility rather than manipulation.

Conclusion

The book of Joel provides a sophisticated theological framework for understanding the relationship between divine judgment and divine mercy. The prophet demonstrates that even the most severe forms of suffering can serve redemptive purposes when understood adequately within the context of a covenant relationship. The locust plague, although devastating in its immediate effects, creates an opportunity for genuine repentance and a renewed relationship with God.

Joel's message remains theologically relevant because it addresses the universal human experience of suffering while maintaining the tension between divine sovereignty and human responsibility. The prophet neither provides straightforward answers to the problem of suffering nor minimizes the reality of divine judgment. Instead, Joel calls his audience to see beyond immediate circumstances to discern the redemptive possibilities that exist even within crisis.

The book ultimately affirms that behind apparent divine harshness lies divine love, and behind divine judgment lies the invitation to return. This theological vision transforms suffering from mere tragedy into potential opportunity, judgment into invitation, and despair into hope. Joel's call to "return to me" echoes across the centuries as both warning and promise, reminding each generation that the gracious and merciful God continues to seek an authentic relationship with his people.

The Old Testament Speaks to the Church

On June 26, 2016, my pastor, Jeff Griffin, Senior Pastor of The Compass Church in Naperville, Illinois, delivered a sermon entitled "Return To Me," drawing from Joel 2:10–13. His pastoral exposition illuminated the practical implications of Joel's prophetic message for contemporary believers navigating seasons of difficulty and suffering. Jeff's sermon provided a hermeneutical bridge between the ancient text and modern Christian experience, demonstrating how Joel's call to repentance and restoration remains relevant for believers confronting hardship in their own lives.

The Relational Nature of Divine Discipline

Jeff's central thesis emphasized God's fundamentally relational character as the theological foundation for understanding divine discipline. Rather than viewing suffering as evidence of divine indifference or cruelty, Jeff encouraged the congregation to recognize that God's disciplinary actions emerge from his desire for an intimate relationship with his people. This relational understanding transforms the interpretive framework through which believers approach their suffering.

When hardship enters a believer's life, the natural human response often involves questioning God's goodness or presence. Jeff's pastoral insight challenges this reactive pattern by encouraging believers to consider an alternative perspective: that suffering may be a sign of God's active involvement rather than his absence. This theological shift requires what Jeff calls "eyes to see," a spiritual perception that recognizes divine love working behind difficult circumstances.

The relational dimension of divine discipline distinguishes it from mere punishment or arbitrary suffering. Where punishment seeks retribution, divine discipline seeks restoration. Where arbitrary suffering lacks purpose, divine discipline serves the redemptive goal of drawing God's people into a deeper covenant relationship. This distinction proves crucial for believers seeking to respond appropriately to their experiences of hardship.

The Imperative of Spiritual Return

Joel's exhortation to "Return to the LORD" assumes spiritual distance as both the source of the people's predicament and the target of divine restoration efforts. Jeff emphasized that this call to return implies a prior departure: the people of Judah had somehow moved away from their covenant relationship with God. For contemporary believers, this principle entails an honest self-examination of their own spiritual trajectory and their positioning relative to God.

The call to return encompasses both recognition and action. Recognition involves acknowledging one's spiritual condition and the reality of separation from God. Action involves deliberate movement toward renewed relationship through repentance, prayer, and renewed obedience to God's revealed will. Jeff's pastoral application emphasized that returning to God is not merely an emotional experience but a comprehensive reorientation of life priorities and practices.

This return must be understood as more than crisis-driven religion, the tendency to seek God only when circumstances become difficult. Instead, Joel's call envisions a fundamental reestablishment of the covenant relationship that will sustain the believer through both seasons of blessing and seasons of trial. The return to God transforms not only the believer's immediate circumstances but their entire approach to living in relationship with the divine.

Authentic Repentance Versus Religious Performance

Jeff's exposition of Joel's phrase "rend your hearts and not your clothing" addressed a persistent challenge in religious communities: the substitution of external religious performance for genuine spiritual transformation. The ancient practice of tearing one's garments as an expression of grief or repentance could easily become a mere theatrical display rather than an authentic expression of heartfelt contrition.

This distinction between heart-rending and garment-rending carries profound implications for contemporary Christian practice. Jeff warned against the tendency to substitute religious activity, such as increased church attendance, more frequent prayer, and additional Bible reading, for the deeper work of heart transformation that God desires. While such activities may accompany genuine repentance, they cannot substitute for it.

Authentic repentance, as Jeff explained, requires engagement of the whole person—heart, mind, will, and action. It cannot remain compartmentalized as merely one aspect of life but must affect every dimension of the believer's existence. This comprehensive approach to repentance reflects the biblical understanding of human nature as integrated rather than compartmentalized, requiring holistic transformation rather than partial modification.

The pastoral challenge lies in helping believers distinguish between authentic spiritual transformation and religious performance. Jeff suggested that genuine repentance leads to lasting change in priorities, relationships, and behavioral patterns, whereas religious performance tends to remain superficial and temporary.

Encountering Divine Grace Through Return

The promise embedded within Joel's call to return involves an encounter with God's true character—merciful, gracious, forgiving, and healing. Jeff emphasized that believers who respond to hardship by returning to God will discover not the harsh judge they may fear but the compassionate Father who desires their restoration. This discovery requires faith to move beyond immediate circumstances toward a more profound truth about God's nature.

The reference to Jeremiah 3:22, "Turn back . . . I will heal your afflictions," illustrates the restorative outcome that awaits those who respond appropriately to divine discipline. Jeff emphasized that God's ultimate purpose in allowing or sending hardship is not punishment but healing. This healing encompasses not only relief from immediate suffering but restoration of the spiritual relationship that provides meaning and purpose for all of life.

The encounter with divine grace transforms the believer's understanding of both their suffering and their God. Suffering is reframed as an opportunity rather than merely a trial. God is experienced as present and active rather than distant and uncaring. The relationship between the believer and God is renewed on the foundation of divine grace rather than human performance.

Jeff's pastoral application provides several practical guidelines for believers facing hardship in their own lives. First, believers must resist the immediate tendency to interpret suffering as evidence of divine abandonment or punishment. Instead, they should consider the possibility that their hardship may represent God's disciplinary love designed to draw them into a closer relationship.

Second, believers facing hardship should examine their spiritual condition honestly, asking whether they have drifted from close fellowship with God. This examination should focus not only on apparent moral failures but on subtle shifts in priorities, affections, and spiritual practices that may have created distance in the divine-human relationship.

Third, believers must commit to authentic rather than performative repentance. This involves a comprehensive life change rather than a temporary religious activity. The goal is not to manipulate God's response but to restore an authentic relationship that honors God's character and serves the believer's ultimate spiritual welfare.

Fourth, believers should approach God with the expectation of encountering grace rather than condemnation. While genuine repentance acknowledges wrongdoing, it is motivated by confidence in God's merciful character rather than fear of divine retribution.

Conclusion

Jeff's exposition of Joel 2:10–13 demonstrates the enduring relevance of prophetic literature for contemporary Christian experience. His pastoral wisdom bridges the gap between ancient text and modern application by focusing on the unchanging character of God and the consistent human need for an authentic relationship with the divine. Jeff's sermon reminds believers that even in seasons of hardship, God's relational love provides both the context for understanding suffering and the pathway toward restoration and healing.

The call to "return to me" echoes across the centuries as both a challenge and a promise: a challenge to authentic spiritual transformation, a promise of divine grace for those who respond with genuine repentance. Jeff's pastoral application ensures that Joel's ancient message continues to speak hope and healing to contemporary believers facing the universal human experience of hardship and suffering.

CHAPTER 29

JOEL: LIGHT AT THE END
OF THE TUNNEL

The book of Joel presents a compelling narrative of divine judgment followed by restoration, using the devastating imagery of a locust invasion to explore themes of repentance, divine mercy, and eschatological hope. This prophetic text, set against the backdrop of ecological catastrophe, offers profound theological insights into the nature of God's relationship with his covenant people and the transformative power of genuine repentance.

Historical Context and Literary Background

The prophecy of Joel comes from a time of unprecedented natural disaster that struck ancient Israel. The text describes a devastating locust invasion along with severe drought conditions that lasted for several years. While locust swarms and droughts were not uncommon in the ancient Near East, Joel depicts these events as particularly intense in both scale and duration.

Joel's account describes successive waves of locusts (Joel 1:4) that systematically destroyed the nation's agricultural foundation. The prophet provides vivid descriptions of ecological devastation: grapevines destroyed, fig trees stripped not only of foliage but of bark itself, leaving branches "white and bare" (Joel 1:7). The accompanying drought created conditions of extreme suffering for both human and animal populations, as evidenced by Joel's description of livestock wandering "confused" and "bleating in misery" due to the absence of pasture (Joel 1:18).

According to Joel's theological interpretation, this natural catastrophe represented divine judgment upon the nation's sins. The calamity catalyzed Joel's prophetic call to national repentance, prayer, and humble submission before Yahweh.

The Call to Repentance

Central to Joel's message is his exhortation to authentic repentance, articulated in the memorable phrase: "rend your hearts and not your clothing" (Joel 2:13). This call transcends mere external displays of mourning, demanding instead genuine internal transformation. Joel's appeal is grounded in his understanding of Yahweh's character as "gracious and merciful, slow to anger, and abounding in steadfast love," one who "relents from punishing" (Joel 2:13–14).

The uncertainty inherent in Joel's appeal, "Who knows whether he will not turn and relent," reflects the prophet's recognition that divine mercy cannot be presumed upon or manipulated through ritual performance. Instead, it acknowledges that repentance creates the possibility for divine compassion to manifest.

National Response and Divine Intervention

Joel's prophetic message prompted a comprehensive religious response. Religious leaders initiated a solemn assembly by sounding the ram's horn, calling all citizens, including infants, to participate in collective fasting and prayer (Joel 2:16). This inclusive gathering demonstrated the communal nature of both sin and repentance within the covenant community.

The priests' intercessory prayer during this assembly reveals the theological stakes involved: "Spare your people, O LORD. Do not make your inheritance an object of scorn, a byword among the nations. Why should they say among the peoples, 'Where is their God?'" (Joel 2:17). This petition recognizes that Israel's suffering reflected not only upon the nation but upon Yahweh's reputation among surrounding peoples.

The text presents Yahweh's response as immediate and compassionate: "the LORD became concerned about his land, and he had pity on his people" (Joel 2:18). This divine response demonstrates the efficacy of genuine repentance and intercession in moving God to action.

Divine Promise of Restoration

Yahweh's promise of restoration addresses both the immediate crisis and its long-term consequences. The divine commitment includes the removal of the locust army, described metaphorically as the "northern army," and its destruction in the surrounding seas (Joel 2:19–20). More significantly, God promises agricultural restoration through the provision of "grain, wine, and oil" and the assurance that Israel will no longer serve as "a mockery among the nations."

The Theology of Celebration

The restoration narrative culminates in a divine call to universal celebration. Joel records Yahweh's invitation to all creation—soil, animals, and people—to "be glad and rejoice" (Joel 2:21–23). This cosmic celebration reflects the comprehensive nature of both judgment and restoration within Joel's theological framework.

The promise of restored rainfall patterns, "early and later rain, as before," signifies not merely agricultural recovery but the restoration of the natural order that sustains life. This meteorological imagery carries profound theological significance, representing the renewal of divine blessing and the reestablishment of the covenant relationship.

Suffering and Hope

Joel's narrative provides key insights into the temporary nature of suffering within the divine economy. The prophet's message shows that although judgment is a necessary correction for covenant unfaithfulness, it is not God's final word. The metaphor of "light at the end of the tunnel" illustrates this theological idea: suffering, no matter how severe, is temporary when accompanied by genuine repentance.

The text's emphasis on divine character, God's mercy, compassion, and reluctance to punish, provides the theological foundation for hope during periods of divine judgment. Joel's portrayal suggests that God's essential nature inclines toward restoration rather than destruction.

Divine Compensation and Grace

Perhaps the most remarkable aspect of Joel's restoration theology is found in Yahweh's promise: "I will repay you for the years that the swarming locust has eaten" (Joel 2:25). This divine commitment to compensation reveals the extraordinary nature of God's grace. The promise encompasses not merely restoration to previous conditions but abundant blessings that exceed prior prosperity.

Joel describes this restoration in agricultural terms: "The threshing floors shall be full of grain, the vats shall overflow with wine and oil" (Joel 2:24). This imagery of overflow and abundance suggests that divine restoration transcends simple replacement, offering instead superabundant blessing.

The theological significance of divine compensation lies in its demonstration of grace rather than justice. The people deserved judgment for their covenant violations; they had no claim upon divine restoration. Yet Yahweh's compassion motivates him to repay losses and bestow blessings far beyond what justice would require.

The Paradox of Prosperity

Joel's restoration theology includes an implicit warning about the spiritual dangers of prosperity. The text acknowledges that while adversity often drives people toward dependence on God, prosperity can foster self-reliance and spiritual complacency. This insight reflects a broader biblical theme articulated elsewhere: "When I fed them, they were satisfied; when they were satisfied, they became proud; then they forgot me" (Hosea 13:6).

The solution to this spiritual peril lies in maintaining a proper theological perspective during times of blessing. Joel suggests that the key to avoiding spiritual complacency involves celebrating "the giver" rather than merely enjoying the gifts. Recognizing God as the source of blessing, "he is the one who gives the autumn rains," provides the necessary foundation for sustained faithfulness during prosperous times.

Conclusion

The book of Joel presents a sophisticated theology of judgment, repentance, and restoration that addresses fundamental questions about divine character and human responses to suffering. The prophet's message affirms that while divine judgment represents a necessary response to covenant unfaithfulness, God's essential character inclines toward mercy and restoration.

Joel's narrative illustrates that genuine repentance opens the door for divine intervention and that God's response to true contrition goes beyond just forgiveness to include abundant blessing and restitution. The text's focus on celebration and gratitude offers vital guidance for keeping spiritual life strong during times of divine favor.

Ultimately, Joel's prophecy offers hope grounded in the character of God rather than human merit. The "light at the end of the tunnel" emerges not from human effort or worthiness but from divine grace that transforms judgment into blessing and despair into celebration. This theological perspective provides enduring insight for communities facing crisis and individuals seeking to understand the relationship between suffering and hope within the framework of divine providence.

The Old Testament Speaks to the Church

The enduring relevance of Joel's prophetic message finds contemporary expression through pastoral application that bridges ancient text and modern experience. This analysis examines the homiletical interpretation and practical application of Joel 2:20–25 as delivered by my pastor, Jeff Griffin, Senior Pastor of The Compass Church in Naperville, Illinois, in his sermon "A Light at the End of the Tunnel" (July 3, 2016). Jeff's pastoral exposition demonstrates how Joel's theology of temporary suffering, divine compensation, and proper response to prosperity provides essential guidance for contemporary Christian communities navigating hardship and blessing.

The Temporality of Suffering

Jeff's primary emphasis centers on Joel's fundamental assertion that suffering, regardless of its intensity or duration, remains inherently temporary within God's redemptive economy. This theological principle emerges directly from Joel's historical narrative, where the devastating locust invasion, though lasting many months and causing extensive agricultural and social disruption, ultimately yields to divine restoration and abundance.

Jeff's application extends this biblical principle to contemporary human experience, acknowledging that while earthly suffering may persist for extended periods, it operates within temporal boundaries established by divine sovereignty. This perspective offers crucial comfort without minimizing the reality or severity of present hardship. Jeff's approach recognizes that the end of suffering manifests in two distinct but related dimensions: temporal relief within earthly experience and ultimate resolution in eschatological fulfillment.

Ultimate Resolution

Jeff's sermon demonstrates sophisticated theological integration by connecting Joel's temporal restoration with the ultimate eschatological promise found in Revelation 21:4. This hermeneutical approach recognizes that while Joel's prophecy addresses immediate historical circumstances, its theological principles point toward complete redemptive fulfillment in the eschaton, where God "will wipe every tear from their eyes. Death will be no more; mourning and crying and pain will be no more."

This eschatological perspective serves multiple functions. First, it provides hope for those whose earthly suffering may not experience the dramatic reversal depicted in Joel's narrative. Second, it establishes the theological framework within which all temporal suffering must be understood: as part of a larger redemptive narrative that culminates in complete restoration.

Third, it prevents misapplying Joel's message as a guarantee of immediate material restoration, while maintaining confidence in God's ultimate redemptive purposes.

The Theology of Repayment

Jeff's exposition of Joel 2:25, "I will repay you for the years that the swarming locust has eaten," emphasizes the remarkable nature of divine compensation that transcends human understanding of justice or fairness. Jeff's application of Joel's message recognizes that God's promise to repay losses is pure grace rather than an obligation, demonstrating a divine character that exceeds human expectations or entitlements.

This theological principle carries profound implications for Christian discipleship. Jeff's emphasis on divine repayment offers comfort to those experiencing loss while simultaneously challenging recipients of blessing to recognize the gracious nature of divine provision. Jeff's approach avoids the prosperity theology error of viewing blessing as earned while maintaining confidence in God's commitment to care for his people.

The diversity of divine blessing, "God's blessings come in different ways," highlights the broad scope of divine grace that appears through material needs, relational healing, spiritual development, and many other forms of divine favor. This nuanced view prevents reducing divine blessing to just material things, while still recognizing the legitimacy of expecting God's tangible care.

Celebrating the Giver

Jeff's treatment of prosperity's spiritual dangers demonstrates careful attention to Joel's implicit warning about the corrupting potential of abundance. Jeff's emphasis on "rejoicing in the giver" rather than merely enjoying gifts provides practical guidance for maintaining spiritual vitality during prosperous seasons.

This application addresses a vital modern challenge: the tendency for material blessings to lead to spiritual complacency or self-reliance. Jeff's statement, "The Lord is the giver, and he is the gift," captures a nuanced theological view that sees God both as the source of blessings and as the ultimate blessing itself. This perspective prevents treating divine relationships as merely instrumental and promotes proper gratitude for material provisions.

Jeff's assertion that people's relationship with God should not be affected by their prosperity articulates an essential principle for spiritual maturity. This stability of relationship, independent of circumstances, reflects the covenant faithfulness that Joel advocates and demonstrates practical wisdom for navigating the spiritual challenges of abundance.

Jeff's application of Joel's message demonstrates several important principles for Christians today. First, Jeff's emphasis on temporary suffering, divine compensation, and proper response to blessing flows directly from Joel's message.

Second, Jeff's message demonstrates pastoral sensitivity by acknowledging the reality of prolonged suffering while maintaining hope grounded in divine character rather than immediate circumstances. This balanced approach avoids both false optimism and human despair.

Third, Jeff's treatment of the spiritual dangers of prosperity addresses an important modern issue often overlooked in popular religious views, known as the prosperity gospel. His focus on celebrating the giver offers practical advice for staying spiritually authentic during times of blessing.

Conclusion

Jeff's application of Joel's message demonstrates the enduring relevance of prophetic literature for contemporary Christian communities. His emphasis on suffering's temporality, divine compensation, and proper response to prosperity provides essential guidance for navigating the complexities of human experience within the framework of divine sovereignty and grace.

Jeff's message offers hope during times of extreme suffering. This hope is grounded in divine character rather than immediate circumstances, providing the foundation necessary for sustained faithfulness through both hardship and blessing.

Jeff's application of Joel's message ultimately demonstrates that the "light at the end of the tunnel" remains not merely a metaphor for temporal relief but a reality grounded in the character and promises of God, whose grace transforms both suffering and prosperity into opportunities for a deeper relationship with the divine giver of all good gifts.

PART 6

ESTHER

INTRODUCTION

ESTHER: FOR SUCH A TIME AS THIS

Among the outstanding women whose stories light up the pages of the Old Testament, few have touched hearts and inspired generations as much as Queen Esther. Her story goes beyond just a love tale to stand as a strong testament to courage, faith, and divine guidance in the face of seemingly impossible odds.

Esther's journey from humble Jewish maiden to Persian queen reads like an ancient fairy tale, but underneath its romantic surface lies a powerful story of survival and sacrifice. When the Jewish people across the Persian Empire faced destruction, God placed an unlikely heroine at the center of power, a young woman willing to risk everything to save her people.

The Heart of Esther's Story

The selection of Esther as queen seems almost accidental—a beautiful young woman chosen from many to replace the deposed Queen Vashti. After months of preparation and beauty treatments, she gained the favor of King Ahasuerus and became queen of the vast Persian Empire. Yet what appeared to be luck would soon prove to be a divine plan.

When Haman, the king's chief minister, plotted a genocidal scheme against the Jewish people, Esther found herself in a unique position to step in. Her adoptive father, Mordecai, challenged her with words that have resonated through history: "Who knows? Perhaps you have attained to royal position for such a time as this" (Esther 4:14).

Faced with Persian law that forbade approaching the king without being summoned, a violation punishable by death, Esther made a choice that defined her character. Despite the mortal danger, she declared, "I will go to the king, though it is against the law; and if I perish, I perish" (Esther 4:16). In that moment, Esther shifted from a passive recipient of royal favor to an active agent of deliverance for her people.

Lessons for Today

Esther's story resonates across centuries because it addresses timeless human experiences: living under oppressive circumstances, facing impossible choices, and discovering courage in moments of crisis. Her life demonstrates that God often works through ordinary people placed in extraordinary situations, using their willingness to act despite overwhelming odds.

When we encounter our own "such a time as this" moments—those critical junctures when our response could significantly impact others—Esther's example challenges us to choose courage over comfort, purpose over safety, and faith over fear.

About This Study Series

This collection of studies on Esther is based on a sermon series delivered by my pastor, Jeff Griffin, Senior Pastor of The Compass Church in Naperville, Illinois. Each chapter reflects one of Jeff's messages, offering a deeper look at the themes and lessons of Esther's extraordinary life.

Whether you are facing personal challenges, seeking to understand God's providence, or looking for inspiration to act courageously under challenging situations, these studies provide biblical wisdom and practical insights.

Study Topics

The series covers the following themes from Esther's life:

God's Grace - Exploring how divine favor positioned Esther for her crucial role.

Our Mission - Understanding how God calls ordinary people to extraordinary purposes.

Our Nightmare - Examining how we respond when facing seemingly insurmountable challenges.

Our Decision - Learning to choose courage and action over fear and passivity.

God's Justice - Witnessing how divine justice ultimately prevails, even through human instruments.

Setting the Stage

Our study on Esther begins with an overview of ancient Susa, the magnificent capital of the Persian Empire, where palace intrigue and political maneuvering set the stage for one of history's most dramatic rescue stories. From this opulent setting emerges a narrative that speaks to anyone who has ever wondered whether their life has a greater purpose or whether God can use them in their current circumstances.

Through Esther's example, we discover that heroism often begins not with grand gestures but with faithful availability to God's purposes, even when—especially when—those purposes require us to risk everything we hold dear.

These studies on Esther aim to bless readers in the same transformative way Jeff's sermons blessed the congregation of The Compass Church. May Esther's courage inspire your own journey of faith and purpose.

CHAPTER 30

THE ROYAL CITY OF SUSA

Before we begin our studies on Esther, based on a series of sermons titled "For Such a Time as This," preached by my pastor, Jeff Griffin, Senior Pastor of The Compass Church in Naperville, Illinois, I want to introduce you to the royal city of Susa, the capital of the ancient Persian empire.

Esther became the queen of Persia when Ahasuerus, also known as Xerxes, the king of Persia, chose her as his wife. Ahasuerus's palace was in the fortress of Susa. The royal city of Susa is unknown to most readers of the Bible. The royal city of Susa was one of the four capitals of the Persian Empire and the winter residence of the kings of Persia (Nehemiah 1:1; Esther 1:2).

The city was located in the ancient Elamite territory, in southwestern Iran, near the Ulai canal (Daniel 8:2). The Ulai, an artificial river, was also known as the Eulaeus by the Greeks. The site of ancient Susa is located in the modern Iranian city of Shush. Susa appears in the KJV as Shushan (Esther 1:2).

Susa was an ancient Mesopotamian city, built around 4000 BC and inhabited by Semitic people. Around 3200 BC, the city received an influx of non-Semitic people whose influence extended across the Iranian plateau. This proto-Elamite culture eventually was absorbed by the Sumerians, and Susa became part of the empire of Sargon of Akkad ca. 2350 BC. The Elamites conquered the city from the Sumerians around 2000 BC, and Susa became an Elamite city until the Assyrians conquered it in the seventh century BC.

Elam appears in the table of nations in Genesis 10:22 and in the oracles of Isaiah (11:11), Jeremiah (49:34–39), and Ezekiel (32:24). The Elamites also appear in the New Testament when the Holy Spirit fell upon the believers (Acts 2:9). All biblical references to Susa in Nehemiah, Daniel, and Esther relate to the Persian period. In 646 BC, Assurbanipal, king of Assyria, conquered the Elamites, and Susa became part of the Assyrian empire. Assurbanipal deported part of the Elamite population and settled them in Samaria (Ezra 4:9–10). After Susa became part of the Assyrian empire, the Elamites ceased being a major political force in the region (Bright 1981:314). Susa was under Assyrian control until Cyrus the Great, king of Persia, conquered Babylon in 539 BC.

After the conquest of Babylon, Cyrus probably made Susa one of the capitals of his empire and gave it as much prestige as Ecbatana, Pasargadae, and Babylon. The royal palace at Susa was built by Darius I, also known as Darius the Great, a Persian king who ruled from 522–486 BC.

The first two years of his reign were marked by political unrest and rebellions throughout the Persian empire. When the political situation was brought under control, Darius set out to reestablish the Achaemenid empire. In addition to building Persepolis as the new capital of the Persian empire, Darius also began substantial construction at Susa, now the empire's second capital. Under Darius, Susa again "became a vital, cosmopolitan city and a locus of interchange between people of the Mesopotamian plain and the Iranian highlands" (Harper et al 1992:215).

The city was also the residence of Ahasuerus (486–465 BC), the king of Persia, who chose Esther as his new queen. Ahasuerus is also known by his Greek name Xerxes I. Ahasuerus's empire extended from the Indus Valley, modern-day Pakistan, to Ethiopia, the area occupied by modern-day Sudan. Ahasuerus finished the construction of the palace that his father had built.

The ancient city of Susa was divided into four areas (Yamauchi 1983:427):

(1) The acropolis ("capital" [Esther 1:2]) was the strong and fortified palace complex within the city where the king kept his residence. Esther 1:2 uses the word "capital" to translate a Hebrew term meaning "fortress." The palace was designed after Assyrian and Babylonian palaces, with outer walls, several inner courts, and surrounding rooms. The Book of Esther mentions the "inner court" (5:1), "the outer court" (6:4), and "the court of the garden" (1:5).

(2) The apadana is the area where the Hall of Pillars, or Audience Hall, was constructed. It features thirty-six columns. According to an inscription on one of the columns, the apadana was burned during the reign of Artaxerxes I (465–424 BC) and was later restored during the reign of Artaxerxes II (404–358 BC).

(3) The royal village, the section of the city where the merchants and the royal functionaries lived.

(4) The village of the artisans, the place where the craftsmen lived.

The site of Susa has yielded numerous archaeological discoveries. Archaeologists have found hundreds of texts, inscriptions, pottery, jewelry, and other objects of art. In addition, three important monuments were also found at Susa: the stela containing the Code of Hammurabi, the Stela of Naram-Sin, and the Obelisk of Manishtusu. The most famous of these, the Code of Hammurabi, is a collection of 282 laws written in Old Babylonian cuneiform. Some of these laws are similar to the laws in the book of Exodus.

During the exile, probably in the Persian period, a sizeable Jewish community developed in Susa. In the last year of Belshazzar (539 BC) Daniel was in Susa when he had the vision of the Ram and the He-goat (Daniel 8:2). Nehemiah served as cupbearer in the royal palace of Artaxerxes I (Nehemiah 1:1). It was at the palace at Susa that Esther lived and became the wife of Ahasuerus and the queen of Persia.

The palace where Esther lived was famous for its splendor and grandeur. When Darius decided to build a palace that would showcase the glory of his reign, he aimed to make it the center of the empire's government. "The whole empire was mobilized to contribute to this vast enterprise, using material and human resources of each province [of the Persian empire]" (Miroschedji 1992:6:244). The palace was lavishly decorated with costly woods, silver, gold, and precious stones. The Audience Hall was adorned with glazed bricks featuring winged bulls, sphinxes, griffins, and other figures.

The ancient city of Susa still has great religious significance in the Muslim world. Shiite Muslims believe that the remains of the prophet Daniel were buried in the village of Shush, the site of ancient Susa. The alleged tomb of Daniel, enshrined within a mosque, has become the focus of religious pilgrimages.

CHAPTER 31

ESTHER: FOR SUCH A TIME AS THIS - "GOD'S GRACE"

The book of Esther offers a unique story within the Hebrew Bible, marked by its lack of explicit references to God while still highlighting deep theological themes of providence, courage, and redemption. Unlike typical biblical stories that often mention God's name, Esther's story unfolds in a context of divine hiddenness, where God's presence is felt through circumstances rather than direct intervention. This theological paradox offers a powerful view of faith under pressure and of divine sovereignty at work through human efforts. The story traces the transformation of a young Jewish woman from a victim of political schemes to a key figure in national salvation, showing how divine grace can operate even within oppressive systems and feelings of abandonment.

The Deposition of Queen Vashti

The story starts with Queen Vashti's deposition. This event highlights the patriarchal power structures of the Persian court and sets the stage for Esther's eventual rise to prominence. King Ahasuerus's order for Vashti to appear before his drunken officials is more than just a royal whim; it represents a serious violation of royal dignity and female honor within ancient Near Eastern cultural norms.

Vashti's refusal to obey the king's summons is an act of principled resistance that goes beyond personal preference. The text shows that she was also hosting her own banquet for the women of the palace (Esther 1:9), indicating her involvement in legitimate royal duties at the time of the king's demand. Her refusal to leave these responsibilities to become a spectacle for drunken courtiers demonstrates both personal integrity and an understanding of the dignity of her position.

The officials' response to Vashti's defiance shows the broader sociopolitical implications of her action. Memucan, one of the king's officials, warned the king that "this deed of the queen will be made known to all women, causing them to look with contempt on their husbands" (Esther 1:16–17). His words reveal the fragility of patriarchal authority when faced with principled resistance. The systemic nature of this concern, reaching to 'all the provinces of King Ahasuerus," indicates that Vashti's act of defiance threatened the empire's core social order.

The deposition of Vashti, while seeming to symbolize the dominance of patriarchal authority, also creates the providential opportunity through which God's redemptive plans will unfold. This initial act of injustice paradoxically serves as the means by which ultimate justice is achieved, highlighting the complex interaction between human sin and divine sovereignty that runs throughout the entire story.

Esther's Entrance into the Royal Court

Esther's entry into the Persian royal court clearly violates personal autonomy and cultural identity, which must be recognized to fully understand the story's theological depth. The king's order for gathering "beautiful young virgins" (Esther 2:2) amounts to state-sanctioned abduction for sexual purposes, a fact that modern readers need to acknowledge to accurately interpret Esther's experience.

Esther's Hebrew name, Hadassah, meaning "myrtle," reflects her original identity within the Jewish community, while her Persian name demonstrates the cultural assimilation imposed on her. This dual naming highlights the broader theme of hidden identity in the story, as Esther must balance her true self with the persona she needs to adopt to survive in the Persian court.

The description of Esther as having both physical beauty and "a beautiful figure" (Esther 2:7) should not hide the traumatic reality of her situation. These women were permanently separated from their families and communities, relying entirely on their ability to please the king sexually. Those who did not satisfy the king's preferences were turned into concubines, never to return to their previous lives or have their own families.

Within this context of systematic exploitation, God's providence begins to reveal itself through seemingly natural circumstances. Esther's positive reception by Hegai (Esther 2:3), the eunuch responsible for preparing the women, serves as the first sign of divine favor operating within an oppressive system. Hegai's provision of better cosmetic treatments, food, and living conditions for Esther shows how God's grace can work through human agents, even within corrupt institutions.

The twelve-month preparation period before meeting the king highlights both the artificial nature of these relationships and the immense pressure on these young women. Six months of oil of myrrh treatment, followed by six months of perfumes and cosmetics (Esther 2:12), created a highly manufactured presentation designed to appeal to royal sensibilities rather than to build a genuine relationship.

Esther's Ascension to Queenship

Esther's eventual selection as queen highlights the connection between personal character, divine guidance, and strategic wisdom. Her choice to follow Hegai's advice instead of insisting on her own preferences shows humility and practical smarts. The text notes that "Esther was admired by all who saw her" (Esther 2:15), using the Hebrew word *ḥēn*, which includes favor, grace, and charm— qualities that go beyond looks to include character and demeanor.

The king's declaration that he "loved Esther more than all the other women" (Esther 2:17) indicates that her appeal went beyond just physical attraction to include qualities of personality and character that set her apart from the other candidates. This genuine affection, even though it developed within a complex power dynamic, forms the emotional foundation that will later enable Esther to influence the king's decisions regarding the Jewish people.

Esther's coronation takes place four years after Vashti's removal, emphasizing both the long process of selection and the time needed for God's redemptive plan to fully develop. The placing of the royal crown on Esther's head stands for more than personal elevation; it represents the appointment of a covenant people's representative at the very center of imperial power.

Divine Hiddenness and Providential Action

The lack of explicit divine references within the book of Esther has sparked extensive scholarly debate about the text's theological purpose and meaning. Ancient translators and scribes grappled with this apparent divine silence, with the Septuagint translators adding extra material that explicitly referenced God's name and actions. Some scholars have identified possible acrostic references to the sacred name (YHWH) within the Hebrew text, suggesting that God's presence was encoded rather than completely absent.

However, the theological significance of Esther's narrative may lie precisely in its demonstration of divine providence working through seemingly natural circumstances. Unlike stories that feature miraculous interventions or prophetic messages, the book of Esther shows how God's sovereignty functions through human choices, political situations, and the interaction of character and chance.

The parallel between Esther's experience and that of Joseph in Egypt supports this providential interpretation. Both stories feature individuals forced out of their communities who eventually gain influence that allows them to save their people from destruction. Joseph's retrospective interpretation of his brothers' actions—"Even though you intended to harm me, God intended it for good, to preserve a multitude of people, as he is doing today," (Genesis 50:20)—applies equally to Esther's situation.

These similar situations reflect the universal human experience of divine absence during times of suffering and uncertainty. Instead of promising constant awareness of God's presence, the story of Esther indicates that divine grace often works beneath the surface of apparent abandonment, acting through circumstances and relationships to fulfill redemptive purposes that only become clear later.

The Old Testament Speaks to the Church

My pastor, Jeff Griffin, Senior Pastor of The Compass Church in Naperville, Illinois, delivered a sermon on October 25, 2020, titled "For Such a Time as This: 'God's Grace." Jeff's sermon addresses a core issue within modern Christianity: the feeling of divine abandonment during times of suffering and uncertainty. His pastoral insights show how Esther's story speaks directly to believers who question God's presence and activity in their lives. Jeff's message goes beyond personal comfort to include broader church-related implications for how the church understands and ministers in times of divine apparent silence.

Jeff's observation that "all of us have experienced the absence of God in our lives" acknowledges a universal human experience that transcends cultural and temporal boundaries. This honest admission serves as a corrective to views that promise constant awareness of divine presence or suggest that faithful believers should never experience spiritual darkness. Instead, Jeff's pastoral wisdom recognizes that seasons of divine hiddenness are normative rather than exceptional, requiring theological frameworks that can sustain faith during extended periods of uncertainty.

Jeff's emphasis on discovering God's presence "behind the scenes" offers a sophisticated understanding of divine providence that operates through natural circumstances rather than miraculous intervention. This perspective challenges contemporary expectations for dramatic divine activity while affirming that God's sovereignty encompasses the ordinary mechanisms of history, relationship, and human decision-making. For Christians struggling with unanswered prayers or unresolved suffering, this framework provides hope without promising immediate resolution.

Jeff's reference to Jack Deere's testimony in *Even in Our Darkness: A Story of Beauty in a Broken Life* demonstrates the pastoral application of Esther's theology to extreme circumstances of loss and trauma. Deere's journey through his father's suicide, his son's suicide, and his wife's attempted suicide represents the kind of comprehensive darkness that challenges conventional religious comfort. Yet Jeff's use of this testimony illustrates how Esther's story provides resources for maintaining faith even within circumstances that seem to contradict divine goodness entirely.

Jeff's conclusion that "in the intersection between providence and obedience, God's grace is always present, inviting us to meet him in the darkest hour of our soul" articulates a mature spirituality that neither minimizes suffering nor abandons hope. This theological framework enables believers to act faithfully within their circumstances while trusting divine sovereignty for outcomes beyond their control.

Jeff's sermon, viewed through Esther's story, highlights several key challenges facing today's church. The experience of divine hiddenness is no longer rare but has become common for many believers living in increasingly secular societies where God's presence is questioned or denied. Esther's story offers a biblical framework for understanding how faith communities can stay true to their identity and mission even when working within hostile or indifferent cultural environments.

The church today finds itself in situations quite similar to Esther's role in the Persian court. Just like Esther, modern Christian communities often work within power structures that are either indifferent or hostile to their core values. The struggle to stay true to authentic faith while effectively engaging with secular institutions reflects Esther's navigation of her dual role as both queen of Persia and member of the covenant community.

Jeff's sermon suggests that the church's current cultural position may itself be providential, positioning believers strategically within secular institutions and communities where they can serve as agents of divine grace.

The concept of being called "for such a time as this" takes on particular significance for Christians who are facing spiritual

317

challenges. Jeff's application suggests that these circumstances may represent opportunities for faithful witness rather than evidence of divine abandonment. Like Esther, the church is called to act courageously within its current context, trusting in divine sovereignty for outcomes that extend beyond immediate circumstances.

Jeff's reference to Deere's experience with multiple family suicides addresses the extreme circumstances that test the limits of conventional religious comfort. Jeff's application suggests that Christians must develop a support system capable of sustaining faith even within circumstances that seem to contradict divine goodness entirely. This requires moving beyond simplistic explanations for suffering toward more sophisticated understandings of how divine grace operates within broken systems and tragic circumstances.

Conclusion

The convergence of Esther's ancient narrative with Jeff's contemporary pastoral insights reveals profound implications for how Christians understand their identity and mission within the current cultural moment. The book of Esther speaks directly to Christians who live in an increasingly secular world where God's presence is questioned, denied, or ignored by the broader culture.

The sermon's emphasis on providence operating through natural circumstances rather than miraculous intervention offers Christians a sustainable approach to faith that neither depends upon dramatic supernatural experiences nor reduces divine activity to mere human effort. This balanced perspective enables congregations to recognize and cooperate with God's activity in the world while maintaining realistic expectations about how such activity typically manifests.

CHAPTER 32

ESTHER: FOR SUCH A TIME AS THIS – "OUR MISSION"

Human beings were created in God's image to live in fellowship with him. This divine design explains why we have an innate need for a relationship with our Creator, a fundamental longing to connect with God. Yet God often works invisibly in our world, which can make him seem absent precisely when we need him most.

The paradox of faith is that God is never truly absent, even when he seems distant. Scripture assures us, "When you search for me, you will find me; if you seek me with all your heart, I will let you find me, says the Lord" (Jeremiah 29:13–14). Only those who genuinely seek will discover his presence.

Esther's Story: Divine Providence in Difficult Circumstances

Esther's life in Persia exemplified profound difficulty and displacement. As a young Jewish woman, she was forcibly taken from her family to live in the king's palace, not by choice, but to serve the king's pleasure with the possibility of becoming queen if she found favor with him.

Esther embodied what we might call "the other," someone culturally and socially different from the dominant society. She carried multiple layers of otherness: she was Jewish in a Persian land, a woman in a patriarchal system, and an orphan without parents. Her cousin Mordecai had adopted her, but she remained fundamentally displaced from her community and her heritage.

In the isolation of the royal harem, Esther likely felt God's distance acutely. This sense of divine hiddenness may explain why God's name never appears in the book of Esther; it reflects the human experience of God's apparent absence during our darkest moments.

Yet the central message of Esther's story is God's providence. While Esther may have assumed God was unaware of her situation, he was actively orchestrating events behind the scenes. God was preparing her for a specific purpose, working through circumstances to position her as an instrument of salvation for her people.

The Ministry of Mordecai

God demonstrates his providence by working through human relationships. People become the channels through which God expresses his presence and love to others. For Esther, Mordecai served as God's chosen vessel to provide what she needed most.

Mordecai lived in Susa, the Persian capital, and his genealogy reveals important connections to Israel's history. As described in Esther 2:5–6, he was "a Jew in the citadel of Susa whose name was Mordecai, son of Jair son of Shimei son of Kish, a Benjaminite." His lineage connected him to King Saul's family—Kish was Saul's father, and Shimei belonged to Saul's clan.

This genealogical detail is intentional, setting up the conflict between Mordecai and Haman, who descended from Agag, the Amalekite king whom Saul had defeated. The author uses this background to show how ancient conflicts play out in new generations.

Mordecai's name, which comes from the Babylonian god Marduk, suggests he may have taken a foreign name for court service, similar to how Daniel and his friends received Babylonian names. This change illustrates how God's people sometimes adapt to foreign cultures while staying true to their faith.

God reached Esther through Mordecai in three distinct ways: through love, comfort, and wise counsel. Mordecai's adoption of Esther demonstrates how God shows love through human relationships. When Esther's parents died (according to tradition, her father died while her mother was pregnant, and her mother died in childbirth), Mordecai stepped in to raise her as his own daughter.

Though no Old Testament law mandated such adoption, the practice was common in the ancient Near East. Mordecai's motivation went beyond legal obligation; God's love moved him to care for an orphaned child. As Esther 2:7 records: "Mordecai had brought up Hadassah, that is Esther, his cousin, for she had neither father nor mother; the girl was fair and beautiful, and when her father and her mother died, Mordecai adopted her as his own daughter."

This reflects our calling as Christians. We become God's means of expressing his love to others, as 1 John 4:12 reminds us: "No one has ever seen God; if we love one another, God lives in us, and his love is perfected in us." When we love people, we make God's love real in their lives.

Despite the restrictions around the royal harem, Mordecai found ways to stay in touch with Esther. Esther 2:11 tells us: "Every day Mordecai would walk around in front of the court of the harem, to learn how Esther was and how she fared."

Mordecai's daily presence demonstrated that he cared deeply. He likely established a relationship with Hegai, the eunuch in charge of the harem, which could have allowed him supervised visits with Esther. Through these visits, he offered encouragement and emotional support during her frightening experience.

Esther found comfort knowing her adoptive father cared about her welfare and remained present in her crisis. Mordecai became the channel through which God provided comfort during her isolation and uncertainty.

This models our role in others' lives. As 2 Corinthians 1:3–4 explains, God "comforts us in all our troubles, so that we can comfort those in any trouble with the comfort we ourselves have received from God." We become portals of divine comfort for people experiencing pain and struggle.

Mordecai's counsel proved crucial for God's larger purposes. He advised Esther to keep her Jewish identity secret when she entered the palace, wisdom she faithfully followed. Esther 2:20 notes: "But

Esther had kept secret her family background and nationality just as Mordecai had told her to do, for she continued to follow Mordecai's instructions as she had done when he was bringing her up."

Even after becoming queen, Esther continued to be obedient to Mordecai's guidance. This obedience positioned her strategically for the moment when she would need to advocate for her people's survival. What seemed like simple, practical advice became part of God's providential plan.

God continues to speak through people who offer wisdom to others. As 1 Peter 4:11 reminds us, "If anyone speaks, he should do it as one speaking the very words of God." When we provide godly counsel to those in need, we become vessels for divine guidance.

Our Mission: Being God's Presence for Others

Esther's story reveals a fundamental truth about how God operates in the world. While he could act directly, he chooses to communicate his love, comfort, and wisdom through people dedicated to being vessels of blessing to others.

This is our mission in the world: to serve as channels through which God reaches people in their times of need. Like Mordecai, we can be the means by which others experience God's presence, even when he seems absent. Through our love, comfort, and wisdom, we make the invisible God visible to those who desperately need to encounter him.

When we accept this calling, we participate in God's ongoing work of providence, becoming part of his plan to bring hope and salvation to people who, like Esther, may feel out of place, alone, or forgotten. In doing so, we realize that we, too, have been placed "for such a time as this."

The Old Testament Speaks to the Church

My pastor. Jeff Griffin, Senior Pastor of The Compass Church in Naperville, Illinois, preached a sermon on November 1, 2020, titled "Esther: For Such a Time as This – Our Mission."

Jeff concluded his message with a powerful dual application that captures the reciprocal nature of God's work through human relationships. He challenged the congregation to embrace two complementary perspectives on how God's providence operates in our daily lives.

First, Jeff encouraged us to actively become doorways, portals through which God can extend his love and comfort to others. This calling goes beyond passive availability; it requires intentionally positioning ourselves as conduits of divine grace. Just as Mordecai served as God's chosen vessel to reach Esther in her isolation and fear, we are called to be the means by which God touches the lives of people around us.

This doorway ministry happens in ordinary moments: when we listen to a friend's struggles, offer practical help to a neighbor in need, or speak words of encouragement to someone facing difficult circumstances. We become portals when we allow God's love within us to flow outward to others, making his invisible presence tangible and real in their experience.

The metaphor of a doorway is especially powerful because it signifies both access and purpose. A doorway provides a means to move from one space to another, and when we serve as spiritual doorways, we help people transition from isolation to connection, from despair to hope, and from feeling abandoned by God to experiencing his care.

Equally important, Jeff urged us to develop sensitivity to when God is using others to speak to us. This requires humility and spiritual discernment, the recognition that God often delivers his guidance, comfort, and love through the people he places in our lives.

God's providence feels more real and personal when we realize he uses spiritual people to meet our needs. This understanding changes how we see advice from mentors, comfort from friends, and wisdom from those who have traveled similar paths. Instead of thinking of these as just human connections, we begin to see them as divine moments when God reaches out to us through his chosen vessels.

This perspective requires us to listen more carefully to the voices around us, particularly those who demonstrate godly character and wisdom. It means being alert to the possibility that God might be speaking through a pastor's sermon, a friend's timely phone call, a colleague's unexpected kindness, or even a stranger's words of encouragement.

Jeff's dual application reveals the reciprocal nature of God's work through human relationships. We are simultaneously called to be vessels through whom God works and recipients of God's work through others. This creates a beautiful cycle of divine providence where the same community of faith serves both as ministers and as those being ministered to.

Sometimes we find ourselves in Mordecai's position, offering love, comfort, and wisdom to someone in need. Other times, we are like Esther, isolated and uncertain, needing God to reach us through others' care. Both roles are vital to understanding how God's providence works within the community of faith.

Jeff's sermon reminds us that we live in our own "such a time as this" moment. Just as Esther was strategically positioned for her generation's crisis, we are placed in our current circumstances, relationships, and communities with a divine purpose. The question is whether we will recognize and embrace our role as both doorways for God's work and recipients of his providence through others.

The beauty of this calling is that it makes every relationship potentially sacred and every interaction a possible encounter with divine providence. When we live with this awareness, we begin to see our ordinary lives as part of God's extraordinary plan to bring his presence, love, and comfort to a world that desperately needs to experience him.

CHAPTER 33

ESTHER: FOR SUCH A TIME AS THIS – "OUR NIGHTMARE"

The book of Esther tells a powerful story of commitment: Mordecai's unwavering dedication to his principles and Esther's courageous loyalty to her people. At its heart, this narrative explores a fundamental question: What price must one pay to live with genuine commitment to a righteous cause? As we examine this ancient account, we discover that genuine commitment often demands extraordinary sacrifice.

The Rise of Haman the Agagite

After the failed assassination attempt against King Ahasuerus (Esther 2:21–23), an unexpected promotion altered history's course. Instead of honoring Mordecai, who uncovered the plot and saved the king, Ahasuerus promoted Haman, son of Hammedatha the Agagite, to the highest rank in the kingdom (Esther 3:1). The text does not clarify this baffling choice. Haman had done no notable service, yet suddenly he was second only to the king in power and authority.

Haman's ancestry carried deep significance. As an Agagite, he descended from Agag, the Amalekite king whom Samuel had executed centuries earlier after King Saul's incomplete obedience to God's command (1 Samuel 15:32–33). The Amalekites had been Israel's ancient enemies since the exodus from Egypt, making Haman's elevation particularly ominous for the Jewish population scattered throughout the Persian Empire.

With his new position came a royal decree: all servants and officials were required to kneel and bow before Haman, their faces to the ground. This command would soon spark a conflict that could threaten the survival of an entire people.

Mordecai's Stand

Among all who served in the king's court, only Mordecai refused to bow. Day after day, he remained standing while others prostrated themselves before Haman. The biblical text states simply that Mordecai would not kneel "because he was a Jew," but this explanation encompasses layers of meaning.

Mordecai's refusal likely stemmed from multiple convictions. As a descendant of those who had suffered under Amalekite oppression, he understood the historical enmity between their peoples. More fundamentally, as a faithful Jew, Mordecai may have viewed the required obeisance as crossing the line from civil respect into worship, something reserved for God alone. The commandment against bowing to idols echoed in his conscience, much as it had for Shadrach, Meshach, and Abednego when they faced Nebuchadnezzar's golden image (Daniel 3:1–30).

Mordecai's commitment to his principles had been forged through years of exile. Like many Jews, he had chosen to remain in Persia rather than return to the devastated homeland after Cyrus's decree. Life in exile offered comfort and opportunity. Jews had established businesses, worked in agriculture, and even gained positions in the royal court. Archaeological evidence from cuneiform tablets reveals that Jews in Susa held significant roles as royal courtiers and interacted with Babylonian economic elites. Yet despite this integration into Persian society, Mordecai maintained his distinct identity and convictions.

The Nightmare Begins

When the king's servants repeatedly questioned Mordecai's disobedience, he revealed his Jewish identity to explain his refusal. This information quickly reached Haman, who erupted in fury. But Haman's rage extended far beyond one man's defiance; he saw an opportunity to address what he perceived as a larger problem.

Approaching King Ahasuerus, Haman painted the Jewish people as a dangerous threat to imperial unity. "There is a certain people scattered and separated among the peoples in all the provinces of your kingdom; their laws are different from those of every other people, and they do not keep the king's laws, so that it is not appropriate for the king to tolerate them" (Esther 3:8).

To demonstrate his commitment to this "solution," Haman offered a remarkable sum—ten thousand talents of silver, equivalent to 375 tons—to finance the extermination. This amount surpassed the annual tribute of an entire Persian province, revealing both Haman's personal wealth and the extent of his hatred. The king, possibly seeing this as a way to solve an administrative problem while boosting the royal treasury, agreed. He removed his signet ring and handed it to Haman, effectively giving him free rein to carry out genocide.

The Weight of Commitment

When news of the decree reached Mordecai, he was devastated. Tearing his clothes and covering himself with sackcloth and ashes, he wandered through Susa's streets, crying out in anguish. His stand on principle had triggered a holocaust that would consume every Jewish man, woman, and child in the empire.

This moment reveals the heavy burden that commitment can impose. Mordecai chose to stand by his convictions rather than compromise, but his choice had consequences that reached beyond his own life. The nightmare he now faced, the systematic destruction of his people, stemmed directly from his refusal to bow.

Yet this crisis also set the stage for God's deliverance through Esther, revealing how individual acts of faithfulness, however costly, can become part of a larger divine purpose. Mordecai's commitment, though it seemed to endanger his people, would ultimately position them for salvation.

The story of Esther reminds us that genuine commitment often leads us into darkness before dawn, through valleys of shadow before reaching the mountaintop. The question remains for each of us: When faced with the choice between compromise and conviction, what price are we willing to pay to stay faithful to what we know is right?

The Old Testament Speaks to the Church

This timeless message from the book of Esther was powerfully proclaimed by my pastor, Jeff Griffin, Senior Pastor of The Compass Church in Naperville, Illinois, in his sermon "Esther: For Such a Time as This – Our Nightmare" on November 8, 2020. Jeff's insights illuminate how Mordecai's ancient struggle speaks directly to contemporary believers facing their own moments of testing.

The Pattern of Faithful Resistance

Jeff drew a compelling parallel between Mordecai's refusal to bow before Haman and the courageous stand of Shadrach, Meshach, and Abednego before Nebuchadnezzar's golden image. Both stories reveal the same essential truth: genuine faith sometimes requires us to stand alone against overwhelming pressure to compromise.

When faced with the blazing furnace, Daniel's three friends declared with remarkable confidence: "If our God whom we serve is able to deliver us from the furnace of blazing fire and out of your hand, O king, let him deliver us. But if not, be it known to you, O king, that we will not serve your gods and we will not worship the golden statue that you have set up" (Daniel 3:17–18). Their words resonate through the centuries as a lesson in commitment; they trusted God's power to save them, yet stayed equally faithful even if salvation did not come.

This same trust in divine providence sustained Mordecai through his darkest hour. Even as he mourned the death decree hanging over his people, he believed God would raise help from somewhere (Esther 4:14). His faith was not based on guaranteed outcomes but on the character of a faithful God who works through human vessels committed to his purposes.

Jeff identified the biggest threat to Christian commitment: not persecution from outside, but indifference from within. While external pressures can actually strengthen faith, spiritual apathy gradually weakens our devotion to Christ. The comfortable exile many Jews experienced in Persia reflects the easy compromise that can define modern Christianity: maintaining cultural identity while avoiding the costly demands of true discipleship.

Authentic Christian living demands our best effort, our most profound devotion, and sometimes our ultimate sacrifice. Like Mordecai, we must be prepared to stand for our convictions even when the cost seems overwhelming. The Christian life should pulse with devotion to Christ, marked by a willingness to sacrifice comfort, security, and even one's own life for God's cause in the world.

Jeff concluded his message by sharing the remarkable journey of Nik Ripken, whose story in *The Insanity of God: A True Story of Faith Resurrected* demonstrates how a commitment to Christ plays out in the world's most challenging contexts. After six grueling years of relief work in Somalia, Ripken and his wife faced a crisis of faith that many believers encounter when God's goodness seems absent from human suffering.

Ripken's haunting questions resonate with anyone who has wrestled with faith in dark circumstances: "Does the gospel work anywhere when it is really a hard place? How does faith survive, let alone flourish in a place like the Middle East? How can good truly overcome such evil? How do you maintain hope when all is darkness around you?"

The Ripkens' spiritual and emotional odyssey, detailed in their book, reveals that authentic faith does not guarantee easy answers or comfortable circumstances. Like Mordecai facing the nightmare of genocide, like Daniel's friends facing the furnace, committed believers often find themselves in situations where faithfulness appears to lead toward destruction rather than deliverance.

Yet it is precisely in these moments that genuine commitment proves its worth. Whether in ancient Persia or modern Somalia, whether facing royal decrees or contemporary challenges, the call remains the same: Will we bow to the pressures around us, or will we stand firm in our devotion to Christ, trusting his providence even when we cannot see his plan?

The book of Esther teaches us that our individual acts of faithfulness, however costly they may seem, become part of God's larger purpose for his people. Mordecai's refusal to bow did not just preserve his personal integrity; it positioned an entire nation for divine deliverance. Our commitment to Christ today may seem small in the face of overwhelming challenges, but God specializes in using faithful individuals to accomplish his extraordinary purposes.

The question that Jeff's sermon leaves with us is profoundly personal: In our own "such a time as this," will we choose the path of comfortable compromise or costly commitment? The story of Esther suggests that our answer to this question may determine not only our own spiritual destiny, but the welfare of those God has placed in our sphere of influence.

CHAPTER 34

ESTHER: FOR SUCH A TIME AS THIS – "OUR DECISION"

The Book of Esther reveals a profound truth about how God works in the world, even when his name is never mentioned. At its heart lies the concept of divine providence, God's active involvement in accomplishing his purposes through human agents who choose to act courageously in pivotal moments.

Understanding Divine Providence

Providence describes how God orchestrates events to fulfill his purposes in the world. John Goldingay, in his work *Old Testament Theology: Israel's Gospel*, explains that "God certainly had an aim, a vision, some goals, and sometimes formulates a plan for a particular context, but works out a purpose in the world in interaction with the human beings who are designed to be key to the fulfilling of those goals" (Goldingay 2003:60). During the Persian exile, when the Jewish people faced complete annihilation, God's chosen instrument of deliverance was an unlikely candidate: a young Jewish woman named Esther.

Though God's name never appears in the narrative, his providential hand is unmistakable throughout. Consider the remarkable chain of events: Esther's placement in Ahasuerus' palace, her favor with the eunuch overseeing the harem, her selection as queen, Mordecai's timely discovery of an assassination plot, and countless other "coincidences" that positioned her to save her people. Each event, seemingly independent, wove together in a divine tapestry of deliverance.

Esther's journey from an orphaned girl to Persian queen represents more than personal success; it illustrates God's pattern of blessing people so they can, in turn, bless others. Her royal position was not only for herself but to safeguard God's people and his salvation plan for humanity (2 Corinthians 5:19).

While some might see these events as fate or coincidence, the biblical worldview acknowledges the hand of God, who created the universe and still cares for his creation and his people. God's providential work guarantees the survival of his people because their preservation is vital to his plan of reconciliation with humanity.

The Looming Threat

The crisis began with a clash of loyalties. When King Ahasuerus elevated Haman to high office and commanded all court officials to bow before him, Mordecai faced an impossible choice. As a devout Jew, he would bow only before God, a conviction that would cost him dearly.

Haman's fury at Mordecai's refusal went far beyond personal offense. In his rage, he conceived a genocidal plot that would eliminate not just Mordecai, but every Jewish man, woman, and child throughout the Persian Empire. His manipulation of King Ahasuerus was masterful and malicious, painting the Jews as a threat to imperial unity and securing royal approval for their extermination.

The royal decree was chilling in its scope: "to wipe out, kill, and destroy all the Jews—young and old, women and children—on a single day, the thirteenth day of the twelfth month, the month of Adar. Their possessions were also to be seized" (Esther 3:13). Sealed with the king's ring and bearing his authority, this edict seemed irreversible and absolute.

Mordecai's Desperate Appeal

News of the decree shattered the Jewish community. Mordecai tore his clothes, donned sackcloth and ashes, and mourned publicly, a demonstration of grief that echoed throughout the provinces as Jews everywhere fasted and lamented their fate. Though the text does not explicitly mention prayer, desperate appeals to God traditionally accompanied these acts of mourning.

When Esther learned of Mordecai's distress from her servants, she was very troubled. Her first response, sending clothes to replace his sackcloth, showed her limited understanding of how serious the situation was. When Mordecai refused her gift, she sent Hathach, a trusted eunuch, to find out what was troubling her adoptive father (Esther 4:5–10).

Mordecai's message to Esther was urgent and clear. He detailed Haman's horrific plan, included a copy of the royal edict, and made a direct plea: she must go to the king, beg for mercy, and plead for her people's lives. The fate of an entire nation rested on her shoulders.

Esther's Initial Hesitation

Esther's response reveals the dangerous reality of her position. She reminded Mordecai of Persian law: anyone who approached the king uninvited faced death unless the king extended his golden scepter. Even as queen, she was not exempt from this rule. Her words carried the weight of genuine fear: "I myself have not been called to come in to the king for thirty days" (Esther 4:11).

Several factors likely influenced her hesitation. Access to the king was tightly controlled, possibly through advisers like Haman himself. The king's absence from her chambers for thirty days indicated their relationship was more formal than personal. Most importantly, approaching the king would require revealing her Jewish identity, something Mordecai had previously warned her to hide.

These were not excuses but legitimate concerns about a course of action that could result in her immediate execution without accomplishing anything for her people.

Mordecai's Response

Mordecai's response to Esther's hesitation was both a gentle rebuke and a prophetic challenge. He demolished her illusion of safety: "Do not think that in the king's palace you will escape any more than all the other Jews" (Esther 4:13). Her royal position offered no protection from Haman's comprehensive extermination order.

Then came his most famous words: "For if you remain silent at this time, relief and deliverance for the Jews will arise from another place, but you and your father's family will perish. Who knows, perhaps you have come to your royal position for such a time as this" (Esther 4:14 NIV). He reminded her that she was blessed not for her own benefit; she was blessed to bless others (Chataira, 2020: 70–75).

This statement reveals Mordecai's deep faith in God's providence. John Wiebe wrote, "When Mordecai appears to affirm to Esther that relief and deliverance will arise for the Jews from another place and that perhaps it was for the purpose of saving her people that Esther had attained royal status, the reader detects a veiled reference to God's providence working behind the scenes" (Wiebe, 1991:409). Though scholars debate whether this refers to divine intervention, another Jewish leader, or Jewish resistance, Mordecai's confidence in ultimate deliverance reflects his trust in God's faithfulness to his covenant people.

Some scholars interpret Mordecai's words as a question rather than a statement: "Will relief and deliverance arise for the Jews from another place?" This rendering suggests that Esther might be the only possible source of salvation, adding even greater urgency to his appeal (Wiebe, 1991:413).

Regardless of the interpretation, Mordecai's message was clear: Esther's position was not accidental but providential. She had been placed in the palace "for such a time as this," to serve as God's instrument of deliverance at the moment of her people's greatest need.

Esther's Transformation

Mordecai's words sparked a deep change in Esther. The obedient young woman who had always followed others' commands stepped into her role as a leader and decision-maker. Her response showed courage, wisdom, and faith: "Go, gather all the Jews in

Susa and fast for me. Do not eat or drink for three days, night or day. I and my maids will fast as you do. When this is done, I will go to the king, even though it is against the law. And if I perish, I perish" (Esther 4:16).

This response reveals several crucial elements of Esther's character development. First, she took command—notice that she gave orders to Mordecai rather than receiving them. As Bush observes, "This is a decisive turning point in Esther's development. Heretofore, though queen, she was nevertheless under Mordecai's authority as his ward. Now she is the one who sets the conditions and gives the commands" (Bush 2018:620).

Second, she understood the spiritual dimensions of her mission. The three-day fast was not merely preparation but a recognition that human effort alone would be insufficient. She needed divine intervention and favor.

Third, she demonstrated remarkable courage with her declaration, "If I perish, I perish." This was not fatalism but faith, a willingness to risk everything for her people's survival.

The Power of Providential Purpose

Esther's story challenges us to recognize how God works through ordinary people in extraordinary circumstances. Her transformation from a reluctant queen to a courageous advocate illustrates several timeless principles.

Providence positions us for purpose. Esther's elevation to queen was not random but purposeful. God places people in specific positions to accomplish his will at crucial moments in history.

Blessing carries responsibility. Esther's royal position was a blessing, but it came with the responsibility to use her influence for the benefit of others, not merely her own comfort and security.

Courage requires choice. Esther had to choose between personal safety and her people's survival. Her decision to act courageously, despite the risks, made her an instrument of divine deliverance.

Faith acts despite uncertainty. Esther could not guarantee the outcome of her appeal to the king, but she acted in faith, trusting that God would honor her courageous obedience.

The Old Testament Speaks to the Church

My pastor, Jeff Griffin, Senior Pastor of The Compass Church in Naperville, Illinois, delivered a sermon on November 15, 2020, titled "Esther: For Such a Time as This – 'Our Decision,'" highlighting strong connections between Esther's decision and the choices Christians face today. His sermon focused on a key truth: Esther deliberately chose to become God's agent of salvation, acknowledging divine providence in her placement in the palace and willingly risking her life to save many, just as Jesus gave his life so that many could be saved.

Jeff illustrated this principle with a remarkable story from his own congregation. A woman in his church held a highly influential position in the business world with substantial compensation. Yet she made a decision that shocked her colleagues and friends: she quit her lucrative job because she believed God had abundantly blessed her not for her own comfort, but to bless others.

Her decision was comprehensive and purposeful. She chose to bless orphans by providing them with a strong Christian home through adoption and foster care. She decided to bless her local church by stepping into leadership roles where her business expertise could strengthen ministry effectiveness. She became a consultant, sharing her professional experience with other churches to help them operate more effectively and reach more people for Christ.

This modern-day Esther understood what Jeff emphasized: Christians are called to become God's agents of blessing to others, serving as distributors of divine favor rather than merely recipients.

Living as Agents of Divine Blessing

The book of Esther reminds us that God's providence often works through human decisions and actions. When faced with "such a time as this," moments that call for courage, sacrifice, and faith, we have the chance to become instruments of God's purposes in the world. Like Esther, we may find that our positions, relationships, and circumstances are not accidental but providential, preparing us to serve God's kingdom when the moment calls for it.

Jeff's challenge resonates across the centuries, from Esther's palace to our present moment: How can we use the blessings God has given us to bless others? This question demands honest self-reflection about our resources, relationships, and opportunities.

Consider your own "palace"—the positions, privileges, and platforms God has placed in your life:

Your Professional Influence: Like the businesswoman Jeff mentioned in his sermon, your career may be more than a means of personal provision. It could be your platform for kingdom impact. What expertise, connections, or resources has God entrusted to you that could benefit others?

Your Relational Networks: Esther's relationship with the king became the pathway for her people's deliverance. What relationships has God given you that could become channels of his blessing to others?

Your Life Experiences: Both your triumphs and trials have prepared you to support others facing similar situations. How can your journey become a source of hope and encouragement for someone walking a difficult path?

Your Material Resources: Every financial blessing, from modest means to abundant wealth, carries the responsibility to be a conduit of God's provision to others in need.

The woman in Jeff's story made a bold decision, but not every calling requires leaving a career. Sometimes God calls us to flourish where we are planted, using our current positions as mission fields. The key is recognizing that whatever blessings we receive—talents, opportunities, resources, relationships—are not accidents but appointments that place us to serve God's purposes in our generation.

The Choice Before Us

Esther's declaration, "If I perish, I perish," echoes through history as a testament to the power of surrendering personal security for a greater cause. Her story, amplified by Jeff's contemporary application, challenges us to examine our own lives with fresh urgency:

What positions has God given you? What influence do you possess? What resources have been placed in your hands? And when "such a time as this" arrives—when God presents opportunities to bless others through the blessings he has given you—will you have the courage to act?

The choice Esther faced in the Persian palace is the same choice we face today: Will we use our blessings primarily for our own comfort and security, or will we risk something significant to become God's agents of blessing to others? Will we recognize that our "for such a time as this" moment might not involve saving an entire nation, but it could include saving a marriage, rescuing a child, strengthening a church, or meeting a desperate need in someone's life?

Like Esther, we must decide. The decision to become distributors of God's blessings rather than merely collectors of them is not a one-time choice but a daily surrender, a continuous commitment to see our lives through the lens of divine providence and purpose.

Jeff's question remains: "How will you be used by God to bless others?" Your answer to that question could determine not only your own spiritual legacy but also the eternal impact you will have on the lives God has strategically placed within your sphere of influence.

The palace doors are open. The king is waiting. The choice is yours.

CHAPTER 35

ESTHER: FOR SUCH A TIME AS THIS — "GOD'S JUSTICE"

Throughout Scripture, God demonstrates a deep commitment to justice. The psalmist describes God as a "lover of justice" (Psalm 99:4), while the prophet Isaiah confirms this divine trait: "For I the LORD love justice" (Isaiah 61:8). This is not just an abstract quality but an active dedication—God steps into human affairs to oppose injustice and judge evil by his righteous standards.

Angelika Berlejung emphasizes this theological necessity: "Divine judgment over each individual is a theological necessity. It is the only way that the power and justice of God are finally proven: justice is established only if the disturbed order is re-established through punishment of sinners and the salvation of the righteous" (2015:287). The book of Esther provides a compelling narrative demonstration of this divine justice in action.

A Queen's Courage

When Mordecai revealed Haman's genocidal plot against the Jewish people, he urged his adopted daughter Esther to intercede with King Ahasuerus. Initially hesitant due to the mortal danger of approaching the king uninvited, Esther faced Mordecai's profound challenge: "Perhaps you were made queen for just such a time as this?" (Esther 4:14 NLT).

This moment of decision would define not only Esther's legacy but also demonstrate God's providential justice. Esther's response revealed both wisdom and courage. She called for a three-day fast among all Jews in the empire, recognizing that divine intervention required divine preparation. On the third day, she donned her royal robes—significantly, not as a mere wife or concubine, but as the Queen of Persia—and approached the throne room with the words, "If I perish, I perish" (Esther 4:16).

The king's favorable reception and extension of the golden scepter marked the first step in God's unfolding justice. Rather than making an immediate plea, Esther demonstrated remarkable strategic wisdom by inviting both the king and Haman to a banquet. The Hebrew text's ambiguity about whether this banquet was prepared for the king, for Haman, or for both, suggests Esther's careful diplomacy in handling this delicate situation.

When offered up to half the kingdom, Esther's humble request for a second banquet revealed her understanding that timing and preparation were crucial. Her response, "Tomorrow I will answer the king's question" (Esther 5:8), set the stage for God's justice to unfold.

The Reversal of Fortune: Haman's Downfall

Haman's character serves as a study in pride leading to destruction. Despite his elevation to honor at the queen's table, his rage at Mordecai's continued refusal to bow consumed him. His boasting to family and friends about his wealth, numerous sons, governmental position, and unique privilege of dining with royalty revealed a man intoxicated by his own importance.

The construction of a seventy-five-foot gallows intended for Mordecai's public execution demonstrates the extremes of Haman's hatred. Yet this very instrument would become the means of his own demise, a perfect example of divine justice turning the perpetrator's evil intentions back upon him.

The king's sleepless night proved pivotal. As court records were read aloud, the oversight of Mordecai's unrewarded service for saving the king's life came to light. In a moment of exquisite irony, Haman arrived at court that very morning, intending to request Mordecai's execution, only to be commanded to honor the man he sought to destroy.

Haman's detailed suggestions for honoring someone he assumed to be himself, royal robes, the king's horse, a crown, and a public parade with proclamation, became the very honors he was forced to bestow upon his enemy. The humiliation of parading Mordecai through the city while proclaiming, "This is what is done for the man whom the king wishes to honor," left Haman returning home "mourning and with his head covered" (Esther 6:12).

Justice Revealed

At the second banquet, Esther finally revealed both her Jewish identity and Haman's treacherous plot. Her words carried both personal appeal and universal principle: "Spare my life. That is my request. And spare the lives of my people . . . we have been sold so that we can be wiped out, killed, and destroyed" (Esther 7:3–4).

The king's immediate outrage —"Who is this person? Where is the person who has dared to do this?"—demonstrated that even pagan rulers can recognize fundamental injustice. Esther's identification of "this wicked man Haman" as their "vicious enemy" sealed Haman's fate.

The Old Testament Speaks to the Church

My pastor, Jeff Griffin, Senior Pastor of The Compass Church in Naperville, Illinois preached a sermon on November 22, 2020 titled "Esther: For Such a Time as This – 'God's Justice.'" This chapter is based on Jeff's sermon.

Jeff's sermon illuminated a profound truth about divine justice through the Esther narrative. While human legal systems operate under the maxim that "justice delayed is justice denied," God's justice operates on a different timeline, one that ultimately proves both perfect in timing and comprehensive in scope.

The situation appeared desperate: evil was prospering, Haman's genocidal plot was advancing, and untold tragedy seemed inevitable for God's people. Yet as Walter Brueggemann observes, when God acts as judge, he "does indeed, enact justice, but it is a justice that is demanding, fierce, and uncompromising" (2005:248). In Esther's account, this divine justice manifests as what Jeff terms "poetic justice"—a complete and artistically perfect reversal that transforms every element of Haman's evil into blessing for those he sought to destroy.

Jeff identified five specific reversals that demonstrate the comprehensive nature of God's poetic justice:

First, the Parade of Public Honor: Haman's elaborate fantasy of royal recognition—riding the king's horse, wearing royal robes, and being proclaimed throughout the city—was transferred entirely to Mordecai. The very man Haman plotted to kill received the exact honors Haman coveted for himself, while Haman was forced to serve as the herald of his enemy's exaltation.

Second, the Instrument of Execution: The seventy-five-foot gallows Haman specifically constructed for Mordecai's public impalement became the instrument of his own death. The weapon fashioned for genocide became the tool of justice, demonstrating how God can turn the schemes of the wicked back upon themselves.

Third, the Transfer of Wealth: All of Haman's possessions, the very wealth he had boasted about to his family and friends as evidence of divine blessing, were confiscated and given to Queen Esther, who placed them under Mordecai's stewardship. The oppressor's resources became the foundation for the oppressed people's restoration.

Fourth, the Symbol of Ultimate Authority: The king's signet ring, which had empowered Haman to issue the death decree against all Jews throughout the empire, was removed from his finger and given to Mordecai. The same authority that had been wielded for destruction was now employed for protection and deliverance.

Fifth, the Position of Governmental Power: Haman's exalted rank as second in the kingdom was stripped away and transferred to Mordecai. The position that had been used to advance personal vendettas and ethnic hatred was now occupied by one who would "work for the good of his people and speak up for the welfare of all the Jews" (Esther 10:3).

This five-fold reversal reveals the comprehensive nature of divine justice. God does not merely punish evil; he transforms every aspect of the oppressor's advantage into blessing for the oppressed. As Jeff emphasized, this demonstrates that God is indeed "a God of justice," fulfilling Paul's promise: "God is just: He will pay back trouble to those who trouble you and give relief to you who are troubled, and to us as well. This will happen when the Lord Jesus is revealed from heaven in blazing fire with his powerful angels" (2 Thessalonians 1:6-7).

God's justice extends beyond punishment to restoration. The reversal of fortunes was complete: Haman's property transferred to Esther, his position to Mordecai, and his power transformed into protection for the Jewish people. Mordecai's elevation to second in the kingdom, his royal robes of "blue and white, with a great golden crown and a mantle of fine linen and purple" (Esther 8:15), symbolized not just personal vindication but divine justice made visible.

The new decree authorizing Jewish self-defense turned potential victims into victors. The establishment of Purim as a perpetual celebration ensured that this demonstration of God's justice would be remembered throughout generations.

Jeff's sermon concludes with a powerful challenge drawn from the final description of Mordecai's legacy: "Mordecai the Jew was second in rank to King Ahasuerus, preeminent among the Jews, and held in high esteem by his many fellow Jews, because he worked for the good of his people and spoke up for the welfare of all the Jews" (Esther 10:3). This verse provides a blueprint for how God's people can serve as agents of divine justice in their own contexts.

Working for the Good of Others: Mordecai's rise to power did not corrupt him or cause him to forget his people's needs. Instead, he used his position to serve their interests. This encourages contemporary Christians to see their roles, whether in business, education, healthcare, government, or community leadership, as chances to promote the well-being of others rather than pursue personal gain.

Speaking Up for the Vulnerable: The phrase "spoke up for the welfare of all the Jews" reveals Mordecai's commitment to advocacy. He did not remain silent when others faced injustice, even when speaking up might have been costly or uncomfortable. Modern believers are similarly called to use their voices on behalf of those who cannot advocate for themselves—the marginalized, the oppressed, and the voiceless in society.

Maintaining Identity While Serving: Significantly, the text identifies Mordecai as "the Jew" even while serving as second-in-command to a pagan king. He never compromised his core identity or convictions for political advancement. This demonstrates that Christians can serve as agents of justice in secular contexts without abandoning their faith commitments.

The Esther narrative challenges every believer to consider Mordecai's haunting question to his adopted daughter: "Who knows but that you have come to your royal position for such a time as this?" (Esther 4:14). Jeff's application suggests that God continues to position his people strategically throughout society, not for personal comfort or advancement, but to serve as instruments of his justice in a world marked by oppression and inequality.

Whether we find ourselves in positions of obvious influence or in seemingly ordinary circumstances, the call remains the same: to work for the good of others, speak up for those who face injustice, and trust that the God who orchestrated Esther and Mordecai's story continues to work through his people to accomplish his purposes of justice and redemption.

Conclusion

The book of Esther shows that although God's justice might seem delayed, it is never denied. Even though God's name is not directly mentioned in the text, his providential hand guides every event. The timing of Esther's rise to queenship, the king's insomnia, the reading of court records, and even Haman's presence at the critical moment all reveal divine orchestration.

Esther's story provides profound assurance that God sees injustice, cares about his people's suffering, and will ultimately vindicate the righteous while judging the wicked. As Paul reminds us, "God is just: He will pay back trouble to those who trouble you and give relief to you who are troubled, and to us as well. This will happen when the Lord Jesus is revealed from heaven in blazing fire with his powerful angels" (2 Thessalonians 1:6–7). The justice demonstrated in Esther's time points forward to the ultimate justice that will be revealed when Christ returns.

The question each generation faces is the same as Mordecai asked Esther: Have we been placed in our roles "for such a time as this" to act as agents of God's justice in our world? The legacy of Esther and Mordecai continues to motivate those who stand against injustice, trusting that the God who values justice will use ordinary people to achieve extraordinary redemption.

Like Mordecai, who became "preeminent among the Jews, and held in high esteem by his many fellow Jews, because he worked for the good of his people and spoke up for the welfare of all the Jews" (Esther 10:3), we are called to be agents of divine justice—working for the good of others, speaking up for those who cannot speak for themselves, and trusting that God's justice, though it may seem delayed, will ultimately prevail.

BIBLIOGRAPHY

Avioz, Michael. "The Motif of Beauty in the Books of Samuel and Kings." *VT* 61 (2011): 1–13.

Beck, John A. "Gideon, Dew, and the Narrative-Geographical Shaping of Judges 6:33–40," *BSac* 165 (2008): 28–38.

Berlejung, Angelika. "Sin and Punishment: The Ethics of Divine Justice and Retribution in Ancient Near Eastern and Old Testament Texts." *Int* 69 (2015):272–287.

Blair, Edward Payson. "Appeal To Remembrance: The Memory Motif in Deuteronomy." *Int* 15 (1961): 41–47.

Block, Daniel I. *Judges, Ruth: The New American Commentary.* Nashville: Broadman & Holman Publishers, 1999.

Boling, Robert G. "Gideon." *ABD*:1013–1015.

Brenton, Lancelot Charles Lee, trans. *The Septuagint Version of the Old Testament, According to the Vatican Text, Translated into English.* London: Samuel Bagster and Sons, 1844.

Bright, John. *A History of Israel.* Philadelphia: Westminster, 1981.

Brueggemann, Walter. *Genesis.* Interpretation. Louisville: John Knox Press, 1982.

———. *First and Second Samuel.* Interpretation. Louisville: John Knox, 1990.

———. *Theology of the Old Testament: Testimony, Dispute, Advocacy.* Minneapolis: Fortress Press, 2005.

Bush, Frederic W. *Ruth-Esther.* Word Biblical Commentary. Grand Rapids: Zondervan Academic, 2018.

Butler, Trent. *Judges.* Word Biblical Commentary. Nashville: Thomas Nelson, 2009.

Cartledge, Tony W. *1 & 2 Samuel.* Smyth & Helwys Bible Commentary. Macon, GA: Smyth & Helwys, 2001.

Chataira, Tekweni. "'For Such a Time as This:' A Clarion Call in a Time of Crisis," *Stimulus* 27 (2020): 70–75.

Clines, David J. A. "The Story of Michal, Wife of David, in its Sequential Unfolding." Pages 129–140 in *Telling Queen Michal's Story: An Experiment in Comparative Interpretation.* Sheffield: JSOT Press, 1991.

Deere, Jack S. *Even in Our Darkness: A Story of Beauty in a Broken Life.* Grand Rapids: Zondervan, 2018.

Endris, Vince. "Yahweh versus Baal: A Narrative-Critical Reading of the Gideon/Abimelech Narrative." *JSOT* 33 (2008): 173–195.

Evans, M. J. *Judges.* Apollos Old Testament Commentary. IVP Academic, 2017.

Goldingay, John. *Old Testament Theology: Israel's Gospel.* Downers Grove, InterVarsity, 2003.

Griffin, Patrick. *David: After God's Own Heart.* Nashville: B&H Publishing, 2018.

Hamilton, Victor P. *The Book of Genesis 18–50.* New International Commentary on the Old Testament. Grand Rapids: Eerdmans, 1995.

Hamori, E. J. *When Gods Were Men: The Embodied God in Biblical and Near Eastern Literature.* De Gruyter, 2008.

Harper, Prudence O., Joan Aruz, and Françoise Tallon (eds.). *The Royal City of Susa.* New York: The Metropolitan Museum of Art, 1992.

Josephus, Flavius. *The Antiquities of the Jews.* Translated by William Whiston.Vol. 1 (Books I–V). Peabody, MA: Hendrickson, 1987 (reprint of 1737 edition).

Klein, Ralph W. *1 Chronicles: A Commentary.* Hermeneia. Minneapolis: Fortress Press, 2006.

Lewis, Theodore J. "Belial." *ABD* 1:654–656.

Malamat, Abraham. "The War of Gideon and Midian: A Military Approach," *PEQ* 85 (1953): 61–65.

Mariottini, Claude F. "Joel 3:10 (H 4:10): 'Beat Your Plowshare Into Swords,'" *Perspective in Religious Studies* 14 (1987) 125–130.

_____. "Potiphera." *ABD*:5:427.

_____. "Introduction to Joel." *The People's Companion to the Bible.* Minneapolis: Fortress Press, 2009.

McCarter, P. Kyle Jr. *II Samuel.* The Anchor Bible. New York: Doubleday, 1984.

Messenger, William. "Calling in the Theology of Work." *Journal of Markets & Morality* 14 no 1 (Spring 2011): 171–187.

Miroschedji, Pierre de. "Susa." *ABD* 6:242–245.

Mourad, Anna-Latifa. "Foreigners at Beni Hassan: Evidence from the Tomb of Khnumhotep I (No. 14)," *ASOR* 384 (2020): 105–132.

Murphy, Kelly J. "Laying Out the Fleece: Reading Gideon's Requests with Reception History," *Word & World* 37 (2017): 241–251.

Niditch, S. (2008). *Judges: A Commentary*. Old Testament Library. Westminster John Knox Press, 2008.

Oppenheim, A. Leo. "The Golden Garments of the Gods." *JNES* 8 (1949): 172–193.

Pedersen, Johannes. *Israel: Its Life and Culture*. Atlanta: Scholars Press, 1991.

Rad, Gerhard von. *Genesis*. Old Testament Library. Philadelphia: Westminster Press, 1973.

Ripken, Nik, with Gregg Lewis. *The Insanity of God: A True Story of Faith Resurrected*. Nashville: B&H Publishing Group, 2013.

Rouse, W. Bradford. "God Sees the Heart: Character and Covenant in the Books of Samuel." *Restoration Quarterly* 50 (2008): 179–194.

Rowe, Ignacio Márquez. "How Can Someone Sell His Own Fellow to the Egyptians?" *VT* 54 (2004): 335–343.

Sachs, Gerardo G. "David Dances – Michal Scoffs." *Jewish Bible Quarterly* 34 no 4 (2006): 260–263.

Soggin, J. Alberto. *Judges*. Old Testament Library. Philadelphia: The Westminster Press, 1981.

Sasson, J. M. *Judges 1–12: A New Translation with Introduction and Commentary*. Yale University Press.

Speiser, E. A. *Genesis*. The Anchor Bible. New York: Doubleday, 1964.

Thompson, John A. "Joel's Locusts in the Light of Near Eastern Parallels." *JNES* 14 (1955): 52–55.

White, Ellen. "Michal the Misinterpreted." *Journal for the Study of the Old Testament* 31 (2007): 451–464.

Webb, Berry G. *The Book of Judges*. The New International Commentary on the Old Testament. Grand Rapids: Eerdmans, 2012.

Webb, B. G. *The Book of Judges: An Integrated Reading*. Sheffield Academic Press, 2012.

Wenham, Gordon J. *Genesis 16–50*. Word Biblical Commentary. Dallas: Word Books, 1994.

Wiebe, John M. "Will Relief and Deliverance Arise for the Jews from Another Place?" *CBQ* 53 (1991): 409–415.

Wolff, Hans Walter. *Anthropology of the Old Testament*. Philadelphia: Fortress, 1974.

Yamauchi, Edwin. "Susa." *The New International Dictionary of Biblical Archaeology*. Edited by E. M. Blaiklock and R. K. Harrison. Grand Rapids: Zondervan, 1983.

www.ingramcontent.com/pod-product-compliance
Lightning Source LLC
Chambersburg PA
CBHW060408130626
46555CB00005B/1999